RELIGION AMONG THE
UNITARIAN UNIVERSALISTS

RELIGION AMONG THE UNITARIAN UNIVERSALISTS

Converts in the Stepfathers' House

Robert B. Tapp

Departments of Humanities and Religious Studies
University of Minnesota
Minneapolis, Minnesota

SEMINAR PRESS   New York and London   1973

SEMINAR PRESS, INC.
111 Fifth Avenue, New York, New York 10003

United Kingdom Edition published by
SEMINAR PRESS LIMITED
24/28 Oval Road, London NW1

LIBRARY OF CONGRESS CATALOG CARD NUMBER: 72-82127

PRINTED IN THE UNITED STATES OF AMERICA

CONTENTS

v

APPENDICES

PREFACE

By focusing in considerable detail upon one small religious group in the United States and Canada, we hope to cast light upon a number of social, psychological, and religious processes within Western society. Religious mobility—the movement of persons into, out of, and between churches—is on the increase. The Unitarian Universalist denomination exemplifies this to an almost extreme degree since 90% of its members are converts.

The subtitle of this book, *Converts in the Stepfathers' House,* is intentionally suggestive. The most familiar allusion will be to a phrase "in my Father's house . . ." spoken by "the Christ" of the Fourth Gospel and attributed to Jesus of Nazareth. There, the metaphorical "house" was an other-wordly place and the "Father" was singular. In our usage here, the house is clearly of this world, the fathers are many, and the kinship is (at least) once-removed.

An intensive examination of one religious group should also illuminate the institutionalization of religiousness. Cyprian, a third-century theologian, argued that "he who does not have the Church for his Mother cannot have God for his Father." That dictum no doubt takes on new meanings in post-Freudian culture, but the familial metaphor has been important throughout the history of Western religions. Readers who know early Christian history will not have to be reminded that there has never been *one* church (not even in the third century!) and that Cyprian was warning the "heretics" in *other* churches that they had better join *his* church.

Far more ancient than the symbolism of the institution as a mothering community is the idea that the temple or building is a house for the god or goddess. The ancient Jews finally succumbed to this pattern and built their Yahweh a "house" in Jerusalem. While that twice-destroyed edifice has not been rebuilt, their literature and that of their Christian offspring abounds with references to religious institutions which are at the same time "homes" for the god and for the faithful followers of the god. Billboard slogans urge Americans to find themselves a "church home," and a presidential candidate has called upon the United States to "come home."

The very presence of these primary mother-father-home symbolisms helps explain both the ferocity of religious disputes and recurring attempts to change the religious institution. Western history, until the seventeenth century, could almost be written in terms of these fights between and within a variety of churches. Sometimes the reformers were "restorationists," seeking to shift the institution back to an alleged primitive purity. At other times, the slogans for change have been more adaptive and futuristic: "New occasions teach new duties; time makes ancient good uncouth."

United States and Canadian Unitarian Universalists have joined a religious institution spawned by the latter mood. The original house and family (mother) had indeed been Jewish-Christian but, as we suggest by reference to stepfathers, a number of basic changes had been made. In this case, the stepfathers came from the eighteenth-century Enlightenment—that curious blend of faith in science, political optimism, rational moralism, and classical paganism that stirred in such diverse men as Kant, Locke, Paine, Voltaire, Condorcet, and Jefferson. Almost all Western religions were affected by Enlightenment, but in Unitarian and Universalist churches this new spirit was welcomed. Thus the founding fathers of Enlightenment took up residence as stepfathers in those churches.

This peculiar religious adaptation embodies a variety of variously labeled strands: secularization, modernism, scientism, progressivism. But since the coming of the stepfathers, the "house" was never quite the same. In recent years an overwhelmingly large number of new converts have moved into this already-transformed institution. What are they doing to what they found? How will interaction between stepfathers and their converts affect the house? How will they settle questions of authority and power? And, above all, how will they make decisions on maintenance and remodeling?

ACKNOWLEDGMENTS

Many books begin with a dedication; we shall instead begin with a recognition of indebtedness to the Committee on Goals of the Unitarian Universalist Association. This ad hoc committee, which I had the privilege of chairing, met for two years to consider long-range denominational planning. The survey research project providing the basis for this book grew out of that harmonious and innovative committee's need for information and resulted in a rich datum of the interpenetration of human creativity, observational experience, and empirical data. We confronted many difficult problems: the operationalizing of questions, the interpenetration of the actual and the ideal, the tension between individual and institutional religion, the bureaucratic impact of empirical information, and the sheer politics of a large, voluntary organization. Committee members were Paul N. Carnes, Ralph Conant, Doris Dodds, Philip R. Giles, Roland B. Greeley, G. Robert Hohler, Michael Kami, Walter R. Kayne, Mason F. McGinness, Harry Meserve, Rosamund Reynolds, Todd Taylor, and Julie Underwood. The Reverend Dana M. Greeley, then-president of the Unitarian Universalist Association, must be credited with sensing the urgency of fact-finding and long-range planning—even though he did not always concur in the plans or take comfort in the facts.

The National Opinion Research Center played a central role in the design, data collection, and first-level analysis stages of this project. Special thanks are due to Paul B. Sheatsley, Director of the Survey Research Service; Seymour Sudman, Director of Sampling (now at the University of Illinois); and Carol Bowman Stocking, who gave daily supervision to both the tedious and creative aspects of these initial stages.

Many parts of this book reflect the counsel of colleagues at the University of Chicago who should be remembered for their share of the strong points and absolved of any responsibility for erroneous interpretations. Peter H. Rossi (now at Johns Hopkins) funded this study in more ways than he realizes. Appreciation is also due James E. Dittes (Yale), Andrew M. Greeley, John F. Hayward (then at Meadville, now at Southern Illinois), William E. Henry, Salvatore E. Maddi, Bernice Neugarten, John Shlien (now at Harvard), Fred L. Strodtbeck, and last, but by no means least, June Louin Tapp. Statistical advice has been received, and, hopefully, not misused, from William H. Kruskal and David E. Wiley.

Research on this scale has required a considerable amount of man/machine dialogue. My direct involvement at one end of this dialogue would have been impossible without the continuing help of the University of Chicago's Computation Center. Their staff, especially Carl N. Hildabrand, Frank K. Bamberger, John Iannantuoni, and Donald Goldhamer deserve special thanks.

My graduate students at Meadville and my undergraduate students at the University of Chicago have been edifying sounding boards for the interpretation of data and concepts in this study. Larry B. Boyd, Frank W. Carpenter, and J. Forrest Whitman helped with early formulations, and Vern Barnet as research assistant has unselfishly seen the project to completion.

Further gratitude must be expressed to those colleagues who commented upon the sections of this manuscript that were presented to the American Academy of Religion, the Society for the Scientific Study of Religion, the International Congress of Psychologists, and the International Congress for Social Psychiatry.

Without the initial funding of the Board of Trustees of the Unitarian Universalist Association, this project would never have begun. In addition to financial assistance provided by the UUA, the eighty churches represented in the survey not only contributed thousands of dollars in postage and secretarial assistance but, above all, made it possible to get the questionnaires into the hands of individual Unitarian Universalists. In addition, a Faculty Research Grant to the author from the Social Science Research Council in 1968-1969 permitted the completion of several crucial phases of the research.

Meadville/Lombard Theological School expanded its curriculum to include courses in the empirical study of religion, and provided a research office and many other supportive services which have facilitated this study. These included the secretarial services of Minerva Bell, without whose expertise the manuscript would not have existed.

Ultimately, most books are also debts to a family which has endured the prolonged absence of the writer from his customary roles. Thus, June Tapp not only functioned professionally, as already mentioned, but covered extra home bases on a number of occasions, and Mara and Kami went to bed unkissed many nights because "Daddy is at the Computer Center."

To all these, this study is offered in grateful if partial payment.

Note: While this book was in press, a study of three Lutheran denominations has appeared: *A Study of Generations* by M. P. Strommen, M. L. Brekke, R. C. Underwager, and A. L. Johnson, Minneapolis: Augsburg Publishing House, 1972. In a number of major conceptual and methodological ways, this analysis of 4745 laymen and pastors extends the review of this volume's Chapter 2. Of particular interest is the parallel use of factor analysis as an empirical technique for exploring the dimensions of religiosity.

Chapter 1

THE UNITARIAN UNIVERSALISTS: A DENOMINATIONAL OVERVIEW

SOME INTRODUCTORY CONSIDERATIONS

While the primary focus of this book will be upon one small religious group, the Unitarian Universalists, a number of larger issues will be found lurking in the near background. To what extent can this be said to be a religious group? What kind of religiousness does it embody, and how does it stand with relation to other religious groups? Is it meaningful to speak of a civil or a secular religion? If so, where does it exist, and how can it be recognized?

Many of these issues have been raised sharply by Thomas Luckmann (1967) who argues that many of the existing studies of religion are really studies of churches. He contends that these reveal, at best, only part of the picture and that an invisible religion also exists in the lives of many persons not connected with religious institutions. The implication here seems to be that religiousness is essentially an individual, psychological phenomenon, and that the more socio-logical perspective, which views religiousness as something that occurs with men in groups, needs correction. Erich Fromm, on the other hand, has argued that religion is inevitably a group phenomenon and that the only term that could be applied to an individual religion would be neurosis (1950).

The dilemma posed by these extreme positions is both conceptual and philosophical. More important, it reflects the thinness of our present empirical knowledge of religiousness. The relatively recent scientific study of religion has

1

been surveyed by Milton Yinger (1970). The classical interplay of theory and data is readily apparent. Until we know what we are looking for, we are not likely to find it, and until we have found several instances of it, we don't really know what it is! One is reminded of St. Augustine trying to philosophize about the nature of time: "I knew exactly what it was until you asked me."

We will typically use the term "religiosity" to denote that which is being explored here. The term commends itself as being less institutionally and historically biased than "religion," and less awkward than "religiousness." Those interested in this conceptual issue (What's in a name?) would do well to consult Wilfred Smith, *The Meaning and End of Religion* (1963), who carefully reviews the historical usages of the term "religion," concluding that we should abandon it in favor of "piety," which will serve to remind us that we must always deal with particular men at particular points in cultural space and time. Their beliefs and behaviors, which of course include historical memories and symbolizations, constitute the actual meaning of any particular religious tradition in any particular period. Thus, to refer to Christianity or Judaism would be to over-reify complex traditions which have actually meant many different things to men in different epochs.

While we share Smith's intent, his label "piety" may encourage biasing presuppositions toward the affective side of religiosity and tempt us to overlook cognitive and volitional aspects. Religiosity, needless to say, is used here as a thoroughly neutral and descriptive construct. Although any author, and probably every reader, makes private judgments regarding good and bad forms of religiosity, the initial task of any scientific inquiry is to describe and explain phenomena rather than judge them. Finally, it should be clear that this book attempts an initial, quantitative, empirical description of one kind of religiosity. It would be surprising if there were not indeed many other kinds of religiosity, within religious institutions as well as outside of them. Nevertheless, we are seldom given the luxury of such a synoptic vision, and must content ourselves with inferences made from whatever is available.

HISTORICAL BACKGROUND

Before turning to Unitarian Universalists in the present, some historical background will be helpful. Rather than undertake a comprehensive treatment here, we will note salient ideological and institutional landmarks and direct interested readers to fuller sources by the use of footnoted references. We shall first deal with ideological themes and then describe their institutionalization.

Ideological Backgrounds

The basic doctrine of universalism appears as a "heresy" at a number of points in Christian history. Most simply, it holds that God is too loving to condemn even the worst of sinners to an eternal punishment. Popularly, this is a "no Hell" idea, although it has often been modified into the belief in a noneternal but after-death place of punishment. As initially preached in America, universalism stressed the lovingness of God, holding that a loving God would not predestine men to Hell. From a strict universalist standpoint, the God of the early American unitarians, whose moral nature required the eventual judgment of morally free and responsible men, was little better than the Calvinist God.

The precise meaning of unitarian is often misunderstood by both outsiders and insiders. Correctly speaking, it is nothing more than a rejection of the Christian dogma of the trinitarian nature of God which held that the three persons of the Godhead (Father, Son, and Holy Spirit) were distinguishable but nevertheless of one substance. The debate relating to this dogma occurred in the third century of the Christian era and, at this distance, can be summarized as a practical/theoretical confrontation. Practical thinkers argued that the Son must be equal to the Father if he is to be the medium of salvation. More theoretical thinkers had difficulty in finding a real distinctiveness for the three persons within such a unity. Various versions of this tension threatened the peace of the Roman empire and political intervention finally forced the somewhat paradoxical formula of resolution. This solution by authority was by no means instantaneous nor, it may be noted, did it claim to be reasonable. Subsequent tensions concerning the relationship of the Son to Jesus of Nazareth in many ways continued some of the same controversies.

During the late middle ages and early Renaissance, the confluence of several currents of thought reopened the issue. The rediscovery of Aristotelian logic gave a sharper meaning to reason. The development of Florence's Platonic Academy, augmented by emigres from the Muslim conquest of Constantinople, revived European interest in Socratic dialectics. Muslim and Jewish scholars in Spain brought freedom and sophistication to scriptural exegesis, and Erasmus' critical New Testament text climaxed classical humanism. These widened resources fostered a developmental study of ideas—from primitive Christianity through the scripture-writing period to the layerings of theological formulations. In Spain, Miguel Servetus committed to writing the view that the Trinity was not scriptural, while the Sozzini brothers made the same announcement at about the same time in Italy. Despite considerable persecution, these ideas prospered for a brief time in Poland and Transylvania.

The significant aftermath of the religious wars of the sixteenth and seventeenth centuries, however, was the creation of a climate of increased toleration for religious and intellectual pluralism (cf. Wilbur, 1949). The major beneficiaries of this were the developing empirical sciences. Yet the very success of the sciences posed sharp problems for European religions. The growing picture of the unity and orderliness of nature raised questions about the role of "supernature." The arguments revolved around discovery versus revelation, and nature versus miracle. Especially in England, morality was seen as anchored in a natural religion which did not rely upon the miraculous, and salvation came to be regarded as the result of human virtue acquired in the exercise of human freedom rather than a result of any divine intervention. This whole system, often labeled Deism, was held to be a reasonable reflection upon a reasonable nature as discovered by the sciences. The function of a god from this perspective was to create and maintain the orderly system.

Two difficulties plagued this position. This god bore scant resemblance to the Jewish-Christian sovereign Deity whose inscrutable operations and decrees preceded (and therefore regarded as irrelevant) the moral behaviors of individual men, and the world described by the sciences was increasingly deterministic and devoid of any place for that same human freedom upon which moral virtue was claimed to depend. Kant had seen this clearly and postulated a transcendental realm where human freedom (if not the Christian God) could be located. Many versions of Romanticism—poetic, philosophical, and religious—developed in these directions during the nineteenth century. But that century, nonetheless, ended in the triumph of Darwinian biology which explained all living phenomena in terms of natural selection, an admittedly incongruous juxtaposition of terms.

Scientific determinism became even less available for religious retranslation when Freud pictured the nonrational substratum of human rationality that had developed all moral and scientific thinking. To be sure, Freud's ideas have never been fully accepted by the physical or even social sciences and, therefore, philosophical and religious thinking has continued to vacillate between variations of rationalism and romanticism.

In England and America, these were blended in specific ways by the precursors and early theologians of Unitarianism and Universalism. This story has been carefully documented by Conrad Wright (1955). Using reason as the clue to interpret both the Bible and human history, these theologians saw a divine (if not fully trinitarian) Jesus as the exemplar of wisdom and morality, and viewed his miracles as both a cosmic approval and a proof of his perfection.

The application of critical historical scholarship to the Biblical traditions was, however, almost coincident with the early Unitarian preaching of Theophilus Lindsey in England and William Ellery Channing in America. This new Biblical scholarship came increasingly to view the miracles as misperceptions. Thus, whatever authority Jesus retained had to rest upon his moral stature. Nineteenth-century thinkers found this hard to absolutize, partly because of the prescientific ideas of first-century Palestine and partly because they were discovering different moral horizons themselves in their enthusiasm with democratic individualism and "self-reliance" (to use Ralph Waldo Emerson's phrase). By midnineteenth century, the classical rationalist orthodoxies regarding Jesus and morality were forced to contend with a Transcendentalist challenge which was almost, at the same time, mystical, individualistic, antiorganizational, and panreligionistic (as in Emerson's enthusiasm for Hinduism). Some of this impact has been traced by William Hutchison (1959). A good treatment of the role of Harvard University in the development of the genteel tradition of Boston Unitarian orthodoxy has been written by Daniel Howe (1971).

The general American religious scene was also transformed by the rise of the social gospel. In the beginning, this was a rejection of the view that religion dealt primarily with individual salvation in favor of a stance that saw redemption occurring in and through the social order. As the movement developed, the definition of problems and solutions drew far more on religious and secular socialist thought than upon a first-century Jesus. In a real sense, education came to be regarded as the means to change human nature and culture, and reformism was increasingly rooted in a sociological vision of society's ills and possibilities. John Dewey both symbolized this approach and exerted a strong influence in Unitarian and Universalist circles, with ministers from both denominations joining him in "The Humanist Manifesto" of 1933. This text provides a programmatic description of nontheistic humanism (Parke, 1957).

Describing thought currents within this religious movement in the last two generations is more difficult, and reliable histories have not yet been written. Controversies have continued between theists and humanists, reflected not only in the official journals (*Unitarian Register* and *Universalist Leader*) but in such related journals as the *Journal of Liberal Religion*, the *Crane Review, Faith and Freedom, Journal of the Liberal Ministry*, and the more partisan *Unitarian Christian, Humanist*, and *Religious Humanism*. The Unitarian and Universalist spokesmen have had to deal with the attack on pragmatism and liberalism made by Protestant neoorthodoxy (most familiar in Reinhold Niebuhr's writings), the rise of first Protestant and then Roman Catholic ecumenism, and the renascence of many non-Western religions. A recent illustration of liberal religious perspectives may be found in the published reports of six study commissions on "The Free Church in a Changing World" (1963).

Unitarian Institutional History

In 1785, King's Chapel in Boston revised its prayerbook removing trinitarian references, and in 1796 the First Unitarian Church of Philadelphia was founded, the first American church making explicit use of that name. Under the system of congregational polity, many of the Congregational parishes of New England were calling ministers of open unitarian persuasion, and a widely read declaration of these ideas appeared in an 1819 sermon in Baltimore, Maryland on the occasion of the ordination of the minister there. In 1825, the American Unitarian Association was founded to provide a focal point for churches with this orientation. In 1852, the Western Unitarian Conference was formed in Cincinnati, later moving to Chicago. This conference came to stand for a broader interpretation of Unitarianism. In 1900, the International Conference of Free Christians and Other Religious Liberals was founded to unite British and American Unitarians with continental Unitarians and other liberals in continental state churches. Beginning in the late 1930s the Unitarians experienced considerable membership growth and, in 1948, they launched a "fellowship" movement to establish lay-led groups where no churches existed. The techniques and impact of this somewhat unique venture have been described by Laile Bartlett (1960).

Universalist Institutional History

In 1770, John Murray emigrated from England and began preaching universalism in the United States. Nine years later, the Independent Church of Gloucester, Massachusetts won freedom from church taxation for its members. In 1805, Hosea Ballou's *Treatise on Atonement* made a sharp break with Christian orthodoxy in a unitarian direction. Universalist congregations tended to band together into local and state conventions and only created a national organization in 1833, not granting it any measure of power until 1866. The numerical peak of Universalist growth came in the early twentieth century. Brief histories of U.S. Universalism have been written by Clinton Scott (1957) and Elmo Robinson (1970), and Ernest Cassara has compiled a documentary history (1971).

Unitarian Universalist Merger

From an observer's standpoint, it would appear strange that these two denominations were unable to merge until 1961. Many of their ministers moved back and forth, both groups lived in the same general intellectual climate, and the stress that each placed on individual and congregational freedom had so pluralized both groups that there was probably more ideological overlap than uniqueness. There were, however, persisting class and regional differences that had overcome previous moves, and until these were transcended or bypassed, merger did not come.

In 1867 the Free Religious Association was created, blending Transcendentalist themes with an inclusive organizational dream (Persons, 1947). This proved far more attractive to non-New England Unitarians than to Universalists, and eventually lost its impetus. In 1908 the National Federation of Religious Liberals was created (which also included Friends and Reform Jews). This met with minimal success and was replaced by a Free Church of America in 1933 which only lasted five years, being unable to attract wide support. Beginning in 1947, a series of joint commissions eventually (1953) established a Council of Liberal Churches which federated the departments of publications, education, and public relations. In that same year, the two youth groups voted to merge. Subsequent commissions, plans, and concomitant denominational assemblies eventually created the Unitarian Universalist Association in 1961. Given the autonomy of the constituent congregations, this merger created a new structure at the top, merged the intermediate district and regional structures, but had no automatic effect at local levels.

DEMOGRAPHIC CHARACTERISTICS OF THE UNITARIAN UNIVERSALISTS

With this brief historical background in mind, we can proceed with the analysis of a questionnaire study of the Unitarian Universalist Association conducted in 1966. Completed questionnaires were obtained from a representative sample of 12,146 members of this denomination living in the United States and Canada. The respondents in the study come from 80 local churches. In most cases, the data presented in this book have been weighted (indicated by the symbol "Nwt" on a table) to equalize the group return rates and to compensate for the stratification of the sampling design. The details of sampling, data collection, and weighting may be found in Appendix A. The questionnaire developed for this study, with the weighted response percentages, is reproduced in Appendix B. We may note here that the sampling, in the absence of a "continental" (meaning U.S. and Canada) mailing list, used the indirect procedure of selecting local churches and mailing questionnaires to all the "legal adult members" of the group selected.

An examination of the questionnaire will show that most of the specifically religious items were designed and pretested to explore this denomination. We will therefore not be able to present direct comparisons to responses of other religious groups. The questionnaire also elicited demographic information which aids in locating the Unitarian Universalists in American religious space. Table 1.1 presents information on those UU (Unitarian Universalist) characteristics where we have comparable data on the overall U.S. population as well as on major religious groups. It will be noted that this table, and some of the other tables in this volume, contain breakdowns for several selected regions. In view of the historical development of Unitarian Universalism already discussed, it will sometimes be instructive to explore regional differences.

Age

Compared to either the U.S. population or membership of most other religious groups, the UUs are underrepresented in the high and low age brackets. It is even possible that the 3% in the youngest category is overstated since the UU cutting point was under 25.

Certain regional variations must be noted. The Canadians have considerably fewer members over 55, and in New England there are fewer members under 45, and 14% over 54. To the extent that age affects patterns of religiosity, we shall have to bear in mind that neither the overall UU denomination nor its New England subgroup resembles the Protestant or U.S. patterns of age distribution.

TABLE 1.1

Characteristics of United States and Unitarian Universalist Populations[a]

| | United States | | | | | | | | | | Unitarian Universalists | | | | |
| | | | Protestant | | | | | | | | | | Region | | |
Item	All	Jewish	All	Baptists	Episco-palians	Lutherans	Metho-dists	Presby-terians	Roman Catholics	No religion	All	Canada	Pacific	Mid-west	New England
Age															
21-24	6	5	6	8	4	6	6	5	7	9	3	3	3	4	3
25-34	24	22	24	24	18	26	22	23	26	15	19	19	19	21	13
35-44	25	32	23	24	30	21	22	22	27	24	33	39	36	35	24
45-54	19	18	21	20	23	21	20	17	17	26	21	23	21	20	22
55-64	14	13	14	12	13	12	14	19	12	11	12	11	9	12	17
65+	12	10	12	12	12	14	16	14	11	15	12	5	11	8	22
Gender															
Male	46	42	45	42	35	46	44	42	46	81	44	47	44	44	38
Income[b]															
Under $3000	25	8	28	44	6	26	31	20	19	32	4	(2)	(5)	(2)	(6)
$3000-$4999	28	19	27	29	19	28	25	26	29	28	9	(8)	(7)	(5)	(7)
$5000-$7499	28	31	27	20	29	30	29	28	34	18	9	(18)	(12)	(13)	(16)
$7500-$14,999	16	31	15	6	35	14	13	20	16	15	52	(57)	(45)	(53)	(47)
$15,000 and over	3	11	3	1	11	2	2	6	2	7	26	(15)	(30)	(26)	(24)

Education															
Eighth grade or less	33	21	33	44	8	35	31	18	34	40	1	2	1	1	2
High school incomplete	20	13	21	24	14	22	20	17	20	20	4	13	3	3	6
High school graduates	28	33	27	21	25	29	28	29	32	18	11	17	8	9	19
College incomplete	10	17	10	7	25	9	10	20	9	10	23	20	28	22	27
College graduates	9	16	9	4	28	5	11	16	5	12	60	48	59	65	45
Occupation															
Professional	9	10	9	5	23	7	10	13	8	15	66	60	63	68	51
Manager-ownership	12	32	12	8	23	11	11	20	11	10	17	18	14	15	25
Salesmen-clerical	10	16	10	7	17	13	11	14	10	5	9	11	9	9	9
Skilled	18	9	17	16	12	18	16	17	22	10	6	9	10	6	11
Semi unskilled	24	10	25	35	10	22	22	15	30	27	2	1	1	2	4
Other	27	14	27	29	12	29	31	21	19	33	1	1	3	2	1

[a] Data in this table, except for Unitarian Universalists, are taken from B. Lazerwitz (1961). Percentages are used.

[b] The U.S. percentages reflect 1956 income. Since the Unitarian Universalist data were for 1965 "family income before taxes," direct comparison would have been misleading. The percentages in the UU "All" column, therefore, reflect the elimination of the Canadian responses, reduction of the cutting points by Bureau of Labor Statistics' indices for these two periods, and a redistribution based on a graph of the reduced intervals. The regional UU percentages, shown in parentheses, have not been corrected, and should not be directly compared to the corrected percentages. It must also be noted that Canadian intervals are in Canadian dollars.

Gender

(We prefer this term to "sex," especially since we will be using the latter term to denote attitudes on sexuality). Only the Lutherans and Catholics have as high a proportion of males as are found in the U.S. population. The UU male/female proportionality parallels the Protestant population and, thus, is slightly more female than the U.S. population. Some regional differences are apparent, with the Canadians being slightly more male, and the New Englanders 14% more female than the overall denomination.

Income

The UUs are clearly concentrated in the higher-income brackets, representing the highest income level ever reported for a total denomination. Four-fifths of the UU families live at income levels enjoyed by only one-fifth of the U.S. population.

As indicated on the table, the regional income percentages have not been adjusted and are therefore not directly comparable to the denominational percentages. It should also be clear that the general dollar income of Canadians is lower, and, therefore, no direct class inferences should be made from these figures. Within the U.S. regions, however, it is quite apparent that the New Englanders are heavily underrepresented in the middle and high brackets (52% as against 66% for the total denomination).

Education

In regard to the number of college graduates, the "all Protestant" group parallels the U.S. figures, and only Jews, Presbyterians, and Episcopalians exceed this percentage. The UUs, however, have a 66% college-graduate membership (in fact, 25% of the UUs hold one or more graduate degrees).

In regional terms, it will be noted that the Canadians show less variation from the denominational pattern on education than on income, indicating the complex relationship of these two measures of social class. While the New Englanders have the largest percentage of members who did not proceed beyond high school and the smallest percentage of members with college degrees, their percentage of college graduates nevertheless exceeds that of any other religious group.

Occupation

A third common measure of social class is occupation. The UUs reported the occupation of the main earner and the U.S. figures are for heads of family, but these should be essentially comparable. As was the case with education, the Unitarian Universalist pattern shown by these figures differs so sharply that systematic comparisons are almost impossible. Of all UUs who are main earners, 83% are professionals, managers, or owners. For the other upper-class religious groups (Episcopalians, Presbyterians, and Jews), the comparable percentages are 46, 43, and 42.

In regional terms, the New England UUs again show the most significant variation from the continental pattern. They are 8% higher in manager or owner families, and 7% lower in professional—science or engineering—families. Midwest UUs are 5% above the denominational average for teachers.

In describing the extremely high proportion of teachers among the UU main earners (13%), we can underscore the disparity in occupational patterns found within this denomination by noting that this is above the U.S. percentage for professionals of all kinds, and above the "all professions" percentages for every religious group except Episcopalians (it is identical to the Presbyterian professional figure).

Type of Employer

As further data upon the possible role that occupation might play in religiosity, the questionnaire elicited the UU main earner's type of employer. This information is shown in Table 1.2. No comparable figures are available for other religious groups, but among the UUs, a slightly higher percentage of Canadians are in government employ. The other group departing from the continental

TABLE 1.2
Additional Characteristics of UU Population[a]

		Region			
			Pacific		New
Item	All	Canada	Coast	Midwest	England
Employer of main earner					
Private enterprise	44	46	42	42	51
Nonprofit organization	14	10	16	17	16
Government	26	33	24	24	13
Self-employed	13	9	15	14	14
Nonemployed	4	2	4	3	7
Place of residence					
Urban	42	51	49	55	5
Suburban	37	37	34	35	42
Other	21	13	18	10	53
Residential mobility					
(years in present community)					
0-5	28	24	30	28	18
6-10	20	25	24	21	14
Over 10	52	51	46	51	68
Marital status					
Single, never married	9	7	7	9	12
Married, never divorced	72	80	62	72	71
Divorced, remarried	8	4	15	8	4
Divorced, or separated	5	5	11	6	4
Widowed	6	3	6	5	9

[a]Nwt = 170, 758 for all, 93,820 for region.

pattern is New England, where 7% more are employed by the private sector, and 13% fewer by government.

Residence

Residential information on UUs concerns their place of residence and their length of residence in their present communities. The overall picture is one of a highly metropolitanized denomination. At least 70% live either in large cities or in their suburbs. Several residential categories from the questionnaire have been collapsed into the "other" category of Table 1.2, since less than 1% of UUs live on farms and only 3% live in open, nonfarm, country.

There are, however, major regional differentiations. The Canadians and Mid-westerners are most heavily concentrated in the large cities, whereas a majority of New England UUs live in middle-sized or small towns, away from the suburbs and cities.

Unitarian Universalists are a highly mobile population in terms of their residence. Almost half (48%) of them have lived less than 10 years in their present communities. Regionally, the Pacific Coast UUs are the most mobile and the New England UUs are strikingly least mobile. These mobility patterns may be partially explained by the large number of professional persons involved in this denomination. The annual migration rates calculated by Bogue (1959) showed that professionals are the most mobile occupational group, and that mobility is highest in persons under forty-five. Both of these characteristics are marked among UUs (but notably absent from the New England section of the denomination, where residential mobility is also lowest).

Marital Status

In order to examine the possible effect of remarriage upon religious patterns, the questionnaire included the category "divorced and remarried." The U.S. figures for 1957, as given by Lazerwitz (1961) were 6% single, 82% married, 8% widowed, 2% divorced, and 2% separated. If the two UU "married" categories are combined, no significant departures from these U.S. figures appear.

On the other hand, in terms of intact first marriages, there are significant regional variations. Marital stability is highest among Canadians (80%) and lowest among Pacific Coast UUs (62%). It may also be noted that among the New England UUs there are slightly higher rates for the single and widowed states. The latter is obviously related to the higher median age of the New England group.

A CONVERT FAITH

Both the title designation of Unitarian Universalism as a "stepfathers' house" and the brief historical sketches given of the two denominations have indicated the change-oriented and marginal status of this movement in relation to the mainstream of Western Protestant Christianity. A new and major element in this dynamic in recent years has been the influx of converts. The Unitarians, at least, experienced considerable growth in actual membership between the 1930s and the time of merger. Lacking accurate figures for these decades, however, we cannot describe accurately the attrition—those who grew up in Unitarian or Universalist families and are no longer members, but there has clearly been a two-way street leading both into and out of the churches in this denomination.

The extent of traffic along the streets leading into Unitarian Universalist churches is shown in Table 1.3. The overall percentage of 89% converts is unprecedented for any established religious group. Almost equally striking is the extent to which New England churches have lagged behind the denomination in recent years. Since we lack accurate membership figures or convert percentages for any previous periods, we would not be justified in inferring that a lower percentage of converts reflects a pattern of higher membership retention. It may simply indicate a relative lack of growth; institutional growth is a function, among other things, of growth-potential in the immediate environment. If we assume a random distribution of "proto-UUs," the New England areas has most fully approached its potential, since 1% of the New England population in 1966 was UU. Less than one-tenth of 1% of the U.S. population was UU, and less than one-twentieth of 1% of the Canadians.

TABLE 1.3
UU Convert Percentages by Region[a]

	Region			
	Canada	Pacific Coast	Midwest	New England
Convert (%)	97	96	94	67

[a]Nwt = 93,820.

This preponderance of converts would normally only be found in a new religious movement, not one that is almost two centuries old. In any explanation of UU religiosity, this looms as a salient and dominant fact, making any comparisons to other religious groups with more stable membership patterns even more difficult.

At this point, we need to make some preliminary assessment of the effect that this high immigration rate has had upon group religiosity. Later on, we will also try to assess the effect that religiosity has upon the converts themselves. It seems reasonable to assume that people join a particular group because they perceive affinities between members of that group and themselves. To the extent that this perception has been correct, the group is able to satisfy the needs that initially moved converts toward it. Where misperception has occurred, a dropping-out can be expected.

Where a group undergoes rapid change, a somewhat similar process of alienation and exit can be expected among the long-time members. This process may
afford a partial explanation for the surprisingly small number of born Unitarian
Universalists who have remained as members.

The data shown in Table 1.4 supports certain generalizations regarding this
immigration-emigration process. This information also makes clearer the connotations of Unitarian Universalism as a "stepfathers' house." The first two items
deal with God and immortality, thus reflecting the belief aspect of UU religiosity. The third item, on the frequency of prayer, reflects religious practice, and
the remaining items on the importance of the Bible and the importance of
worship reflect an institutional component of religiosity. On each of these
representative items, the born UUs are markedly more traditional than the
converts or the overall denomination. On most of the items this contrast is most
extreme between the born UUs and the new converts. The born UU is half again
as likely to believe in immortality as the new convert, and three times as likely
to pray often. He is considerably more likely to hold traditional beliefs about
God, and twice as likely to want traditional Biblical teachings in his church
school and regard worship as an essential function of his church.

TABLE 1.4

Traditional Beliefs, Behaviors, and Values of Born UUs and Converts[a]

Item[b]		Converts: years of membership			
	Born	0-2	3-10	11+	All
God as "supernatural being" or "ground of being"	43	25	20	27	26
Immortality—affirmed as personal	17	11	8	11	10
Prays often	21	7	8	14	11
Bible—want more in church school	66	33	37	45	42
Worship—very important in a church	57	25	30	42	36

[a]Nwt = 165,376.

[b]Actual questions may be found in Appendix B, items P-1, P-9, P-3, D-6, L-2.

Putting this another way, it is very doubtful if many of these converts would
have become Unitarian Universalists if the beliefs and practices of UU religiosity
were being characteristically determined by those born into and remaining with
the denomination. Given the high proportion of converts, of course, this has not
been the case, and the new converts resemble the overall denominational pattern
far more closely than they resemble the pattern of the born UUs.

Yet another way of describing the situation is that the movement away from
traditional Protestant religiosity, as reflected in these items of belief, practice,

and institutional expectation, has been more rapid in the overall denomination than among those who were born into, and have remained with, Unitarian Universalism.

The data presented in this table do not sustain any generalizations regarding the effects of length of membership among the converts. Age is a confounding element in this, and we will examine this issue of socialization more closely in later chapters.

THE PATHS OF CONVERSION

At first glance, it would appear that the Unitarian Universalist converts provide an opportunity for a study of religious mobility. It is far more difficult to ascertain whether they are persons who are religiously moving from "house to house" or are those who have, religiously, "found a home." A frequently-voiced UU self-criticism is that their churches provide some kind of half-way house. *Newsweek*, commenting on the first release of this survey data, put this succinctly in labeling UUs "atheists who have not shaken the church habit" (1967). There is also the normal institutional anxiety among UUs that their children are not remaining to become Unitarian Universalist adults.

Adequate research on these issues would be possible but extremely complex and expensive since it would involve tracking down those who have ceased to remain church members. There are no extensive studies of these processes in any religious group, and therefore no bases on which we could establish normal church turnover. In the case of UUs, the issue is further complicated by wide variations in the meaning of church membership. In some instances it involves subscribing to a set of affirmations or even being voted upon by the present membership, in others it simply involves signing a membership book.

A further complication is the distinction that must be drawn between identification and affiliation. Previous studies have shown that individuals retain their institutional identification long after personal endorsement of the stance of that institution has subsided. Probably to a lesser degree, individuals reach a personal religious commitment (identification) prior to institutional affiliation. While the former generalization would probably be true across the religious spectrum, it seems more likely that the second generalization would be more operative on the liberal end of the spectrum. That is to say, persons may come to essentially liberal values as the result of education or common cultural exposure and not feel any strong necessity of immediate affiliation with a religious institution embodying those values. Persons who come to more conservative religious commitments, in contrast, would be more likely to feel the press for institutional affiliation. We will, in a later chapter, explore some aspects of the identification issue. At this point we are concerned with the more formal issue of affiliation.

Although we lack information on the "exit paths" of the Unitarian Universalists, we can nevertheless describe the "entrance paths" of present convert members. The questionnaire contained two separate questions, one dealing with "your family religion during your childhood" and the other with "your own religious preference before joining the Unitarian Universalist Church." Table 1.5 presents this information on the UU converts. Several of these categories deserve

TABLE 1.5

Religious Backgrounds of the Converts[a]

Type of religion	Life stage	
	Childhood	Pre-conversion
Liberal Protestant	32	42
Fundamentalist Protestant	25	7
Liturgical Protestant (Lutheran or Episcopal)	14	9
Catholic (Roman or Eastern Orthodox)	7	3
Reform Jewish	2	2
Conservative or Orthodox Jewish	2	1
Mixed (Catholic/non-Catholic)	2	—[b]
Mixed (Jewish/non-Jewish)	1	—[b]
Other	6	5
No organized religion	10	32

[a]Nwt = 146,006.

[b]Not applicable.

explanation, since their definition was shaped by the peculiar nature of the UU group and by the necessity of creating categories broad enough for use in a U.S. and Canadian study. The Liberal Protestant designation appeared on the questionnaire with no further qualification, as was the case with the Fundamentalist Protestant designation. Two other designations appeared with illustrative denominations: Liturgical Protestant (Lutheran, Episcopal) and Catholic (Roman or Eastern Orthodox). In choosing between a list of designations that would provide specific denominational labels or one that would provide a somewhat more ideological characterization, the latter alternative was selected. Knowing that a person has been a Methodist or a Baptist, for instance, would give precise denominational information but almost meaningless ideological content since churches in those two denominations vary from extremely liberal to extremely fundamentalist. Similarly, the Liturgical Protestant designation included Lutherans (who tend to be conservative) and Episcopalians (who tend to be liberal). Nevertheless, both of these groups share the commitment to a highly ritualized form of worship. It seemed more desirable to know this about the background of UUs in understanding their present attitudes. The Liberal Protestant designation is admittedly even more vague (especially since some UUs would presently consider themselves to be liberal Protestants). It was assumed that the adjective "liberal" had sufficiently common meaning for present UUs so that their characterization of their own background would select it if the fundamentalist or liturgical characterization did not apply. During the pretesting of the questionnaire, an additional category of Conservative Protestant was employed, but it led to excessive overlapping with the present designations.

Examination of this table suggests that, in terms of the American religious census, those of Protestant background are overrepresented, ex-Catholics are underrepresented, and ex-Jews are normally represented. In the general pattern of Protestant churches, the first two generalizations would be expected, but not the third.

The disparities shown in this table between childhood religions affiliation, as well as the particular paths of conversion, can be better understood by examination of the prior religion/family religion ratio, as shown in Table 1.6. Reading this table without the decimal points, we see that of every 100 persons whose family religion was Unitarian Universalist, 90 report that their previous religion was UU. Out of every 100 persons whose family religion was Liberal Protestant, 78 came directly to a Unitarian Universalist church and 18 report an intermediate period of no organized religion. Thus the ratios on the diagonal of this table represent the persons for whom Unitarian Universalism is a second religion, while the ratios off the diagonal represent the immediately prior religious affiliations of those converts for whom Unitarian Universalism is at least a third religious affiliation.

The data on this table further show that the path of direct conversion is powerfully related to the closeness of the family religion and present UU religiosity. Thus 78 (out of 100) ex-Liberal Protestants made a direct conversion, while only 23 ex-Conservative or Orthodox Jews converted directly. Of the Liturgical Protestants, 51 came directly, while only 26 of the Fundamentalists followed the direct path.

In every case of conversion, at least 18 went through an intermediate period of no organized religion. In the case of the ex-Reform Jews, this rose to 50. These data also show the significant role that Liberal Protestant churches have played in preparing the prospective convert for Unitarian Universalism. Forty-one of the fundamentalists, and the same number of those born in families with no religious affiliation, report an intermediate religious affiliation of Liberal Protestant. These figures suggest an indirect answer to the Unitarian Universalist anxiety that we have mentioned regarding the "half-way house." Whatever may happen to those who cease their UU membership, it is clear that other churches, especially the Liberal Protestant churches, function as half-way houses into the churches of Unitarian Universalism.

TABLE 1.6

Paths of Conversion: The Prior Religion/Family Religion Ratio[a]

Prior religion	Family religion						Conservative/		
	UU	Liberal Protestant	Fundamentalist Protestant	Liturgical Protestant	Catholic	Reform Jewish	Orthodox Jewish	Other	No religion
Unitarian Universalist	.90								
Liberal Protestant		.78	.41	.20				.23	.41
Fundamentalist Protestant			.26						
Liturgical Protestant				.51					
Catholic					.43				
Reform Jewish						.44	.26		
Conservative or Orthodox Jewish							.23		
Other								.33	
No organized religion		.18	.25	.24	.41	.50	.48	.31	.37
Percent	*12*	*28*	*21*	*12*	*6*	*2*	*2*	*5*	*9*

[a]Ratios less than .10 not shown; Nwt = 146,006; respondents from mixed Catholic/non-Catholic (2%) and mixed Jewish/non-Jewish (1%) backgrounds not shown.

SELF-ASCRIPTION—A COMPREHENSIVE UU INDEX

While Chapter 2 will discuss, in detail, general measures of religiosity and specific measures of UU religiosity, we are introducing here the construct of self-ascription which provides a comprehensive measure of Unitarian Universalist religiosity. The prevalence of converts within this denomination, and the apparent meaning of their new religious orientation for these persons, has suggested this conceptualization.

Every individual goes through a set of self-labelings. These can be discovered through the use of "Who am I?" statements, as indicated by a wide social science literature. It is clear that these responses are always made within a particular context. That is to say, the first responses given by a person at his place of employment will probably be related to his vocation, whereas his first responses at a family picnic might turn out to be more familial. Perhaps less obvious is the role that "significant others" play in such responses. These are the reflections of himself that the individual receives from those around him. Thus, "Who are they?" and "How am I related to them?" are auxiliary aspects of the basic Who am I statement. The questionnaire invited a yes/no response to the query "Would you personally define your own religion as Christian?" While most Americans would quite readily respond affirmatively to this, a surprising 58% of the UUs responded negatively. This self-labeling appears to reflect the perceived deviance or marginality of their present religious orientation within the larger American religious context.

An additional form of self-labeling might be termed the "Where am I" statement. Such statements would be especially relevant for persons involved in voluntary associations, serving to particularize the significant others. In other words, these statements would specify the web of group relationships in which a person had become involved. To the extent that alternative relationships were available, these would indeed be voluntary. The UU respondents, for instance, would probably not view their U.S. or Canadian citizenship as a realistically voluntary matter, but certainly would so regard their church membership. One item of the questionnaire further specified the directionality of this denominational affiliation by asking "Which one of the following best describes where you would prefer the U.U.A. to be theologically ten years from now?" Four response-categories were listed. The first two—"closer to liberal Protestantism" and "closer to the ecumenical movement within Christianity"—reflect an organizational directionality toward Christianity. The other two responses—"closer to an emerging Universal religion" and "closer to a distinctive, humanistic religion"—were felt to connote, at least for UUs, an organizational directionality away from Christianity.

The Self-Ascription Index was based on the responses to these two items. This index was ordered from right to left as indicated in Table 1.7. Persons describing themselves as Christians and wanting their denomination to move toward Christianity were given a "Right" designation. Those labeling themselves as not Christian and wanting the denomination to move away from Christianity were designated "Left." Respondents giving a mixed, inconsistent, response to these somewhat parallel items were designated "Center."

TABLE 1.7
The Self-Ascription Index as Ordered from Right to Left[a]

Item: "Which one of the following best describes where you would prefer the U.U.A. to be theologically ten years from now?"	Item: "Would you personally define your own religion as Christian?"		
	Yes	No	Percent
Closer to liberal Protestantism	Right (5.7)[b]	Center (0.6)	6.3
Closer to the ecumenical movement within Christianity	Right (4.5)	Center (0.3)	4.8
Closer to an emerging universal religion	Center (18.4)	Left (18.0)	36.3
Closer to a distinctive, humanistic religion	Center (13.9)	Left (38.7)	52.6
Percent	*42.4*	*57.6*	*100.0*

[a]Nwt - 160,800.

[b]Figures in parentheses are percentages of total weighted sample within each cell.

Some explanation of this ordering and labeling of the Self-Ascription Index is in order since it involved certain terminological peculiarities in Unitarian Universalist usage. With many, or even most, American religious groups, a liberal/conservative continuum would be both useful and acceptable. Most UUs, however, appear to regard the designation liberal as essentially synonomous with their religious position, and employ conservative in designating most other religious groups. Thus, characterizing some group of UUs as conservative might not prove acceptable to them or reflect their own usage. At the time the Unitarians and Universalists merged, there was widespread approval for calling the new denomination "The Liberal Church" or "The United Liberal Church." This would appear to have been dropped in deference to Canadian sensitivities and the realization that the United Liberal Church (in Canada) reflected a merger of denominations that the UUs viewed as conservative. Nevertheless, liberal religion is one of the most frequent self-designations found in UU literature.

Somewhat similar terminological peculiarities led to the two separate "away from Christianity" categories. As indicated in the historical sketch, the UUs for several decades have implied a nontheistic orientation when they spoke of humanism. Many of them were no doubt fully aware that outside of UU circles there existed movements of literary humanism as well as of Christian humanism. More importantly, for purposes of this questionnaire, a number of UUs are exponents of a theistic non-Christian, or more-than-Christian, universal religion. Finally, some of the nontheistic humanists view their religion as universal. Therefore, any single category which combined universal and humanist would have been biasing.

The peculiarities of Unitarian and Universalist history also argued against the use of an orthodox/unorthodox ordering of this index. In their beginnings, both the parent denominations were unorthodox in relation to orthodox Christianity. Since unorthodoxy can only be meaningful in relation to some clearly denoted orthodoxy, it would only be confusing to speak of unorthodoxy within an already unorthodox denomination.

For all of these reasons, we have chosen the neutral right/left/center designation to order the Self-Ascription Index. These designations are readily understandable, and have the additional merit of not being characteristically used by UUs to label themselves. In the case of the "left" UUs, we have already used the somewhat awkward adjective "posttraditional" to describe the initial results of the survey (Tapp, 1967a). This label seemed to give further definition to the clear meaning of Unitarian Universalism for a significant majority of its present membership as a religious movement that was no longer Christian and that was, indeed, moving yet further away from its Christian origins.

This Self-Ascription Index, proposed here as a comprehensive measure of UU religiosity, has several advantages. The items comprising the index are conceptually straightforward and would appear to be semantically stable over the foreseeable future. Thus, replication of research within this denomination is facilitated. In addition, the underlying attitudes and values reflected in the responses would appear to be chronologically indeterminate, thus permitting the index to be used both as an independent and as a dependent variable. In subsequent chapters, we will describe the meanings of self-ascription (treating it as independent variable) and of the sources of self-ascription (treating it as a dependent variable). This alternating usage will minimize the temptation to treat self-ascription as either a cause or effect. In reality, it is probably both, and the immediate task is to see the ways in which it functions. Given the family religious backgrounds of the UUs, for instance, we might decide that since posttraditionality (leftness on self-ascription) appeared at a particular conversion point in each individual's life, any data prior to that point might prove potentially causal. We need to remind ourselves, however, that such an ideological conversion may well have been reflective of underlying attitudes and values present since childhood.

Turning now to the distribution of the Unitarian Universalist population in terms of the Self-Ascription Index, we find that 10% are right and 57% are left. If we contrast the born UUs and the converts, the contrast is far more striking. This information is contained in Table 1.8. It now becomes clear that those who have inherited the "stepfathers' house" are almost equally divided between right, center, and left on self-ascription, whereas the converts are overwhelmingly (60%) posttraditional or left on self-ascription, and only 8% of the converts are presently right-wing. Putting this more directly, twice as many of the convert UUs are posttraditional in contrast to the born UUs.

TABLE 1.8

Self-Ascription as Related to UU Status and Region

Self-Ascription	UU Status (Nwt = 160,800)			Region (Nwt = 93,820)			
	All	Born	Convert	Canada	Pacific	Mid-west	New Eng-land
Right (Percent)	10	31	8	4	4	5	32
Center (Percent)	33	38	33	27	25	30	41
Left (Percent)	57	31	60	70	71	65	27

Table 1.8 also contains information on the variations in self-ascription within the selected regions. It is clear that there is a basic constancy in the frequency of posttraditionality throughout the UU denomination except for New England. We may speak of the saliency of right-wing religiosity among the New England UUs, noting that the New England pattern on self-ascription closely corresponds to the pattern for all of the born UUs.

A final observation may be appropriate here in regard to the effect of the weighting system that has been used on these tables. The system, designed to compensate for differentials in the return rates of the 80 churches as well as for the type-of-church stratification of the sample, is explained in Appendix A. Without the use of weighting, 7.8% of the UUs are right-wing (in contrast to the 10.2% reported on this Table) and 58.4% are left-wing (in contrast to the tabulated 56.7%). Thus, the weighting system produces a very minor ideological correction, reducing posttraditional religiosity by 1% and increasing right-wing religiosity by 2%.

Chapter 2

RELIGIOSITY: THEORETICAL
AND EMPIRICAL APPROACHES

This chapter will explore some contemporary attempts to analyze the complexity of religiosity, and will present analyses of overall Unitarian Universalist religiosity. This will provide a fuller justification for the subsequent use of the Self-Ascription Index as the primary measure of UU religiosity. Before turning to the specific analyses, however, it will be well to review certain philosophical and terminological considerations that are important at this stage in the scientific study of religion.

SOME PHILOSOPHICAL CAUTIONS

The author has a number of biases which will be apparent to close readers, but some of these can be made explicit at the outset. Religion has been one of the most pervasive aspects of man's cultural evolution, at least thus far in human history. No viable culture has persisted without the development of ideas, institutions, elites, valuations, and ways of behaving that must be called religious. In most cultures, these religious systems have been quite central, and attempts to describe those cultures which overlooked or failed to do justice to their religions have been less than satisfactory.

The study of religions, then, does more than simply increment the fund of human knowledge—although that alone would be a sufficient justification.

Knowing about religion may provide a key to a number of aspects of a culture or society: its memories, its dreams, its fears, its anxieties. The study of religion over a span of time may also provide important understandings of mechanisms of stability and innovation.

It is precisely at this point that a major conceptual roadblock appears. The cultural analyst may be able to delineate Religion A, Religion B, and Religion C, but he falters in trying to extract some common essence of Religion-as-such. But if there is no general phenomenon, how can one recognize the specific instances? What do, for instance, Christianity, Buddhism, Shinto, and Confucianism share? Not a belief in a god or gods, not an insistence upon an institution or church, not even an insistence that some morality or ethic should characterize the true believers. Yet such alleged common denominators have appealed to scholars in the past, and many laymen today (as well as dictionary writers) still build such Procrustean beds. Our own linguistic habits may trick us here, and we may keep trying even though our critical intelligence says no. In part, this is because, as twentieth-century men, we cannot seriously deny the right of other men to call themselves religious and therefore cannot deny that their collective behaviors constitute a religion. Thus, we measure without a yardstick. Or, more precisely, we measure with yardsticks known to be culturally-generated and culturally-biased, simply because absolute yardsticks are not available.

This problem is no less acute if we simply look at one religion over some time-period (i.e., Religion C_1, C_2, C_3...). Is Christianity possible without the Biblical view of creation? Scholars may note that the first two chapters of Genesis embody two quite incompatible accounts, but theologians, preachers, and believers have usually defended something which they took to be the Biblical view against a variety of heresies and unbeliefs. Certainly an overwhelming majority of Christians in 1859 would have felt that one had to choose between the faith and Darwin. In an earlier age, Copernicus had posed what was felt to be a similar dilemma. Yet the clear fact today is that most Christians have so accommodated to evolution and heliocentric planetary motion that they have repressed their memory of erstwhile defenders of the faith.

If Western religions (and we must certainly include Judaism here) could assimilate Copernicus and Darwin, can we be sure that they will necessarily boggle at Marx, Freud, or the man-like machine, or even the "death of God"? The point here is basically quite simple, but also quite painful, and we therefore evade it by a number of devices. Change is a characteristic of the human condition, indeed of the whole physical-chemical environment in which we live (or, more precisely, which lives in us). Threatened and confused by change, we render it more manageable by ordering, labeling, and judging it. Some processes are evolutionary, some devolutionary. Some are progressive, some reactionary. Some are developmental and others retrogressive. Judgments like these turn out to be very much a function of where we have chosen to stand. For the man who identifies with religion C_7, religion C_8 appears to be secularization. For the man at C_8, $C_1 \ldots C_7$ appear to be fossilized orthodoxies. This is a way of schematizing the familiar religious dialectic of liberalism and orthodoxy.

Even more tantalizing is the question: "Once a C, always a C?" That is, are some changes so deviant that we no longer have a variant but a mutant, a new species? The answer to this must be yes, or we will have to insist that all religions are simply derivations from some primal unity. The biological metaphor may be suggestive but it raises broader problems when applied culturally. We can perhaps recognize extreme variations when they appear, but we can never know in advance their viability, their adaptability, their survival power. George G. Simpson has argued that modern evolutionary biology has a "postdictive" rather than predictive wisdom (1964). At a given point in time, one can only look backward and note which forms have survived. That, after all, is the biological meaning of adaptation—survival through the reproductive stage. This is clearly postdiction. No biological wisdom permits certainty today as to which present species will make it into tomorrow.

The stuff of human history, then, is a constantly changing environment (physical, but preeminently cultural) in which changing forms, some random and some planned, jostle for niches in which to survive. The fact that this constantly varying population is a major part of the environment would, by itself, make prediction as to viable and unviable forms impossible.

Given this perspective, the intriguing form of any religion is always its present form. About its future, we can only guess, although there is a process of critical extrapolation which is much more reliable than the free play of random hunches. The difficulty enters when we realize that there can be no understanding of the present of any religion without an understanding of its past. This is difficult because almost all of us confuse the past as we remember it with the real past. Our whole enculturation as humans has conspired to do this. As we become aware of the confusion, we label and try to find ways of uncovering the "real" past—scientific, objective, transubjective, universal, absolute. The valid reminder of the existentialists is, of course, that it is always some particular self that creates these perspectives and that the personal dimension can therefore never be fully escaped. The positivistic rejoinder is that there is still a vast difference between naive subjectivity and broader, more critical, perspectives.

Within a particular system, this is the struggle between traditionalism and historicism. Americans, for instance, have received the memory of Lincoln as the great emancipator. Historicist reconstruction reveals his racism, however, and sharply qualifies the traditional past. So is the past-as-remembered transformed. In similar fashion, it took almost nineteen centuries for critical scholarship to achieve the freedom, imagination, and source mastery to show that primitive Christianity had been dominated by an expectation of an imminent world-end. The depths at which these beginnings had been hidden reveals the power of traditionalism to reconstruct the remembered past in keeping with the desire of the present.

Looking at this process the other way, the present of any religion tells us much about that religion as we watch it deal with its (remembered) past. What it chooses to retain, what it forgets, what it distorts, what it revives—are all key clues for understanding and explanation. Assuming the general correctness of the constant environmental change described above, every viable religion is involved in this kind of adaptation, and claims that some structure has been once and for all revealed should only make us look more closely for the footnotes that reflect an inevitable revisionism of the memory.

THE DENOMINATION AS AMBIGUITY

Moving from the preceding level of generalization to the level of empirical studies of religion in America moves us directly into the ambiguous status of the denomination. At first glance, this institution is a clearly definable legal organization. Under closer scrutiny, however, some of this clarity recedes. There have, for instance, in American history, been several branches of Lutheranism which have been distinguishable only by the ethnicities of their members. Should each of these sociological institutions have been regarded as a denomination or should a hypothetical, informal, composite Lutheran denomination have been employed as a construct?

Even more confusion has resulted from the attempts to employ the Max Weber/Ernst Troeltsch typological distinction between church and sect. Admittedly, these were ideal types, but they were also most relevant for the European situations in which a state church existed and alternative kinds of religiousness emerged in contradistinction. The contrast between the church with its large and nominal membership and the sect with its small, rigorously committed membership throws little light upon the nature of the denomination in America. Some of the very small denominations are quite church-like, and some of the large denominations remain sect-like.

The issue of inclusiveness or exclusiveness of denominational membership is only loosely related to the varied political patterns of American denominations. Some are structured along very centralized patterns while others are simply loose associations of essentially autonomous local churches. Further confusions emerge if we try to group denominations in meaningful ways in relation to their belief structures or ritualistic patterns. The confusion becomes complete when we try to group a large set of denominations as "Protestant," or to designate the tremendously varied agglomeration of Roman Catholicism as a denomination. Given these difficulties, what meaning could possibly be attributed to such a super-conglomeration as Christianity or Judaism? If we designate such large groupings as religions or traditions, the implication is that all the groups in the set have more in common with each other than with groups in some other religious set, and this is patently untrue.

In view of these many difficulties, we shall here follow the simple expedient of ordinary language and regard a denomination as neither more nor less than an institution legitimated by law and by the designation of insiders and outsiders. We shall be hesitant, without far more evidence than is now at hand, to assume that every Protestant denomination is a species-member of a Protestant genus or a Christian familia.

The present study is therefore a denominational study of adult members of the Unitarian Universalist Association in the United States and Canada. Judged by a number of external indicators, these individuals are by no means typical of the broader American society, either United States or Canadian. In education, income, occupational status—the traditional measures of social class—they clearly stand at the upper end of the curve. To be sure, we could justify a detailed examination of any religious group simply on the grounds that, like Mt. Everest, it is there. If the group is, in addition, an influential group, or, as may be the case with the Unitarian Universalists, a group that in many ways embodies trends that are bound to become more dominant within a culture, then there is an added justification for closer examination.

If facts such as income, education, and social status represent the externals, an individual's religion may well represent the internal. If we come to know something about a person's religion, we know a good deal about the ways in which he organizes his values, gives meaning to certain ideas and feelings, and assesses his place in society and even in cosmic history. Saying this does not imply that only religious people have such concerns. Surely there is an internal dimension to every individual. It only means that there may be some merit in looking closely at the shared internal dimensions of the group of persons who cluster about some religious movement at some point in history.

Furthermore, the high percentage of converts found within Unitarian Universalism makes them unique among the religious groups of America. They may for this very reason afford us what the biologist might call a pure strain of a species. Most studies have indicated that religious mobility is on the increase in our society. Recent figures on church attendance have shown a decline, which represents a kind of out-mobility. Studies of religious intermarriage indicate an increase, and this could be seen as a form of transmobility. In earlier, more settled periods of religious life in America, the psychologists of religion such as Coe, Leuba, and Starbuck focused upon the religion of the adolescent, contending that this was the period when religiosity was most intense. This is probably true for those who remain within the religious group of their childhood. For converts, it is more likely that the period of intense religiosity comes during the period of conversion. At a later point, we will argue that the UUs have gone through a period of latent religiosity, referring to that interval between their alienation from their childhood religiosity and their affiliation with a group reflecting their new, second religiosity.

It is just because the UUs have come to their present position from more traditional forms of religiosity that we need, as a background for our more intensive study of UU religiosity, to examine in detail what has been discovered about more traditional religiosity.

SOME TERMINOLOGICAL ISSUES

In addition to the ambiguities just discussed, current studies of religion employ a bewildering variety of terminologies, often conveying unwarranted implications of methodological sophistication in conceptual precision where these are not in fact present. In referring to the data in this study, we shall employ the following conventions: An "item" refers to a specific questionnaire item and a "category" is the particular response that an individual makes to an item. We will infer behavior and attitudes from such responses, although in the strictest sense these responses are not themselves religious behaviors or religious attitudes but, rather, much more restricted kinds of verbal behavior or behavior with a pencil. In many cases, the response-categories are arranged in Likert-type patterns. When such an ordering of responses is possible, we shall treat and sometimes refer to items as "variables." When two or more variables are combined and alleged to reflect some complex attitude or behavior, we shall typically speak of an "index."

When dealing with the statistical results of factor analyses, we shall speak of "factors." And, finally, on the highest level of generality, whether based upon statistical factors or not, we shall speak of "dimensions" of this particular kind of religiosity. It is hoped that the possible repetitiveness and artificiality of such a vocabulary will be justified by the conceptual precisions that it facilitates. In reporting the findings of authors whose terminology differs from these conventions, rather than attempt to translate, we will put such terminology in quotation marks, and, when alternative terminologies are on occasion used to facilitate comparison of the UU data to other findings, we will indicate this deviant usage by quotation marks.

MULTIDENOMINATIONAL CONSTRUCTS AND APPROACHES

Quantitative Empirical Studies

A major landmark in the study of religiosity was Gerhard Lenski's Detroit study in 1958 (see, especially, his revised edition, 1963). Focusing upon two presumed kinds of religious orientation, Lenski was surprised to find that doctrinal orthodoxy and devotionalism were only weakly related. Lenski's sample was relatively small, and most of his generalizations are based upon comparisons of Protestant, Catholic, and Jewish responses. His main concern, actually, was not in analyzing religiosity as such but, rather, in assessing the influence of what Max Weber had called "the Protestant ethic"—the blending of a commitment to work and a number of forms of individualism. In the Detroit sample, a religious factor was indeed found and it operated in the expected ways: Protestants and Jews expressing positive attitudes toward work whereas Catholics were negative. Our concern here, however, is with his stress upon the "necessity for differentiating between the various elements of what is so often subsumed under the single heading, 'religiosity.' "

A multidimensional model has been proposed by Charles Glock (1960), hypothesizing five "core dimensions." Glock and Stark (1965) used a parallel labeling system for this model to build a bridge between conventional usage and research language:

> Religious Belief (The Ideological Dimension)
> Religious Practice (The Ritualistic Dimension)
> Religious Feeling (The Experiential Dimension)
> Religious Knowledge (The Intellectual Dimension)
> Religious Effects (The Consequential Dimension)

Questions exploring these dimensions were included in a sample of Northern California church members and a national sample of adult Americans. The two samples are described in Glock and Stark (1965) and some comparative analyses are presented in Stark and Glock (1968).

In their most recent work, these authors describe the operationalization of the first four hypothesized dimensions. Admittedly proceeding in analytic rather than empirical fashion, they developed seven indices to serve as primary and secondary measurements of the dimensions. In correlations on these seven measures, plus two additional measures of church involvement and intrachurch friendships, they are reported separately for Protestants and Catholics, using Pearson's *r*. In a footnote, the authors indicate that the pattern of correlations within each denomination was similar to the overall Protestant pattern.

From this empirical analysis, the authors conclude that the "best single measure" of religious commitment is their "orthodoxy" index. Nevertheless, it must be noted that the average intercorrelation of orthodoxy with all the other indices is .382 among Protestants and .272 among Roman Catholics. By any current standards, these are relatively low figures. The average of all correlations was .272 for the Protestants and .2 for Catholics. The authors draw a number of conclusions from this data, but for our purposes the most significant conclusion is the clear multidimensionality of religiosity that has been established. In addition to this finding, we must note that the "consequential dimension" of religious "effects" was not operationalized or included in the empirical analysis. An "ethicalism index" based upon the importance of doing good and loving the neighbor (which would appear to be consequences of religiosity) was employed as a secondary measure of the "belief dimension" and found to have the lowest correlation with the other indices. In fact, among the Protestants it was negatively correlated to orthodoxy.

A somewhat different approach to the problem of dimensionality was made by Glock in his analysis of the Episcopalians (Glock, Ringer, and Babbie, 1967). The data for this study had been collected in 1952. At that time, no questions on belief were included since the denominational sponsors had felt that this might "offend respondents." In their analysis, the authors developed the concept of involvement, measuring this in its ritual, organizational, and intellectual aspects. Women were more involved than men, and this involvement varied through the lifecycle, reaching its lowest level in the early years of marriage. The involvement of men followed a somewhat similar U-shaped curve, but did not move up as rapidly in the later years, indicating a "growing divergence between men and women." The authors also examined the church as "a family surrogate" and as related to social status. They concluded that "the church may serve as an alternative gratification for those deprived of social status just as it serves those deprived of family ties."

An approach to the previously hypothesized "consequential" dimension was made through a "political permissiveness" index based upon respondents' willingness to have the church become involved in social and political affairs. This was found to be unrelated to the index of involvement, thus confirming a "comfort" hypothesis regarding the role of the church. A positive relationship between involvement and permissiveness would have confirmed a "church" hypothesis and a negative relationship would have pointed to a "Marxian" hypothesis. Measures of the belief in religious and denominational efficacy were also developed which were found to be strongly related to involvement but unrelated to specific social attitudes. The authors conclude that this data yields further confirmation of the multidimensionality of religious commitment.

During 1964-1965, a national survey was undertaken of members of the United Church of Christ, which merged the Congregational Christian and Evangelical Reformed denominations. The first report of these findings was made by Yoshio Fukuyama (1966), comparing subsamples of Great Plains and metropolitan respondents. This analysis explored an earlier four-dimensional model of religiosity: intellectual, institutional, doctrinal, and devotional. It may be noted that Glock credits Fukuyama with having originally suggested that "intellectual" dimension. A "Social Acceptance" index was created from responses to a Social Distance scale. Comparing this to belief items, Fukuyama found a negative relationship and concluded that "the more accepting an individual is of traditional Christian beliefs, the less accepting he is of Negroes in his social relationships." Social acceptance was, however, found to be positively correlated to measures of "religious knowledge," "devotionalism," and "frequency of church attendance." It was also found to decrease with age and length of church membership. This study also found that social acceptance increased with education, occupational status, and income.

Analysis of the overall sample has now been published (Campbell & Fukuyama, 1970). This fuller analysis follows a somewhat different analytical schema. "Religious orientation" is treated as an "intervening variable" between social factors and "consequential social attitudes." The authors now view religious orientation or "church participation" as a composite of "organizational involvement," "religious knowledge," "devotional orientation," and "belief orientation." Thus the "experiential dimension" has been replaced by a measure of "organizational involvement," and the putative "consequential dimension" has been separated from the religiosity syndrome. We may note that Glock has not yet reported the full operationalization of all of his dimensions, and that only one small-scale study exists suggesting their relative independence (Faulkner & DeJong, 1966).

Campbell and Fukuyama, contending that their four indices of church participation measure various styles, found that the six possible interrelations were all positive. On the basis of chi-square computations, these relationships were listed, beginning with the highest correlation:

1. Belief Orientation and Devotional Orientation
2. Organizational Involvement and Religious Knowledge
3. Organizational Involvement and Devotional Orientation
4. Religious Knowledge and Devotional Orientation
5. Organizational Involvement and Belief Orientation
6. Religious Knowledge and Belief Orientation

At several places in their study, the authors express their distrust with complex statistical manipulations of qualitative data at the present stage of the sociology of religion, and the above ranking is therefore justified by percentaged contingency tables (data for the highest and lowest pairings are presented).

The authors then proceed to explore the impact of social factors upon these various styles of church participation to see if these are related to conditions of "social privilege" and "social deprivation." On the variables of age, sex, education, socioeconomic status, and rural-urban differences, the most privileged are also the most involved. This pattern is only reversed in relation to race and former denomination. The Index of Belief Orientation was even more strongly related to the social factors in a way to support the deprivation hypothesis. Traditional beliefs are stronger among the older respondents, the females, the less educated, the poor, and the rural. A similar pattern was found with the index of Devotional Orientation. In the case of the index of Religious Knowledge, the relationships were more ambiguous, and no clear pattern emerged.

Campbell and Fukuyama conclude that their indices represent four different modes of religious orientation, and that "people of privilege prefer organizational religion" and "people of deprivation find devotional and traditional beliefs more helpful." Having established this relationship, they turn to their information on a number of questions of public policy, and particularly attitudes toward the racial crisis. Recognizing that the treatment of these variables as "consequential" may imply an unwarranted causality, their strategy of analysis here, as we have already indicated, is to discover whether social factors are sufficient to account for the attitude items. To test this, they treat the four styles of church participation as intervening--variables. In the white American population, for instance, racism has been found more strongly associated with deprivation than with privilege, and the same distribution was found in the United Church of Christ respondents. Relationships of the four participation indices to racism were then examined in terms of the already established patterns that they had in respect to privilege/deprivation. Organizational Involvement and Religious Knowledge related negatively to racism (as expected) and Belief Orientation related positively to racism (as expected). Devotional Orientation, however, related negatively to racism despite the fact that it had been found to be a measure of deprivation rather than privilege. The authors then examined these patterns as related to the social factor by holding each of the latter constant. Finding the pattern in most cases unaffected, they conclude that the style of church participation "appears to have an influence upon racial attitudes independent of the influence of the socially conditioning factors related to church participation." Above all, this is true in the case of devotional orientation.

Similar procedures were followed with a wide number of "public policy" items and with items relating to "individual conscience" and "collective social responsibility." Summarizing these results, Campbell and Fukuyama regard Organizational Involvement and Religious Knowledge as styles of church participation that reinforce the respondent's position in the social order. Belief Orientation, contrary to the findings of other studies, is not found to have a consistent role; and with Devotional Orientation, some items even reverse the expected orientation.

Jeffrey Hadden conducted a mail survey of ministers of six Protestant denominations (1969). Respondents were asked to characterize their own theological position (fundamentalist, conservative, neoorthodox, or liberal). He also developed a Biblical Ritualism Index from six doctrinal statements. These two measures were found to be closely correlated, and he found that theological conservatism and political conservatism (as evidenced by a Republican Party preference) were strongly correlated. The clergy reversed the tendency within the general population where Republicanism is positively related to social status. The higher the status of the congregation, the less likely for the minister to be a Republican. Hadden explains this in terms of the higher educational levels demanded of clergy by higher-status congregations, and the fact that the higher-status seminaries in America have been "centers of liberal theology and progressive political thought."

A further refinement of the religiosity model has been suggested by N. J. Demerath, III, who made a secondary analysis of questionnaire data from urban congregations in five Protestant denominations (1965). Demerath's study typically focuses upon the Lutherans as representing a central position within this five-denominational spectrum. A more descriptive, less analytical, write-up of this Lutheran data may be found in Kloetzli (1961).

Reviewing the literature on class and religion in America, Demerath notes that, at least among Protestants, church attendance and membership have tended to increase as class status increases. Thus, the measures of religiosity in conventional use may be of dubious value in dealing with low-status religiosity. While basically accepting Glock's four-dimensional schema, he suggests that it should be modified in view of church-sect theory. Ideologically, the church-type person will derive more of his orientation from secular values and goals whereas the sect-type person will use traditional beliefs as a screen through which values and goals must pass. Experientially, the sect-type will stress the spontaneous rather than the ritualistic. Consequentially, sectarian religiosity will lead the believer away from the secular world rather than toward it. Finally, on the behavioral dimension, the sect will place less stress upon ritual and regular church attendance, and more stress upon intimate, small groups and upon private devotions. In effect, Demerath has created eight dimensions of religiosity if we are to understand a dimension as some measurable variable upon which an individual may have a high or low score. Within this model, the pure sect-type person, if his religiosity were unidimensional, would be expected to have high scores upon four of the dimensions and low scores upon the remainder. Sunday attendance, parish activity, and organizational involvement outside the church are measures of church-like behavior. Friendships in the church, viewing religion as an aid and reward, and preferring a minimal role for the minister in public affairs provide an index of sect-type religiosity. Persons with high scores on both of these indices are termed "totally involved" and those with low scores on both are given Joseph Fichter's label "dormant parishioners." The two middle groups, with score reversals on the two indices, are regarded as "pure church" and "pure sect" types. This subdifferentiation also correlated with high and low economic status (measured by education, occupational prestige, and income data on the Lutherans). Further elaboration showed this relationship to be unaffected by subjective class estimates, age, and sex.

Demerath then proceeded to a contextual analysis of individual parishes. Within each of the four class categories differentiating individuals, the frequency of church-like religiosity was found to be higher within high-status parishes than low-status ones. This was confirmed by a reverse pattern in frequency of sect-like religiosity. In this regard, Demerath found parallels to this Lutheran pattern among his Congregationalists, Presbyterians, Disciples of Christ, and Baptists. With regard to denominational differences, he discovered that different rank orderings resulted from scales of status and church-like commitment, whereas in the case of sect-like commitment there was an almost complete isotropism.

The final large-scale denominational study to be noted was made of the United Presbyterian Church in the U.S.A. (Whitman, Keating, & Matthews, 1966). The primary focus of this study was to assess, after twelve years of use, a new curriculum in religious education. A conceptual structure regarding communication variables was developed, including social context, social role, skill, motivation, and belief. While the analyses reported thus far discuss some of the interrelations of these variables, the primary concern was with "How well is the message getting across?" In the course of these discussions, it became clear that there are significant differences within these subgroups in regard to "orthodoxy" (here defined as agreement with the curricular thesis, but not basically dissimilar to items used by other investigators of belief). The clergy were the most orthodox, and the young people least so. The study also found the orthodoxy and devotionalism were not significantly related. While some measures of social value were included in the questionnaire, the published material does not yet include analysis of these in relation to belief systems. Very slight relationships were found between belief systems and education and social class.

The various studies discussed thus far tell us many things about American religious groups, some things about ways in which their religiosity may be described, but relatively little about the composite nature of religiosity itself. These studies also indicate the dominant role played by the several multidimensionality models proposed by Charles Glock. This multidimensionality has either been assumed in these studies, or in some cases has been confirmed, although by relatively limited analyses.

As a somewhat complementary approach, let us examine an application of factor analysis to the problem of religiosity. In theory, this provides us with a statistical technique to reduce some large number of correlated variables to a smaller number of uncorrelated variables. Factor analysis is presumably a blind empirical technique to elicit constructs from data rather than imposing them. Quite obviously, techniques of this kind are limited by the scope and quality of the data. Unless information on a suspected factor is present in the raw data, it can never emerge in any statistical manipulation of that data. Reviewing the literature and questionnaires that had been used in religious studies, Morton King found eleven different dimensions in common usage (1967). Using items felt .to represent each of these dimensions, questionnaire responses were obtained from members of six Methodist churches in Texas. Factor analysis, and a subsequent cluster analysis, yielded a nine-dimensional model. The application of item-scale analysis later expanded this to an eleven-dimensional model (King & Hunt, 1969). These two models are reproduced below, with roman numerals indicating the first version and arabic numerals designating the current version:

I. Creedal Assent and Personal Commitment
   1. Creedal Assent

II. Participation in Congregational Activities
   2. Church Attendance
   3. Organizational Activities

III. Personal Religious Experience
   4. Personal Religious Experience

IV. Personal Ties in the Congregation
   5. Church Work with Friends

V. Commitment to Intellectual Search Despite Doubt

VI. Openness to Religious Growth
   6. Orientation to Religious Growth and Striving

VIIa. Dogmatism
   7. Orientation to Religious Security or Dogmatism

VIIb. Extrinsic Orientation
   8. Extrinsic Orientation

VIIIa. Financial Behavior
   9. Financial Support

VIIIb. Financial Attitude

IX. Talking and Reading about Religion
   10. Talking and Reading about Religion
   11. Religious Knowledge

The authors note that their new scales 7, 8, and 9 are border-line, and should be used cautiously "until better defined, or abandoned." A revised version of this new questionnaire has been used with members of four Protestant denominations: a new Methodist sample, Disciples of Christ, Presbyterians (U.S.), and Lutherans (Missouri Synod). King states that these findings agree closely with their earlier ones, and that "the scales derived separately for each denomination are similar, but not identical [private communication]." The authors' original intention was to provide means of measuring the various dimensions of religiosity when such dimensions had been derived by empirical procedures with actual religious denominations. They tried to minimize the parochial content in order to produce an instrument that could not only be used in studying different denominations but could even be used with other than Protestant or Christian religious groups.

The preceding summary of approaches to the dimensionality issue has been included here as a background to the analysis of UU religiosity. More comprehensive and detailed surveys of this literature have been made by James Dittes (1969, 1971) and Bernard Spilka (1971). We must note, however, that neither the correlational examination of hypothesized dimensions (characterized by Glock's researches) nor the extraction of dimensions by factor analysis directly resolves the unidimensionality/multidimensionality issue. Either of these approaches may fail to include sufficient input data. King, for instance, has not included items of personal and social morality. In such cases, important relationships remain unexamined.

The absence of clear statistical criteria also raises problems. Glock, for instance, decided to view any two dimensions as distinct unless their correlation produced a 50% proportional reduction of error. Since this is estimated by squaring Pearson's r, and none of his dimensions met this criteria, he viewed all of them as distinct. There are, nevertheless, problems in the use of r with qualitative data and, as indicated in Appendix A, the analysis of UU religiosity in this book will use Kruskal and Goodman's gamma, which also serves directly as a measure of the proportional reduction of error. In the case of factor analysis, apart from the general controversies revolving around the use of various rotational techniques to clarify factor structures, there remains the central commonplace that factors are an artifact of factor analysis. Each successive orthogonal factor is constructed to maximize the reduction of the residual variance. Thus we might give the same questionnaire items to two different groups, find that the first three factors counted for, say, 75% of the variance, and still discover that the item-loadings on these factors so differed that the actual qualities of the factors differentiated the groups. In other words, factor analysis helps build models but does not give direct tests of any single model across groups. After considerably more testing, it may turn out that the use of oblique rotational techniques to clarify factor structures will prove more useful in building religiosity models which are regarded as quasidimensional rather than either clearly unidimensional or multidimensional.

UNITARIAN UNIVERSALIST RELIGIOSITY

Some Conventional "Dimensionalities"

We have just described in some detail the general configurations of more traditionally religious groups in America and some of the conceptual techniques that have proved fruitful in studying such groups. In the discussion of the Self-Ascription Index in Chapter 1, we noted the prevalence of posttraditional religiosity among Unitarian Universalists. To what extent can concepts used to study more traditional religious groups be applied to the UU groups, placing it within the larger context of American religions? Such general considerations were present in the earliest stages of this research. Thus, some of the items finally used in the questionnaire are identical to those used in previous survey research, others resemble those used by other investigators with an expansion of the response-categories, and some were clearly designed for this particular population and would have little or no applicability to more traditional groups.

Items in the questionnaire had been designed to permit operationalization of several "dimensions" in use at that time. In the initial analysis which we will now present, the relations of three of these dimensions and two specifically UU dimensions were examined.

The Belief "Dimension"

Measured by an item on theism, this somewhat parallels other investigators' measurement of orthodoxy or creedalism. Responses to this God question are displayed in Table 2.1. This question received more care in the design and pretesting stages than any other question used. The intent was to produce a set of response categories that would be ordered along an unarguably conservative–liberal continuum, that would appear mutually exclusive to most respondents, that would be equally free of biasing terminology, and that would differentiate or distribute this particular population in a reasonably normal way.

TABLE 2.1

Unitarian Universalist Responses to the Theism Item[a]

Item: "Which one of the following statements comes closest to expressing your beliefs about God?"	Percent
" 'God' is a supernatural being who reveals himself in human experience and history"	2.9
" 'God' is the ground of all being, real but not adequately describable"	23.1
" 'God' may appropriately be used as a name for some natural processes within the universe, such as love or creative evolution"	44.2
" 'God' is an irrelevant concept, and the central focus of religion should be on man's knowledge and values"	28.0
" 'God' is a concept that is harmful to a worthwhile religion"	1.8
Percent	100.0

[a]Nwt = 166,257.

The Behavior "Dimension"

While recognizing that religious behavior may have both public and private aspects, a Ritualism Index was constructed from the combination of two items felt to reflect the separate aspects—an item on the frequency of prayer (the private side of ritualism) and an item on the importance of a group experience of worship during the Sunday service (the public side of ritualism). The joint distribution of responses on these two items, and the right-to-left coding system used to order the index, is presented in Table 2.2. It may be noted that this index also distributed this particular religious denomination in a reasonably normal curve.

TABLE 2.2
The Ritualism Index as Ordered from Right to Left[a]

	Item: "How important to you are the following aspects of attending church service: Group experience of participation and worship?"			
	Very important	Somewhat important	Not important	Percent
Item: "How frequently do you pray?"				
Often	RR (5.7)[b]	R (4.0)	C (1.6)	11.3
Occasionally	R (7.7)	C (11.6)	C (5.1)	24.3
Seldom	C (5.6)	C (13.6)	L (8.8)	27.9
Never	C (5.1)	L (14.2)	LL (17.2)	36.5
Percent	*24.0*	*43.3*	*32.7*	*100.0*

[a]Nwt = 162,419.

[b]Figures in parentheses are percentages of total weighted sample within each cell.

The Church Activity "Dimension"

Some measure of church activity has become a standard analytical tool in studying religiosity, and it seemed important to include such information. While the frequency of church attendance has been used for such a measure in many studies, this particular ritual behavior did not seem to be viewed by UUs as efficacious or mandatory (many of their churches, for instance, close for the summer). There is certainly nothing within the UU pattern comparable to attendance at Mass or obligatory confessions for Roman Catholics, for instance. During the pre-testing stage of the questionnaire, items attempting to measure membership and office-holding within church organizations were discarded, as were items measuring denominational, regional, or district involvement. For these reasons, this dimension is operationalized by the direct estimates of church activity as indicated in Table 2.3. Granting the subjective bias of such self-estimates, the variation in organizational patterns and institutional expectations of the UU group seemed to make it the best available measure of intrachurch activity.

The Self-Ascription "Dimension"

Some of the reasons for the creation of a Self-Ascription Index were discussed in the last chapter in connection with Table 1.6. It is clear that in dealing with UUs, we are dealing with religiously marginal persons who see their own religion as different from the religion of the vast majority of their neighbors. On a number of occasions, denominational literature has described this movement as a fourth faith evolving out of, but distinct from, Judaism, Catholicism, and Protestantism. It therefore seemed important to describe and analyze the meanings of the UUs' sense of being "differently religious," a term first used by Dorothy Spoerl to describe UU youth (1961). This need was further confirmed by the fact that 59% of the UUs did not define their own local church as Christian and that 56% did not feel that others in their community would generally regard that church as Christian.

Despite the apparent usefulness of a belief dimension in differentiating most religious groups, it seemed possible that such a cognitively-based measure would prove less than adequate with Unitarian Universalists. It has almost become a commonplace among observers of the religious scene that the meaning of religion is increasingly a matter of life-style rather than of belief. To the extent that life-style may be indicated by the labels that a person is willing to accept for himself and the organizations with which he is willing to relate, the Self-Ascription Index should measure this.

TABLE 2.3
The Church Activity Item[a]

Item: "How active has your participation generally been in your local church?"	Percent
Very active	21.6
Moderately active	39.5
Slightly active	29.2
Inactive	9.6
Percent	99.9

[a]Nwt=167,165.

The Moral Privatism "Dimension"

In the historical development of liberal Protestantism in America, two somewhat paradoxical elements emerged. On the one hand, the impact of the "social gospel" transformed the social problems of the culture into the central concerns of the church, on the grounds that religion must be relevant. On the other hand, the stress upon individual freedom of conscience that has characterized the rise of democracy has increasingly privatized moral matters. An index to measure this paradoxical juxtaposition was constructed from responses to items on nonviolent civil disobedience and on the justifiability of sexual intercourse between unmarried persons, as indicated in Table 2.4. This index has also been ordered from right-to-left.

TABLE 2.4
The Moral Privatism Index as Ordered from Right to Left[a]

| Item: "Sexual intercourse between unmarried persons" | Item: "Which of these statements comes closest to your feelings about nonviolent civil disobedience?" | | | |
	Disapprove under any circumstances	Approve when laws are unjust	Other	Percent
Is never justifiable	R (10.3)[b]	C (7.8)	(1.1)[c]	19.2
Is justifiable for engaged couples	C (1.5)	C (3.7)	(0.6)[c]	5.9
Is justifiable if there is mutual affection	C (3.5)	C (13.3)	(1.5)[c]	18.3
Should be left to free choice	C (12.4)	L (37.6)	(6.0)[c]	56.0
Should be encouraged	(0.1)[c]	(0.4)[c]	(0.1)[c]	0.6
Percent	*27.9*	*62.7*	*9.4*	*100.00*

[a] Nwt = 159,281.

[b] Figures in parentheses are percentages of total weighted sample within each cell.

[c] These cells excluded from ordering procedure.

While a number of other dimensions of religiosity have been suggested in the literature, operationalizations and empirical tests have typically been confined to indices paralleling the first three that were constructed here—belief, ritualism, and church activity. It seemed even less possible, with Unitarian Universalists, to hypothesize a "religious knowledge" dimension. There was, for instance, an absence of agreed-upon instructional materials. Tests of biblical knowledge or knowledge of church history seemed irrelevant since these are no longer accorded any special place by many UU groups. Several items about Jesus were included in the questionnaire in order to estimate exposure to historical critical studies, but these seemed inappropriate as measures of religious knowledge in the sense that previous investigators had used the term. The "don't know" responses on them had very high frequency and also cut completely across any conservative/liberal breakdowns. Therefore, the first analyses of posttraditional religiosity were based upon the five dimensions just described (Tapp, 1967). The matrix of association between the five dimensions first used to explore Unitarian Universalist religiosity is presented in Table 2.5. Within this group, Self-Ascription is the most comprehensive measure, and is closely associated with Belief and Ritualism and strongly associated with Moral Privatism. Belief is also strongly associated with Ritualism and shows a lesser association with Moral Privatism. It will be noted that Church Activity shows only a slight relationship with Ritualism and almost no relationship with the other measures.

TABLE 2.5
Association of Five "Dimensions" by Gamma

Dimension	Dimension				
	B	R	CA	SA	MP
Belief (B)	1.00	.59	−.01	.59	.37
Ritualism (R)		1.00	.15	.51	.31
Church activity (CA)			1.00	−.04	−.02
Self-Ascription (SA)				1.00	.49
Moral Privatism (MP)					1.00

Insofar as these findings can be compared to studies with more traditional religious groups already reported, the most striking aspect of the Unitarian Universalists is the close relationship between Belief and Ritualism. If we were to employ the 50% proportional reduction of error criterion suggested by Stark and Glock, we would conclude that Belief, Self-Ascription, and Ritualism measure one rather than three dimensions.

A Factor Analytic Approach

While the foregoing analysis permits some comparisons between mainstream and UU religiosity, and while it permits certain inferences regarding relative multidimensionality, it may suffer from the same intuitive limitations that have plagued previous studies. Until we know more of the taxonomy of religions, we will be better advised to continue the present methodological vacillation, sometimes approaching a group as if it were a subspecies of a known genus and sometimes approaching it as if it were a totally unknown and therefore not yet classified organism.

As an alternative analysis, therefore, forty-five items were selected from the available data for factor analysis. Earlier examinations had suggested that these items reflected a variety of religious beliefs and values, personal and social beliefs and values, and institutional attitudes and expectations. Demographic items were excluded. While none of the response-scales were collapsed, responses such as "other" or "don't know" were excluded to preserve the meaningful ordering of the categories. The items selected are reproduced in Appendix C, where these modifications have been noted.

For computational simplification as well as to permit subsequent ecological examination of individual church milieux, each of the 80 churches entered the factor analysis as an individual. Successive integers were assigned to the ordered categories of each response-scale, and the mean score for each church on each item was subjected to a principal components factor analysis.*

For each of the first ten factors of the initial principal components analysis, there was at least one item loading that factor greater than .35. The first factor accounted for 36% of the variance, and the first ten factors accounted for 83% of the variance. To clarify the relationship between these factors, and in view of the present lack of consensus on the desirability of the rotation of factor loadings (cf. Humphreys, 1968), the initial loadings were orthogonally rotated, by item, using varimax, biquartimax, and quartimax procedures. The ten new factors extracted by varimax as well as by biquartimax rotation received the highest loadings from the corresponding ten initial factors. On the quartimax rotation, the ordering of initial Factors VIII and V were interchanged. Closer analysis by item indicated that not only had the rotated factors received similar loading by the initial factors, but that the individual items with high loadings retained those loadings upon the rotated factors. The varimax rotation seemed to produce the greatest clarification of item loadings, and subsequent discussion will be based upon this technique.

Each of these ten factors obtained by varimax rotation contained at least one item with a loading of .72 or higher. On this criterion, the ten factors accounted for 39 of the original 45 items. There was a discernible coherence in the content of items in the seven factors with multiple items above this criterion level. For these 39 items, it can be noted that the rotation procedure did not shift any items from those factors where they had loaded highest in the principal components analysis initially performed.

When each of the total 45 items was assigned to the factor where the highest loading occurred as the result of rotation, the basic coherence of the factors was retained, and the minimum loading by an item was .52.

In the presentation of these results in Table 2.6, certain conventions have been used. Within each factor, items are listed in the order of their loading of that factor. The content of an item has been paraphrased to indicate the overall direction of Unitarian Universalist response (as an example, item 1—the God question—is here paraphrased as "nontheism"). In the column containing the loadings of each item on the factor, the + and − signs have been omitted. In the actual computation, such signs show the direction of response and, since linearity within each item has been assumed, the point of interest lies in whether the items loading any particular factor are "signed" in the same conceptual direction. Since the questionnaire randomized the direction of the liberal/conserva-

*I am indebted to Professor David Wiley of the University of Chicago for suggesting this somewhat unorthodox procedure which transforms group qualitative responses into a summarized value for a continuous variable. This procedure seemed justified in establishing the pattern of overall Unitarian Universalist religiosity, although it only takes account of between-groups variance.

tive answers in order to minimize the effects of response set, any apparent anomaly in the sign of a loading within a factor would require interpretation in terms of the response direction of that item. To avert this cumbersome procedure, such items are noted by footnote *c* on the table.

The apparent brevity of Table 2.6 also requires explanation, since it is customary to present the loadings of an item on all factors rather than just one. In this case, however, this full matrix has been omitted. Using .50 as the minimum criterion of significance for the loading of an item on a second factor, only four such loadings occurred, three of which indicated some overlapping of

TABLE 2.6
Ten Factors of Unitarian Universalist Religiosity

Item Number	Loading[a]	Content[b]
		I. Personal Beliefs, Styles, and Values
23	.91	Privatism on nonmarital sexuality
35	.90	Post-Christian denominational thrust
25	.88	Permissiveness on contraception[c]
2	.85	Nonuse of personal prayer
1	.84	Nontheism
10	.84	Personal religion not Christian
24	.84	Privatism on extramarital sexuality
34	.83	Theological self-designation as liberal[c]
36	.81	Against increased Biblical material in church school
15	.78	Gambling a low-order social problem
11	.75	Nonbelief in personal immortality
12	.70	Nonaffirmation of transhuman power for goodness
42	.69	Doubtful of truth or contemporary value of Jesus' teachings
21	.68	Permissiveness on grounds for divorce[c]
22	.66	Permissiveness on abortion[c]
6	.56	Worship as low-order church function
14	.53	Drug addiction as low-order social problem
18	.52	Jesus' eschatology reduces contemporary relevance of his teachings[c]
		II. Social-Ethical Values
28	.83	Social action as high-order church function
17	.81	Racial integration as high-order problem for church action
38	.81	Denominational peace activities have high priority
16	.80	Poverty as high-order problem for church action
18	.74	Prefer doveish policy in Viet Nam[c]
32	.70	Approve ministerial participation in demonstrations
33	.69	Social value self-designation as liberal
19	.68	Approve selective conscientious objection
20	.59	Approve nonviolent civil disobedience

(Continued)

TABLE 2.6 (Continued)

Ten Factors of Unitarian Universalist Religiosity

Item Number	Loading[a]	Content[b]
		III. Church Sociality Values and Participation
29	.85	Fellowship as high-order value in ideal church
4	.81	Fellowship as high-order church function
26	.69	Church activity and participation high
5	.59	Celebrating common values as high-order church function
		IV. Psychological Development Values
31	.89	Personal psychological development as high-order church function
37	.71	Favor increased psychological development material in church school
		V. Aesthetic-Reflective-Worship Values
8	.73	Music and aesthetic satisfaction as high-order church function
7	.69	Reflection as high-order church function
27	.65	Public worship as high-order church function
		VI. Religious Knowledge (A)
39	.72	Jesus in Jewish prophetic tradition[c]
40	.62	Doubtful that Jesus broke with Judaism to create a new religion
9	.58	Motivating to serve others as low-order church function
		VII. Intrasectarian Humanism
43	.81	Jesus did not see himself as Messiah or Christ[c]
13	.70	Human potential is stronger for love than evil
		VIII. Religious Education Stress
30	.78	Religious education as high-order church function
		IX. Religious Knowledge (B)
44	.85	Jesus' Messiahship a creation of the early church
3	.68	Intellectual stimulation as high-order church function
		X. Church as Actual Source of Friendships
45	.83	Few close friends in church

[a]Based on orthogonal varimax rotation, by items, of principal components solution. Using .50 as a minimum criterion, four of these items also loaded second factors. Items 20, 32, and 33 loaded Factor I (.57, .50, and .56, respectively) and item 6 loaded .53 on Factor III.

[b]The content of these items, as indicated in the text, has been paraphrased for brevity in this table. The directions of these paraphrased responses embody the response-quality for the majority of Unitarian Universalist responses on the questionnaire. The actual content of the items, as modified for factor analysis, will be found in Appendix C.

[c]Item loaded this factor with the opposite sign from other high-loading items, but this seeming reversal was the result of the alternation of response direction in the questionnaire.

Factors I and II. These isolated instances are therefore indicated in footnote *a* of the table.

In view of the empirical merits of the factor analytic procedure, and the conceptual clarity of the factors extracted with this sample, we are here provided a basis for describing the dimensions of this kind of religiosity. We shall, in fact, regard the first five factors as dimensions without resorting to any item-juggling or rearrangement.

Dimension 1. Personal Beliefs, Styles, and Values

The items comprising this dimension, loading high on Factor I, reflect traditional theological beliefs, a number of personal moral values, and certain values regarding the function and cultural stance of the church. This is a considerably wider range than the first factor or dimension that was initially proposed by King, "Creedal Assent and Personal Commitment." It is even wider than the amended first factor suggested on the basis of his subsequent analyses, ' Creedal Assent." Three measures of traditional belief (items 1, 11, 12) appear here. The two items creating the Self-Ascription Index (10, 35) also appear here. Item 2, prayer frequency, loads this factor, suggesting that ritualism or devotionalism is not a separate dimension within this population. It is interesting to note that item 34, the self-designation of theological position on a liberal/conservative spectrum, appears in this dimension confirming the contention of psychologists such as Gordon Allport that direct ideological questions and self-reports are reliable.

Insofar as a rough distinction can be made between an individual's personal morality and his social morality, almost all the items dealing with personal ethics and values are in this first dimension. All five items on sex (21-25) are included, as well as the gambling item (15). That such ethical items appear in this first dimension would indicate that at least some of the supposed consequential elements of religious belief and commitment are not, within this population, separate from the actual beliefs and commitments.

Recognizing that the items comprising Dimension 1 are a selection drawn from an already-selected and limited set of items, we may nevertheless perceive some of the outlines of the religiosity most common to most of the Unitarian Universalists.

The most striking aspect of Dimension 1 is the extent and coherence of posttraditionality that it reveals. There is a clear disaffiliation with Christianity, its Biblical sources, its God-beliefs and immortality beliefs, its reliance upon Jesus, its encouragement of the ritual of prayer. The content of item 35 suggests the positive side of this in the UUs' desire that their denomination reflect a universal or humanistic religiousness.

Almost equally striking is the consistent privatism or individualism exhibited on the items dealing with sexual morality and with other levels of moral behavior which, while often falling within the criminal statutes, reflect victimless crimes—abortion, gambling, drug-addiction.

Dimension 2. Social-Ethical Values

Loading high on Factor II are those items dealing with social values and the responsibility of the church for social change. These items, together with the personal-ethical items of Dimension 1, constitute what Glock has hypothesized as the consequential aspect of religion. Again it will be noted that the self-designation on the liberal/conservative continuum of social issues and values represents an accurate estimate of this dimension. We may also note here that none of these items appear on King's original or amended listing of dimensions. That they distributed here between the first and second dimensions would indicate that this population differs considerably from the Methodist group that he studied.

We must note the consistent and coherent liberal direction of these items as they loaded Factor II. As distinct from the moral value items in Factor I, these items all deal with "social" ethics where the rights of other persons are involved. In contrast to the personal-morality situations, there clearly are victims here, whether or not behavior toward them is socially defined as criminal. Racism, war, poverty, all of these reflect other-inflicted rather than self-inflicted kinds of misery.

Dimension 3. Church Sociality Values and Participation

The two items exploring the fellowship function of church-going (4, 29) load this dimension heavily, and the self-estimate of activity within the local church (26) also appears here, indicating that this need for a community of common values is a major dimension of religiosity.

Dimension 4. Psychological Development Values.

Whereas the previous dimensions have indicated needs for shared beliefs and values within a community, this dimension points to a more idiosyncratic value of personal development. This desire for maturity is an inward aspect of religion. With more traditional populations, questions relating to spiritual growth or Christian perfection might explore the same dimension.

Dimension 5. Aesthetic-Reflective-Worship Values.

This dimension, comprising the items loading Factor V, is distinct from Dimension 4. The personality needs reflected here are equally inward and personal but point to a communal context and illuminate an important religious function. The distinctiveness of this dimension is indicated by the extremely low loadings of these items on Factor IV (-.09, .22, -.20, respectively).

Dimension 6. Educational Function of the Church.

Item 30, on religious education, loads Factor VIII, and indicates this dimension. Given the convert-status of this group and the fact that many members join these churches during the years when they enroll their children for religious education, the emergence of this dimension may be predictable. This emphasis on education apparently cuts across most other ideological elements.

Dimension 7. The Church as Source of Personal Friendships

The loading of item 45 on Factor X deserves some comment. This item might have been expected to load Factor III, Church Sociality Values and Participation, but the loading there was only -.35. This apparent discrepancy between the desirable and the actual probably reflects the social, geographical, and religious mobility of these respondents. Within this population, at least, those who have more close friends in their local church are typically the less-mobile persons who live outside of the urban or suburban areas.

Dimension 8. Intrasectarian Affirmations.

Factors VI and IX, both characterized here as Religious Knowledge (A) and (B), require special comment. We have already indicated the difficulties of delineating religious knowledge among mainstream religious populations, and the increased difficulties in doing this with Unitarian Universalists. The several items on Jesus which were finally included in the questionnaire were typically cast in paired form to assess logical and historical consistencies. One of these pairs appears on Factor VI. To the extent that Jesus is asserted to have remained in the Jewish tradition, he could not have founded a new religion, and vice versa. The logical consistency (i.e., negative correlation) of such responses may be examined. It is less clear whether a high agreement with the first assertion, that Jesus remained in the Jewish tradition, should be viewed as a judgment reflecting the acceptance of some particular sectarian interpretation of past events, or simply viewed as a creedal statement at variance with a mainstream Christian creedal statement. This same ambiguity holds for item 44 which loaded Factor IX. Is the belief that Jesus' divinity was a posthumous imputation simply a Unitarian heresy, or is it a historical judgment? In either case, should it be described as religious knowledge? King's analysis of Methodists, as noted, did not initially show a religious knowledge factor, although his subsequent item-scale analysis yielded a homogeneous set of five items, three of them being simple identifications of Biblical authorship and the remaining two being non-controversial descriptions of church history. The coefficient of homogeneity was admittedly low on these items and only rose slightly when another composite index was included.

It hardly seems useful to make much of the assimilation of essentially trivial factual information. The real issue would seem to be the kind of historical-creedal-mythological assertions that religious individuals make, the inferences they draw from them, and the uses to which they put them. To some extent, Factor VII reflects this. Within this population, a rejection of the Messiahship of

Jesus is positively correlated with a humanistic assertion that man's potential for love can overcome his potential for evil, and these two items load together on this factor. We prefer to regard such items as "Intrasectarian Affirmations." These two affirmations, for instance, have typically gone together in the history of this religious group, and yet they do not, singly or together, reflect anything like a simple historical judgment or a clear bit of human knowledge. It may nevertheless be the fact that to put them together in this particular way is an indication that one has interiorized certain assertions characteristic of this particular religious group. Insiders may say that they know these things to be the case, but from the standpoint of outsiders, that would be less than knowledge. From the fact that such items load separate factors, we may conclude that they must be distinguished from the more central belief items of Dimension I, and regarded, at most, as secondarily-creedal. Since only confusion would result from combining the items loading Factors VI, VII, and IX into an index for this dimension, our subsequent analyses will be based upon responses to item 44, Jesus as divinized by the early church, treating this item as prototypical of an index to measure this dimension.

UU RELIGIOSITY—IN SUMMARY

On the basis of the foregoing analysis and discussion, it is conceptually and empirically necessary to employ an eight-dimensional model to describe UU religiosity:

1. Personal Beliefs, Styles, and Values
2. Social-Ethical Values
3. Church Sociality Values and Participation
4. Psychological Development Values
5. Aesthetic-Reflective-Worship Values
6. Educational Function of the Church
7. The Church as Source of Personal Friendships
8. Intrasectarian Affirmations

The shared qualities and characteristics of any particular group might, of course, not be unique—the group might simply be a good sample of some larger population. In the UU case, however, we have indirect evidence that this is not the case with respect to American religious groups. Dimension 1 embraces too many qualities that are multidimensional in other religious groups. While it is theoretically possible that the UUs are simply a sample of the nonchurchmember population, differing only in one organizational variable, such an assumption strains credulity. Even on the basis of demographic elements, the UUs show every evidence of uniqueness.

We shall therefore regard the model as an accurate, if limited, representation of shared attitudes and behaviors of that group of adult Americans who are

Unitarian Universalists. In Chapters 3-7, we will employ the Self-Ascription Index as a measure of Dimension 1 of the model and explore the meanings and sources of UU religiosity. Then, in Chapter 8, we will return to the fuller model and explore ways in which the UUs are differentiated in their composite religiosity.

Chapter 3

THE MEANINGS OF SELF-ASCRIPTION

In this chapter, and the succeeding three, we shall attempt a fuller description and explanation of Unitarian Universalist religiosity, using the Self-Ascription Index described in Table 1.7. This index not only distributed the sample into three conceptually meaningful groups, but it also showed high levels of association with the other intuitively derived measures and is comprised of two items with high loading on Dimension 1, Personal Beliefs, Styles, and Values. We have already suggested that those designated "left" by this index may be regarded as posttraditionally religious persons. Therefore, describing the total sample in terms of the index also affords a direct description of this particular kind of religious position. The "percent of total" figures given in many of the tables of Chapters 3 through 6 will perform the double service of describing overall responses for the whole sample and permitting an assessment of variations within related ideological positions.

Readers who have glanced ahead will notice that the self-ascriptions appear in the tables of this chapter as column headings and are shifted to row headings for Chapter 5. A common convention in the social sciences is to analyze the relationship of two variables by regarding one as independent and the other dependent, placing the independent variable in the columns of a table. This comes very close to suggesting that changes in the independent variable may cause changes in the dependent variable. There are few more thorny issues in the philosophy of science than this problem of causation. David Hume long ago reminded us that no one had ever seen a cause. All we ever really can observe is the interaction of events. If they are close enough to each other in time or space, we may become tempted to supply the notion of causation. But the issue can be extremely complex. Even when there is no doubt about temporal succession (being born male or female obviously precedes the acquisition of any particular ideology), and even when this preceding, independent, variable describes significant differences (if, for instance, women are rated more conservative than men), we have by no means established that femaleness causes conservatism. Or, to take a more ambiguous example, suppose we find that political conservatism is closely correlated with religious conservatism. How could we decide which to label independent and which dependent? Only if we could observe a group of individuals over a period of time, and if we could account for all possible extraneous factors, and if we observed one kind of conservatism typically developing before the other, would we be ready to suggest causation. Those 'ifs' are all big enough to make this a utopian dream.

Our justification for reversing the arrangement of tables when we reach Chapter 5 is a more pragmatic one. Most of the data will be percentaged, for ease of comprehension and comparison. Since a given numeral can represent a row percentage or a column percentage (but not both), we will be suggesting in this chapter that the best way to understand the meanings of self-ascription is to know what percentages of right, center, and left self-ascribers answer a particular question in a particular way. The columns of this chapter, allowing for rounding errors, each total 100%. In Chapter 5, however, where we shall be exploring the sources of self-ascription, it will be more useful to know what percentages of young and old, rich and poor, male and female comprise each type of self-ascription. Thus the columns of the tables in Chapter 5 will still total 100% but the bottom rows of these tables, labeled "percent of total," will represent the column marginals and thus show the percentage of the total sample contained within that column.

TRADITIONAL RELIGIOUS ASPECTS OF UNITARIAN UNIVERSALISTS

We shall begin by looking at a number of elements in the belief, value, and style structures of the Unitarian Universalists. For convenience, we will be regarding these as elements of their religiosity. There is a sense, of course, in which almost any individual in our society, religiously affiliated or not, would be found to hold to some cluster of beliefs about God, man, and the world. Since we lack data on this, the best we can do is explore these affirmations within particular religious groups as we are doing here, being alert to the degrees to which such affirmations are shared within the group. At the present time, that is the most that we can say. It is theoretically possible that similar sharings and consensus occur throughout the whole society.

Personal Beliefs and Attitudes

Since the historic origins of both Universalists and Unitarians were in Protestant Christianity, it will be interesting to examine the continuing influence of this heritage upon present beliefs. For all Christians, the core belief has historically been the God-belief. In many ages, this was so taken for granted that controversies revolved instead around beliefs about Jesus or the nature of the church and its leadership, but this should not obscure the centrality of the basic theistic affirmation. Let us therefore look first at this issue.

God

Unitarian Universalist literature since 1920 is filled with references to a humanist-theist debate. In more recent years, one often finds the assertion that this is no longer the real issue, and that individual freedom of belief has both pluralized the theistic affirmations and shifted the focus of liberal religiosity from God to man. The distribution of God-beliefs within present Unitarian Universalism indicates the accuracy of such a judgment, empirically if not philosophically. Table 3.1 indicates the way these beliefs are influenced by self-ascription. We have already indicated in Chapter 2 that the five categories of this God-question were designed to be mutually exclusive and to be ordered from right to left. In the case of the total Unitarian Universalist population, a normal distribution does indeed occur, with a small group at either extreme and the largest group in the middle. Examination of Table 3.1 indicates the close correlation of these responses with the Self-Ascription Index. Those who are "Right" on self-ascription cluster in the right half of the God-scale and, conversely, those who are "Left" on self-ascription cluster in the left half of the God scale. This latter group, representing 57% of present Unitarian Universalists, we will hereafter refer to as the "posttraditionals."

TABLE 3.1
Theism as Related to Self-Ascription [a]

Meanings of God	Self-Ascription			Percent of total
	Right	Center	Left	
Percentage who answered:				
Supernatural	11	4	1	3
Ground of being	52	29	13	23
Natural	32	52	42	44
Irrelevant	5	15	41	29
Harmful	less than .5	1	3	2

[a]Nwt = 158,550.

If we try to attach customary philosophical or theological labels to particular responses that people made, a new level of ambiguity emerges, but it seems worth the effort. Clearly those persons who describe God as "a supernatural Being who reveals Himself in human experience and history" may be termed "traditional supernaturalists." This is the response that one would expect from most orthodox Christians or Jews in most periods of Western history. The second response, that God is "the ground of all being, real but not adequately describable," reflects a position that has recently been popularized by Paul Tillich, but which is actually rooted in certain German idealistic philosophers and in certain aspects of Western mysticism. We could describe this as "sophisticated theism." Those familiar with Tillich's writings will know that he consistently refused to call himself either a theist or an atheist and preferred this more neutral formulation. Some readers may recall that David Hume had suggested, two centuries ago, that those mystics who denied that God could be described in terms of any attributes were actually atheists in disguise. Nevertheless, in view of the four alternatives that were rejected by those who chose this response, our appellation "sophisticated theists" seems justified. The third response, that God "may appropriately be used as a name for some natural processes within the Universe such as love or creative evolution" was modal for the whole population as well as for the center and left self-ascription groups. In the wording of this alternative, a different verb form was inadvertently used and this may confound these responses somewhat. Whereas the other four alternatives all started out "God is . . ." this middle response said "God may appropriately be used." This more permissive verb form might have made the option more appealing. Granting this difficulty, we would label this response "evolutionary deism," indicating its affinities for the various kinds of "natural religion" that have been popular since the eighteenth century and also for the incorporations of evolutionary theory into liberal theology that began in the last century. The fourth response, that "God is an irrelevant concept and the central focus of religion should be on man's knowledge and values " was designed to reflect "religious humanism." Some forms of humanism which have made an impact in the Unitarian and Universalist past have put a heavy stress upon knowledge and the sciences, whereas other forms have been more concerned with man and his values. Nevertheless, it seemed better to lump these two forms of humanism into a single response in designing this question. Some of these humanists have been agnostic and argued that the God-issue was unknowable and, therefore, not worth debating. Others have been more aggressively antitheistic, arguing that the God-issue must be resolved before one could turn effectively to human values. The fifth response, that God "is a concept that is harmful to a worthwhile religion," we can designate as "religious atheism." No doubt there are many in the American population who would regard religion itself as harmful to man.

But we are dealing here with members of a religious group who happen to be antitheistic, and it seems necessary to describe them by the adjective religious.

Immortality.

This traditional Western religious belief is overwhelmingly rejected by the Unitarian Universalists, as shown in item 1 of Table 3.2. The "Center" percentages have been omitted from this and many subsequent tables. In analysis of the data, this center group remained in the center in almost every relationship (in the few instances where this was not the case, notice will be taken or the full percentages reported). The Center percentage can, of course, readily be calculated as $C\% = [Total\% - (.10\ Right\% + .57\ Left\%)]/.33$. We will also limit tabular presentations to single category-responses in most cases where the interrelation is sufficiently linear to preclude misinterpretation. Readers interested in the full set of category responses can turn to Appendix B. The final self-ascription column on many of the tables contains the remainder of Left minus Right

TABLE 3.2

Immortality, Transhuman Goodness, Human Love, and Progress,
as Related to Self-Ascription

Item	Percent of total (Nwt)	Self-Ascription		
		Right %	Left %	L% minus R%
1. "Is immortality, in the sense of a continued personal existence of the individual after death, part of your belief system?" "No"	90 (157,298)	70	95	25
2. "There is a power that works in history through man that transforms evil into good." "Disagree"	60 (155,712)	36	70	34
3. "Man's potential for 'love' can overcome his potential for 'evil.'" "Agree"	89 (144,356)	90	88	−2
4. "There has been progress in the history of human civilization." "Agree"	95 (159,067)	97	95	−2

percentages, facilitating direct comparison of the magnitude and direction of right-wing and posttraditional differences.

Even among conservative UUs, only 30% affirm personal immortality. Among posttraditionals, this drops to 5%. Some contemporary Protestant theologians have stressed that personal immortality is a Hellenistic rather than Jewish or Christian belief, and that the historical affirmation within these two religious traditions is more properly an expectation of an eschaton, an end of history. It seemed doubtful that this theological argument had had much impact among UUs and there was no attempt within the questionnaire to probe this. What is clear, in the immortality item, is that a central element in earlier Western religiousness as well as in the traditions of eighteenth-century natural religion has attenuated almost to the point of disappearance within this group.

Goodness in History

A number of items in the questionnaire reflected affirmations that had been characteristic of Universalists and Unitarians in their historical development. At one point in the research design, it seemed desirable to identify the respondents in terms of whether their backgrounds were Unitarian or Universalist. Further consideration ruled this out, however. No doubt the population does contain a number of old-line Universalists and old-line Unitarians. But a large block of the present denominational membership is, in a real sense, both. Although their formal merger did not occur until 1961, a joint denominational hymnal had been published in 1937, common curricular materials in religious education had been developed since the 1930s, and there was a free flow of ministers between the two denominations. Thus the sectarian distinctiveness suggested by a saying of the last century, "Universalists think that God is too good to damn man, and Unitarians think that man is too good to be damned" would seem today to have lost much of its distinctiveness.

An historical Universalist affirmation, flowing from the belief in the universal lovingness of God, held that the power of love was such that eventually the evil in history would be transformed. The actual question used did not specify this power working for goodness as a Divine power, since that would have con-founded responses in terms of the high or low theism of the respondents. Instead, the question probes a kind of "crypto-theistic" affirmation regarding meaningfulness and goodness in history. These results are also shown in Table 3.2, as item 2. Whatever historic consensus there might have been around this affirmation is clearly now gone, with only 40% still affirming it. It should be noted that only 30% of the posttraditionals maintained the affirmation, and in this they almost exactly reverse the division within the far right group. This is thus an affirmation on which there is considerable polarization which is closely related to self-ascription.

Love Versus Evil in Man

A somewhat similar affirmation of religious liberals, focusing upon the individual rather than upon the larger, natural-historical situation, has been an affirmation of human goodness. During the Enlightenment, Condorcet wrote of the "infinite perfectibility" of man. The results of the question designed to explore this appear in Table 3.2, item 3.

Progress

Yet another way of affirming the eighteenth-century faith in human goodness and the possibilities of social change is to affirm a belief in progress. The results of a general question on this are shown as item 4 of Table 3.2. If Christian orthodoxy, at least in its Augustinian forms, has argued that human history is ambiguous and indeterminate, and that the reign of goodness and justice can only occur by divine action at the end of history, then religious liberals have been heretics in their historical affirmation of progress. It will be seen that they persist in this particular "heretical orthodoxy." The very slight defection from this almost-complete consensus that appears among the posttraditionals may be an indication of a pendulum swing or it may be an indication of a rejection of this heretical orthodoxy.

This belief in progress has a high-enough consensual status to be viewed as central in the Unitarian Universalist "latent creed." For this very reason, specification is required. The questionnaire therefore included six frequently adduced supports for belief in progress, and asked those respondents who did believe in progress to check the three arguments most supportive of their own beliefs. Table 3.3 presents the results of this specification. Since respondents were asked to check the three strongest supports for their belief in progress, the column percentages will not total 100, and two alternative methods of presenting the

TABLE 3.3

Criteria Justifying Belief in Progress, as Related to Self-Ascription

Criterion	Percent including criterion			Variance from chance (%)			Nwt
	R	C	L	R	C	L	
Growth of science and knowledge	88	89	86	0	1	−1	140,216
Increase in moral sensitivity	42	46	42	0	2	−2	69,512
Emergence of a world community	44	51	51	−1	0	1	80,872
Elimination of poverty and disease	42	35	37	2	−2	0	58,647
Increasing rationality of man	37	38	39	0	0	1	62,319
Increase of leisure time	18	14	13	3	1	−4	22,428

data have been used. The first three columns indicate the percentages within each self-ascription group including that particular criterion. Thus, 88% of the right-wing group included the first criterion on the growth of science. Columns 4 through 6 show the variations from a chance distribution that occurred for each item. Since the Self-Ascription Index designates 10% of the denomination as right-wing, we would expect to find that same percentage of all the persons who included the first criterion coming from the right-wing group if being a right-wing UU made no difference in the inclusion of this item. Any variations from this expected percentage are given in these columns as the differences in percentage between a chance distribution and the actual distribution. Thus the variance of 0% for the right wing on the growth of science criterion indicates that 10% of those including this item were right-wing. Allowing for rounding, the sum of the variances on each item will be 0.

Inspection of this table reveals that the overall denomination and the three self-ascription groups placed these six criteria in essentially similar rank orders, and were also in general agreement on the relative importance of each item. The first item, the "growth of science and knowledge," is placed at the top of the list by each group. There is far less consensus on the remainder of the items. Each group puts the "emergence of a world community" in second place, but these concluding percentages drop considerably. It may be noted that 51% of the posttraditionals included this item whereas only 44% of the right wing listed it. All groups were agreed in placing the "increase in moral sensitivity" in third rank. We may note that 42% of the right wing included the "elimination of poverty and disease," making this their fourth criterion, whereas it was ranked fifth by the overall denomination and by the posttraditionals, only 37% of the latter group including it. Finally, we may note that all groups were agreed in viewing the "increase of leisure time" as the least important criterion of those listed.

The Religious Role of Science

In view of the centrality of the belief that science and knowledge are central in human progress, and the general affinity of religious liberalism for the ideas of the sciences, it seemed important to test this religious appropriation of the sciences further. A general question was devised to assess the overall impact of the sciences on liberal religion. From the results presented in Table 3.4, item 1, it can be seen that Unitarian Universalists overwhelmingly view science as strengthening rather than weaking liberal religion. The posttraditionals are even more convinced that this is the case. It should be noted that the question explores the impact of science upon liberal religion, and, therefore, these answers may be read as reflecting the individual respondent's feeling of the importance of science for his own religious beliefs. Many of these same respondents would undoubtedly say that science had had the overall effect within our culture of weakening more orthodox religions.

TABLE 3.4

Impact of Science upon Liberal Religion and Human Values, as Related to Self-Ascription

	Percent of Total	Self-Ascription		
Item	(Nwt)	Right %	Left %	L% minus R%
1. "How do you think modern science affects religious beliefs?"				
"Strengthens liberal religion"	79 (158,332)	71	80	9
2. "Which one of these statements comes *closest* to your feeling about the relation of modern science to human values?"				
"Science is ethically neutral"	56 (157,279)	54	58	4

The relationship of the sciences to moral and ethical stances is much more complicated. Early Unitarians and Universalists drew much of their inspiration from the Enlightenment which had viewed science and reason as essentially synonymous and had looked forward to the time when all human problems would be resolved by the superior means. This belief in the overall moral as well as intellectual competence of the sciences is often termed "scientism." During the nineteenth century, a number of antiscientistic currents appeared. Perhaps the most notable in terms of its influence on Unitarians and Universalists was that transplantation of German Romanticism known as Transcendentalism. Ralph Waldo Emerson, in leaving the Unitarian ministry, reminded his rationalistic colleagues that "understanding" was higher than "reason." Since 1920, various forms of positivism have been current in intellectual circles. They have shared a common commitment to distinguish between "fact" and "value." The sciences deal only with facts, and values are selected and rejected by men on nonfactual, emotive grounds. More recently, there has been a popularization of existentialist ideas in intellectual and religious circles which, starting from quite different assumptions than the positivists had started, come to similar conclusions regarding the relationship of science and value. From an existentialist standpoint, it is man's act of "willing" that creates the total world of meanings, including a subsidiary world of scientific theories.

As an indirect assessment of the impact of such anti-scientistic thinking, respondents were asked whether they saw science as helping in matters of value choice or as ethically neutral. The responses are shown in the second item of Table 3.4. Clearly, the Unitarian Universalists are quite divided on this question. The posttraditionals are less confident than the total group, and certainly less than the conservative wing, that science is helpful in choosing values.

Theological Self-Designation

We have now looked at a number of items dealing with personal beliefs and attitudes as they related to the Self-Ascription Index and found that in almost every case the responses to items correlated with the right/center/left designations of self-ascription in predictable and meaningful ways. In more technical terms, we have been involved in a series of validations, a spiralling process by which we test whether some single item or index actually measures what it claims to measure. Thus far, self-ascription would appear to have a high validity. This study also attempted to investigate the value of straightforward self-designations, using terminology that was assumed to have a reasonably shared, conventional usage within this particular religious group. Readers may wish to examine the whole of Question L-11 in Appendix B. The overall question is headed "Within our churches we frequently use the labels 'liberal' and 'conservative.' Below, please make a check mark in whichever of the six places between liberal and conservative best describes the position of the person or group in the statement." Our concern here is with the fifth item within this question: Your own position on theological issues and values. Responses to this question are shown in Table 3.5. The most obvious thing shown by this data is that "liberal" is a highly-acceptable theological self-designation for Unitarian Universalists, with 80% of the respondents checking the two boxes at the liberal extreme of the spectrum. It is equally clear that this self-designation correlates very closely

TABLE 3.5
Theological Self-Designation, as Related to Self-Ascription[a]

Own position on theological issues	Self-Ascription			Percent of total
	Right	Center	Left	
Percentage who answered:				
Liberal	19	40	65	52
—	23	34	26	28
—	23	17	7	12
—	17	6	2	4
—	10	2	1	2
Conservative	9	2	Less than .5%	2

[a]Nwt=155,154.

with the designation made by the Self-Ascription Index. Only 42% of the right wing designated themselves as liberals, where 91% of the left wing so described themselves. It should also be noted that very few of the Unitarian Universalists, even those that we have categorized as right-wing, are willing to designate themselves as extremely "conservative" on theological issues and values. This is clearly a parochial Unitarian Universalist usage of the liberal and conservative labels, but it amply justifies our preference throughout this book for the right-center-left terminology which might at first glance have seemed more applicable to political than to religious views. It is precisely because so many of the Unitarian Universalists, regardless of their own orientation within the denominational group, describe themselves as "religious liberals" that we moved in this direction. It will also be clear in the next chapter, where we discuss the social values of the UUs, that the same respondents use the terms liberal and conservative with a rather different yardstick, as it were, when they think in social rather than theological terms.

Religious Identity

Yet another way of expanding our understanding of present Unitarian Universalists is to examine the ways in which they see themselves related to other religious groups and to the Christian tradition which has dominated past Western history. We have already found that 57% of contemporary Unitarian Universalists do not regard their own personal religion as "Christian." Let us turn to the questions of religious distance and of beliefs about Jesus.

Religious Distance

The questionnaire contained a list of thirteen religious groups, and the respondent was asked to indicate "How close, religiously, you feel to each." A four-point scale, from very close to very distant, was provided along with a "don't know" box. The results are summarized in Table 3.6. The percentages in this table represent the combined responses of "very close" and "somewhat close.' It will be seen that Unitarian Universalists as a whole feel closest to Quakers and Reform Jews (62 and 59%, respectively). Lesser percentages, 43 and 41, feel close to Congregationalists and Ethical Culturists. It is interesting to note that the greatest distance is felt between religious liberals and Muslims and Fundamentalists (4 and 3%, respectively).

There is great differentiation between the affinity feelings of the right-wing and left-wing UUs. This is true both in rank order and in order of magnitude. Over half of the right wing feel close to Congregationalists and Quakers (in that order), while the majority of the posttraditional left wing feel close to Quakers, Reformed Jews, and Ethical Culturalists. Both wings agree with each other and with the total denomination in designating the groups from which they feel most distant.

TABLE 3.6
Religious Distance, as Related to Self-Ascription

Item	Percent of total (Nwt)	Self-Ascription		
		Right %	Left %	L% minus R%
"How close do you feel, religiously, to each of the following groups?" "Very close" or "somewhat close" to:				
1. Methodists	20 (155,339)	39	13	−26
2. Congregationalists	43 (156,373)	69	32	−37
3. Episcopalians	14 (155,731)	27	9	−18
4. Roman Catholics	5 (156,343)	10	3	−7
5. Fundamentalists	3 (155,355)	7	2	−5
6. Quakers	62 (156,575)	56	63	7
7. Lutherans	6 (155,154)	15	3	−12
8. Christian Scientists	11 (155,855)	18	7	−11
9. Ethical Culturists	41 (155,095)	15	50	35
10. Orthodox Jews	7 (155,081)	8	6	−2
11. Reform Jews	59 (157,042)	47	63	16
12. Muslims	4 (155,600)	3	5	2
13. Buddhists	23 (156,140)	9	27	18

Another way of viewing this data is to look at the differentiating effect that self-ascription has regarding these other religious groups. There is a 37% differential between the right and left UUs in feelings of distance from Congregationalists, and 35% and 26% differentials in distance feelings from Ethical Culturists and Methodists.

While these figures in general further validate and expand the meanings of the Self-Ascription Index, it should be recognized that there are both regional and urban factors that may be operating. Among all the respondents, the "don't know" percentage ranged from 2 on Roman Catholics to 40 on Ethical Culturists. Since these seemed to be honest and meaningful responses, they were not excluded from the bases on which the percentages shown in the table were calculated. This strategy necessarily lowered the percentages distributed among the specific close/distant responses, but seemed preferable to the artificial inflation of responses that would otherwise have resulted. The procedure was further justified on the basis of differentials between right-wing and left-wing "don't know" percentages. The maximum spread here occurred with the Ethical Culturists but represented only an 8% variance from the mean response with that group. Since Ethical Societies, as they are now known, are confined to a few large cities, not all UUs have had equal chance to meet or know them. Parenthetically, it may be noted here that the Ethical Societies (represented by the American Ethical Union), the American Humanist Association, and the Unitarian Universalist Association pooled personnel for a common Washington legislative office in 1970.

The regional elements that must be recognized include the unequal geographical distribution of many of the groups in this list, as well as regional variations within many of the other denominations. Local Methodist and Congregational churches, for instance, may run the theological gamut from very conservative to very liberal.

As a final observation, the differential distances felt from Muslims and Buddhists should be observed. Not only did the overall group feel much closer to Buddhists, but there was a significant differentiation between right- and left-wing UUs in regard to Buddhists that did not appear in regard to Muslims. Social distance scales have occasionally been devised that include fictitious groups as a means of detecting stereotypical response sets. A response of automatic closeness, which has characterized political liberals in some earlier studies, is apparently not operative here in terms of the responses to Muslims and Buddhists. Neither of these, of course, is a fictitious group, but they are clearly groups that have historically been distant from the Western religious mainstream. Thus any xenophiliac prejudices within the Unitarian Universalist left wing would have lessened the distance from both groups. Since it did not, we can assume that postjudice rather than prejudice is operative.

Returning to the level of generalization from this data, let us imagine a large circle in which the Unitarian Universalists are at the center and these thirteen other religious groups are randomly placed around the circumference. We ask the UUs to turn around, looking successively at each surrounding group, adjusting that segment of the circumference-boundary to reflect their feelings of distance from that group. If they feel quite distant, they will move the boundary in. By this procedure, we will end up with an irregular polygon that is actually a religiometric profile of Unitarian Universalism. The longer sides of this polygon will point to the groups with whom the UUs feel close and at the same time permit us to describe the content of Unitarian Universalism as having a large component of the characteristics of such affinity groups. Conversely, the short sides of the polygon indicating maximal religious distance will also indicate the minimal presence of certain qualities within UU religiosity. Quakerism and Reform Judaism, sectors where the UU profile is largest, have both been characterized by an intense concern for ethical religion which has been coupled with a strong stress upon the individual's freedom of belief. If we constructed separate profiles of the right and left self-ascription groups, they would be quite similar in these two sectors. The third dominant sector for the posttraditional, left group would be the Ethical Culture, reflecting a similar emphasis of ethical religion. The right-wing UU profile would have its most dominant sector in the direction of the Congregationalists with a noticeably salient sector toward the Methodists. The Ethical Culture sector would be quite small. This right-wing profile is somewhat more difficult to comprehend since it has certain affinities with the theological patterning of mainstream Protestantism, but at the same time has a large Reform Jewish sector.

If we look at the smaller parts of the four UU profiles, however, this differentiation is absent. The Muslim and Fundamentalist sectors are very small. Both of these groups have been characterized by an inflexible dogmatism, and it may be inferred that this is a negative theological value for all forms of Unitarian Universalists. Similarly, the Roman Catholic sector is quite small. We may assume that this similarly reflects a rejection of dogmatism if we recall that the data was gathered in 1966 before the potential liberalizations of Vatican II were widely apparent.

Beliefs about Jesus

A further understanding of Unitarian Universalist religiosity may come from an examination of beliefs about Jesus. Not only has Jesus of Nazareth been the central figure in the reflections of Christian theology but Unitarianism, in Europe, in England, and in the United States emerged from a critique of Christian dogmas regarding Jesus. The early Unitarians denied the doctrine of the Trinity which had held that Jesus-as-the-Son and God-as-the-Father were identical in all important respects. This early Unitarianism, it should be noted, was based upon Biblical argumentation and not upon what subsequently emerged as historical, critical scholarship. Since the time of Theodore Parker in the last century, American religious liberals have been in the forefront of those who labored to rethink their theological positions in the light of critical scholarship. These themes have been sounded not only from Unitarian and Universalist pulpits, but also have been quite central in the curricular materials prepared for

church school usage. Judaism and Christianity have been viewed as humanly-pro-
duced religions that grew out of historical experiences. The miraculous and
supernatural elements of these religious traditions were typically considered in
the broad context of comparative religion, implying that such ideas were a
natural product of the imaginations of earlier generations of men. By a similar
logic, Christianity was seen as having emerged rather slowly out of Judaism and
as retaining a number of continuities within the ancestral faith. From this
theological framework, dogmas about Jesus and doctrines about the uniqueness
of the Christian church were viewed as speculative constructions of later generations of Christians rather than as necessary articles of faith. The early theologians among the Unitarians and Universalists, while rejecting the full trinitarian
identification of Jesus with God, nevertheless viewed Jesus as a divine man who
was quite different from ordinary men. This special nature of his was the basis of
his authority; and his ability to perform "miracles," for instance, was seen as a
proof of this authority. By the middle of the nineteenth century, this situation
was rapidly changing. Biblical criticism was undermining belief in the uniqueness
of Jesus' birth or in the veracity of the miracle-stories. By 1900, many thought-
ful liberal Christians were even doubting the historicity of the various post-
crucifixion stories. Along with this process, and in some ways perhaps in
compensation for it, there was developed an emphasis upon the personal char-
acter of Jesus and the moral value of his teachings. Thus, the basis for his
continuing authority shifted from a metaphysical one to a presumably historical
one.

To assess the assimilation of such understandings of Jesus and to explore the
roles that he played in contemporary Unitarian Universalism, eight statements
were included under the general heading "In the past hundred years, historical
scholars have made a number of varied estimates of Jesus." For each statement,
respondents were asked to check a four-point agree/disagree scale or "don't
know" box. The eight statements were numbered consecutively, although, by
design, the first six were conceptually paired so that a respondent with histori-
cal-biblical knowledge would agree with one statement and reject the other. The
data is presented in Tables 3.7-3.10. In these tables, the four-point scale has been
collapsed into the simpler agree/disagree form, and the "don't know" percentages are given.

The first pair of statements, shown in Table 3.7, attempted to explore the
issue of continuity versus discontinuity in the relationship of Christianity to
Judaism. It was felt that the consensus of historical scholarship would agree with
the first statement and disagree with the second. A majority of the overall
Unitarian Universalist group, as well as majorities within the right- and left-wing
subgroups did agree with the statement that Jesus was essentially in the tradition
of the Jewish prophets. On the second statement, however—that Jesus broke
with Judaism and created a new religion—only the posttraditionals behaved in

TABLE 3.7

Estimates of Jesus' Relationship to Judaism, as Related to Self-Ascription

Item	Percent of total (Nwt)	Right %	Left %	L% minus R%
			Self-Ascription	
1. "Jesus was essentially in the tradition of the Jewish prophets."	(156,401)			
Agree	63	64	64	0
Disagree	15	16	15	−1
Don't know	22	21	21	0
2. "Jesus, breaking with Judaism, created a new religion."	(155,980)			
Agree	44	58	38	−20
Disagree	42	29	48	19
Don't know	14	14	14	0

the predicted or "correct" way. The overall group was almost evenly split on this question, and twice as many right-wing UUs agreed with the statement as disagreed with it. From these reponses, certain tentative inferences may be drawn about the nature of posttraditional religiosity. Whereas the posttraditional person does not regard himself as a Christian, he is deeply involved with the ethical side of religion as developed by the Jewish prophets. He places Jesus in this tradition, and rejects the idea that Jesus either broke with Judaism or founded a new church. While this may reflect a simple historical judgment, it may also reflect his preference for, and affinity to the more ethical types of religious denominations as indicated in the posttraditional estimates of religious distance that were just discussed.

The next pair of statements, shown in Table 3.8, attempted to explore feelings about the contemporary validity of Jesus' teachings. This might appear to be a rather arcane issue, but several considerations led to its inclusion. On the one hand, as already indicated, the longstanding Unitarian Universalist stress upon the humanity of Jesus led this group to make much of the authority and value of his moral teachings. Church school materials produced for the denomination have focused almost completely upon Jesus as a moral teacher and example. In the controversies that have revolved around the "corrosive" impact of biblical scholarship, relatively few questions have been raised concerning the reliability of accounts concerning Jesus attitudes on moral and ethical matters. One would therefore expect the traditional UU to retain this high estimate of the continuing usefulness of such teachings.

TABLE 3.8

Estimates of the Effect of Jesus' Eschatology and the Contemporary Value of his Teachings, as Related to Self-Ascription

Item	Percent of total (Nwt)	Self-Ascription		
		Right %	Left %	L% minus R%
3. "Jesus' belief in the end of the world so affected his teachings that their value for modern man is limited."	(156,398)			
Agree	23	9	29	20
Disagree	57	71	50	−21
Don't know	20	21	21	0
4. "Jesus' teachings are as true and useful now as then."	(157,401)			
Agree	67	88	57	−31
Disagree	24	8	33	25
Don't know	8	4	10	6

On the other hand, there has been considerable controversy since about 1900 regarding Jesus' eschatology and the conditioning effect it might have had upon some of his other attitudes. Some scholars have argued that Jesus expected the world to end, by divine action, within his own lifetime. Others have urged that he saw the divine cataclysm as coinciding with his own death. There is little doubt in scholarly circles today that the primitive Christian community lived in expectation of an imminent end to the present age and the consequent establishment of a "kingdom of God." The apostle Paul's attitude toward marriage as well as certain views within the early church regarding possessions and wealth make more sense from this perspective. The fact remains, however, that the time-table of this first-generation Christianity was wrong, and that the world did not end within their lifetime. Later Christians, including the writers of the four gospels, were all involved in the rethinking that was necessitated by this disappointment.

The research design for the questionnaire assumed that Unitarian Universalists might be familiar with this problem, not only because of their concern with the teachings of Jesus and their commitment to historical, biblical scholarship, but also because of their strong interest in Albert Schweitzer. No doubt, many of them first became interested in Schweitzer because of his humanitarian activities in Africa, or his contributions to musicianship and musicology, or his receiving of the Nobel Peace Prize. But Schweitzer was also a philosopher and theologian.

Beacon Press, the denominational publishing house, widely distributed several anthologies of Schweitzer's work which made clear his wide interest in these areas. His famous *Quest for the Historical Jesus*, published in 1902, was the foremost (if not the first) book to raise starkly the eschatological question. Schweitzer argued there that the center of Jesus' teaching was the imminence of the kingdom of God, and that since he had been incorrect in his expectations, many of his other teachings must be relegated to the first century. In more recent years, Rudolf Bultmann's writings have been widely publicized, holding that the basic conceptions of Jesus and primitive Christianity belong to the ancient world and have no direct, modern relevance.

The third statement on Jesus in the questionnaire attempted to explore the assimilation of such notions. While a majority of the UUs disagreed with the idea that Jesus' teachings were flawed by his eschatology, it is noteworthy that 29% of the posttraditionals agreed with the statement as contrasted with only 9% of the right-wing UUs. This differential could, of course, simply reflect the operation of an anti-Jesus and pro-Jesus prejudice, rather than any assimilation of the results of historical scholarship.

To some extent, statement 4 throws light upon this. It must be noted that the "don't know" response dropped from 20% on statement 3 to only 8% on this question, and varied more markedly between the posttraditionals and the others. We must therefore be cautious in any direct comparisons of the magnitude of agreement on the two statements. Nevertheless, it can be noted that the percentage differential between posttraditional and right-wing agreement with statement 3 was 20, while the difference between the percentages agreeing with statement 4 was 31. It seems reasonable to postulate that statement 4 is a better indicator of the presence of prejudicial feelings regarding Jesus since it makes no specific reference to recent historical findings and since a sharply lower percentage of the respondents appear in the "don't know" row. If we compare the differential responses on these two statements, taking the posttraditional response as a base, the difference on statement 3 is 69% and drops to 58% on statement 4. We therefore conclude that the posttraditional response on these two statements reflects more than the operation of a consistent anti-Jesus biasing.

Viewing these two statements in more general terms, we may conclude that the strongest form of the initial hypothesis, that the impact of historical studies would reduce the contemporary relevance of Jesus teachings for Unitarian Universalists, is not confirmed. The hypothesis would have led to a majority agreeing with statement 3 and disagreeing with statement 4, whereas actually a majority of UUs behaved oppositely to the way that had been predicted. The responses of the posttraditionals shifted in the direction suggested by the hypothesis, but not sufficiently to confirm it. Since there is no reason to assume that the posttraditionals have had any greater exposure to historical scholarship or have more successfully assimilated it, we should probably view their differential estimate of the relevance of Jesus' teachings as reflecting their religious stance.

As already indicated, the earliest strands of Unitarian thought were anti-Trinitarian. Some of the Universalist fathers also rejected Trinitarianism. Nevertheless, they all proceeded along the lines of Arius, a third-century thinker who was eventually declared heretical. The Arians held that Jesus was metaphysically of intermediate status, being less than God but nevertheless more than man. Within such a tradition, it would not be at all unusual to regard Jesus as a Messiah (in Greek, a Christ) and, therefore, to regard him as "divine." With few exceptions, the words ascribed to Jesus in the New Testament indicate that he thought of himself in this manner. The anti-Trinitarian arguments that have appeared at various times in Christian history and that played such a central role in the early development of Unitarianism and Universalism took these biblical passages for granted and simply argued that the full doctrine of the Trinity—which not only metaphysically identified the Son with the Father but extended this identification to the Holy Spirit—was absent from the early church or the biblical materials and was a speculative product of later Christian thinkers.

During the last century, some historical scholars asserted that Jesus had not viewed himself as a Messiah (and obviously therefore not as divine in any special sense). It would be a fair estimate that contemporary New Testament scholarship is rather evenly divided on this issue.

To explore the assimilation of these ideas, the two statements shown in Table 3.9 were included. Statement 5, that Jesus thought of himself as a Messiah or Christ, is a reasonably straightforward test of the assimilation of critical ideas, since the New Testament tradition, as we have indicated, is overwhelmingly supportive of the statement. That only 39% of the UUs accepted the statement indicates the assimilation of such ideas. It may be noted that only a slightly larger percentage of right-wing UUs accepted this statement. In the light of this, the interpretation of statement 6 is somewhat more difficult. Evidently, the respondents did not regard a claim to Messiahship as identical with a claim to divinity, since 81% of them felt that this latter status was "created" by the church after Jesus' death. If Jesus had claimed to be a Messiah and if this had been regarded as a claim to divine status, the early church would have been maintaining a tradition rather than creating one. Statement 6 may therefore be regarded as a measure of the classical "orthodox heresy" of liberal religion, and it should be noted that the heresy is shared more fully by the posttraditionals.

The UUs, as expected, did not reject statement 5. Insofar as that statement measures critical knowledge, the lack of any sharp differentiation on the basis of self-ascription further confirms the suggestion that we made in interpreting responses to statements 3 and 4, that critical scholarship has been equally assimilated across the UU ideological spectrum. Regarding statement 6, the

TABLE 3.9

Estimates of Jesus' Self-Conception and Divinity as Related to Self-Ascription

Item	Percent of total (Nwt)	Self-Ascription		
		Right %	Left %	L% minus R%
5. "Jesus thought of himself as a Messiah or Christ."	(156,812)			
Agree	39	43	39	−4
Disagree	36	34	35	1
Don't know	25	23	26	3
6. "After Jesus' death the church created the idea of his 'divinity.' "	(157,615)			
Agree	81	73	83	10
Disagree	9	16	8	−8
Don't know	10	12	10	−2

overall response conformed to what might have been predicted, but the ideological differentiation suggests that the posttraditionals are even more faithful to an "orthodoxy of heresy."

The final two statements on Jesus, shown in Table 3.10, were not designed to be interpreted in correlative fashion, but simply to explore two additional but separate attitudes. Statement 7 is a paraphrase of Rudolf Bultmann's assertion that we can know "little or nothing" about the life or teachings of Jesus.

There is a consensus of agreement with such skepticism among Unitarian Universalists, but it is not shared by the right wing. The contrast between the 57% agreement of the right wing and the 80% agreement of the posttraditionals is sufficiently greater than the acceptance by these two groups of statement 5, and suggests that this statement measures more than biblical knowledge, and that these responses reflect ideological differences.

Statement 8, that Jesus may never have lived, reflects a total rejection of the reliability of the biblical traditions as well as a rejection of the preponderant weight of scholarly opinion. That 23% of the posttraditionals accept this statement further indicates the operation of ideological elements in the attitudes of this group toward Jesus.

Religious Practice

Holding beliefs was the first form of religious behavior that we discussed, followed by our discussion of identification, the holding of beliefs about relationships to others. We now turn to the more conventional meaning of

TABLE 3.10
Estimates of Biblical Reliability and Jesus' Historicity as Related to Self-Ascription

Item	Percent of total (Nwt)	Self-Ascription		
		Right %	Left %	L% minus R%
7. "Trustworthy historical records are so scanty that we can really know little about Jesus."	(158,339)			
Agree	74	57	80	23
Disagree	19	36	14	−22
Don't know	7	7	7	0
8. "Jesus may never have lived."	(158,153)			
Agree	19	8	23	15
Disagree	70	85	64	−21
Don't know	11	7	12	5

religious behavior, what is often called religious "practice." The distinction is often drawn between the private and the public, or communal, forms of practice. We have already cited Glock's current use of the adjectives devotional and ritual to cover these two aspects. The available data on the Unitarian Universalists does not permit a clean distinction between these two, but does let us examine the meanings of prayer for them and the values of church attendance.

The Functions and Frequency of Prayer

The questionnaire listed six common descriptions of prayer under the heading "Which of the following describes the purpose or function that prayer fulfills for you?" The list also provided for other descriptions to be listed in the margin. Less than 2% of the respondents expanded the list in this fashion, and an examination of their additions has indicated too much variety or overlapping to expand the original category list. The question also included a final category called "I do not find the term useful," and 34% of the respondents checked this. Since the question was intended to evoke personal meanings of prayer and not simply definitions of what people thought others might mean by it, additional meanings were not tabulated when checked by respondents who also checked this last category. Responses on the functions of prayer are presented in Table 3.11. Since multiple answers were possible on this question, two forms of presentation are used in this table to assist in understanding the significance of these functions for UUs. The first three columns contain the percentages of each self-ascription group that circled that particular function. Thus, 40% of the right wing would include "communion with God" as a function or purpose that prayer fulfills for them while only 4% of the posttraditionals would include this function. The next three columns contain the variances from chance in the selections made by each group.

TABLE 3.11
Functions of Prayer for UUs, as Related to Self-Ascription

Function	Percent including function			Variance from chance (%)			Nwt
	R	C	L	R	C	L	
Communion with God	40	17	4	24	13	−38	19,081
Petition	19	10	4	16	12	−27	11,867
Intercession	23	13	4	16	15	−32	14,119
Meditation	53	51	30	4	10	−14	62,682
Autosuggestion	6	11	8	−3	11	−8	13,922
Communion with inner self	34	40	26	1	9	−11	50,276
No use for concept	7	17	49	−8	−16	24	54,774

For that 64% of the Unitarian Universalist population finding prayer to be meaningful, "meditation" is the most frequently listed function, followed by "communion with inner self." "Autosuggestion" and "petition" are least frequently cited. It is evident from this data that the practice of private prayer rather sharply separates the right-wing and the posttraditional groups. For all practical purposes, the 51% of the posttraditionals who engage in personal prayer include only meditation and communion with innner self as meanings of their practice. By way of contrast, 93% of the right wing find a personal meaning in prayer. They would agree with the overall denomination and the posttraditional group in placing the highest rank order upon meditation, but depart quite sharply from the overall denomination or the posttraditional, or even the center group in listing "communion with God" in second place. It is also clear from the right-wing responses that the several traditional meanings of prayer such as intercession and petition are still functional for them.

Immediately following these items in the questionnaire was the direct question "How frequently do you pray?" Responses to this question are presented in Table 3.12. We may assume that essentially the same individuals who did not find prayer a useful term responded "Never" on this question and the distributional percentages would indicate this to be the case. From the overall pattern of responses on this table, it is clear that the Self-Ascription Index differentiates UUs in terms of the frequencies with which they engage in prayer, and that prayer is far less frequent for the posttraditionals than for the right wing. If we assume that the connotations of the previous question on the functions of prayer carry over into these responses on the frequency of praying, we are led to the somewhat surprising conclusion that within the majority group of UUs (the posttraditionals), 78% report that they seldom or never engage in "meditation."

TABLE 3.12
Frequency of Prayer, as Related to Self-Ascription

Item	Percent of total (Nwt)	Right %	Left %	L% minus R%
		Self-Ascription		
"How frequently do you pray?"	(159,330)			
Often	11	30	5	−25
Occasionally	24	39	17	−22
Seldom[a]	28	24	26	−2
Never	37	8	52	15

[a]Center group was 32%.

Church Attendance Values

While it was important to understand the meaning of UU religiosity by uncovering the functions of communalism, the exploration was difficult because of the wide variety of practices and terminologies. A number of Unitarian Universalist groups declined to refer to themselves as "churches." In some cases, this practice stems from the early congregational emphasis upon the local parish in New England practice. In other cases, the motivation is quite opposite and reflects the desire to separate the group from conventional religiosity. Similarly, the word "worship" is not universally used by UUs. In 1964, the denomination published *Hymns for the Celebration of Life*. This seemed a clear attempt to find a substitute for the more traditional word "worship."

A list of seven "church attendance values" was included in the questionnaire, with three-point very important/not important scales, under the general heading "How important to you are the following aspects of attending church service?" The responses to these values are presented in Table 3.13. In terms of rank ordering of the "very important" percentages, there is general agreement between the posttraditionals and the right wing with the overall denomination on the first three values. "Intellectual stimulation" is not only the most important value for all groups, but its salience is underscored by the magnitude of these responses. Seventy-five percent of the denomination view this as very important, whereas the second most important church attendance value, "personal reflection," was only viewed as very important by 49%, followed by "fellowship" with 45%. The Unitarian Universalists gave the lowest ranking to the value of "group experience of participation and worship" (24%), and accorded essentially the same ranking to "motivation to serve others" (32%), "music-aesthetic satisfaction" (31%), and "celebrating common values" (30%).

TABLE 3.13
Functions of Church Attendance, as Related to Self-Ascription

Item	Percent of total (Nwt)	Self-Ascription		
		Right %	Left %	L% minus R%
"How important to you are the following aspects of attending church service?" "Very important"				
1. Intellectual stimulation	75 (158,606)	62	78	16
2. Fellowship	45 (158,153)	44	45	1
3. Celebrating common values	30 (154,420)	26	30	4
4. Group experience of participation and worship	24 (156,427)	38	18	−20
5. Personal reflection	49 (156,356)	56	45	−11
6. Music-aesthetic satisfaction	31 (157,357)	43	28	−15
7. Motivation to serve others	32 (156,803)	36	29	−7

In examining the effects of self-ascription, it will be observed that intellectual stimulation is relatively more important to the posttraditionals and that worship is considerably less important to the posttraditionals than to the right wing (18 as compared to 38%). Music, personal reflection, and the motivation to serve were also of less importance to the posttraditional group. Self-ascription makes no noticeable differentiation in regard to celebrating common values or fellowship.

On the basis of this description of the religious practices of the Unitarian Universalists, it has become apparent that we can use conventional categories of "ritualism" or "devotionalism" only with the most radical redefinition. We could always say that devotion is whatever the members of some religious group do in their private moments, but in this case we would have to say that Unitarian Universalist devotion consists of nonpraying. Similarly, we could redefine ritualism as the perceived functions of collective religious behavior and conclude that the Unitarian Universalists "ritual" consisted of a weekly gathering for intellectual stimulation and fellowship. Since behavior that is repeated serves some function, and since the functions here are clearly articulated by the Unitarian Universalists, it seems justifiable to apply the term ritual to these functions of their common life together.

SUMMARY

In terms of the traditional theological doctrines of Protestant Christianity, Unitarian Universalists are clearly dissenters. Moreover, their dissent or unorthodoxy has a consistency about it. Many of the belief areas we have examined in this chapter, it will be recalled, figured heavily in creating Dimension 1 of UU religiosity—Personal Beliefs, Styles, and Values. In times past, liberal religionists and their critics have had occasion to characterize the belief side of this religiosity as holding that "There is at most one God." (Both have sometimes forgotten that this *mot* comes from Tom Paine's *Age of Reason* where it stood as an affirmative summation of eighteenth-century Deism.)

It will not be enough, however, to rest the description of a religious group by noting the presence or absence of traditional doctrines. When they are found to be absent, we must see what has taken their place. By way of illustration, consider that view of God as morally inscrutable in his judgments and dealings with men which is often labelled "Calvinism." When that view goes, is it replaced with the vision of a God who is moral, just, and loving (in the ordinary human meanings of those words), or does the whole idea of a "Transcendent Being" who is somehow related to men and their destinies simply disappear?

The earlier alternative has been the characteristic pattern within Jewish and Christian history, and has usually been correlated with alternative views of human nature. At the beginning of the second century, a Roman named Marcion tried (unsuccessfully) to expunge all references to the "vengeful Jewish God" and rely only on those traditions setting forth the "loving Christian God." St. Augustine, two centuries later, engaged in lengthy polemic with a British monk, Pelagius, who saw human nature as capable of turning toward God and goodness. Augustine, to win his battle, was forced into some extreme defenses of divine sovereignty and human sinfulness. In many ways, these same issues resurfaced in the controversy between Luther and Erasmus concerning "free will." A century later, a pious Calvinist by the name of Arminius, sent to refute the heresy of human freedom, ended up as a convert and lent his name to the most prevalent Protestant version of free man/moral God thinking. That version of the "heresy" not only became central in Methodism but was a major force in early Unitarian and Universalist thinking.

If, however, these earlier forms of UU religiosity held to a clear doctrine of human nature which was coupled with a clear doctrine of a Cosmic Being, their modern successors have moved sharply away from the latter. The current affirmation seems to be that nature and human nature is capable of being morally ordered, without reference to any personalized transcendance. In this sense, the UUs have moved through or beyond the stage of simply privatizing doctrines once held to be enforceable by the community. It will be recalled that Glock found many of the Congregationalists had ceased to be certain about a personal God. In a very influential characterization of the stages of "religious evolution," Robert Bellah has suggested that such a privatization characterized the "modern stage" (1964).

The contemporary UUs would also appear to have moved beyond the substitution of natural science for religion that characterized deism and some early versions of humanism. They seem more likely to look to the social and psychological sciences as sources of human wisdom, although this study was not able to examine the extent of their feeling that these sciences are an embodiment of reason.

In terms of religious identity, UU religiosity regards itself as liberal and describes this by a quite consistent set of affinities for similar denominations. This sense of coherent separateness also appears in relation to Jesus. It will be remembered that these responses were made at the height of the "death of God" controversy. The radical Protestant writers who were at the center of this movement quite typically replaced the "dead God" with a "reconstituted Jesus" (cf. Langdon Gilkey's extensive summary and critique, 1970), and thus felt that they could remain "Christian." In the posttraditional form of UU religiosity, God belongs to a metaphysical past and Jesus to an historical past, and neither, therefore, function as foci.

On the third issue with which this chapter was concerned, religious behavior, we were forced to a redefinition of ritual as the coming together for intellectual stimulation and personal reflection. Quite clearly, these functions are not exclusively ecclestiastical functions in our society. Yet, it is equally clear that the broad cultural offerings do not fully satisfy the Unitarian Universalists and they turn to their churches with some sense of unmet and specifiable need.

The elements of belief, identity, and behavior just summarized are only a part of overall UU religiosity, however, as we characterized it in Chapter 2. We have barely mentioned the whole range of personal and social values, and must now turn our attention in that direction.

Chapter 4

VALUE ASPECTS OF UNITARIAN
UNIVERSALIST SELF-ASCRIPTION

In many ways, the preceding chapter describing religious beliefs, identity, and practices has already been dealing with values. There is a real sense in which traditional religious persons have held it valuable to believe in God or to pray. Conversely, it is valuable to the UU posttraditionals to hold alternative beliefs and engage in alternative practices. In the philosophical framework of this book, beliefs are simply a form of internal behaving.

We shall, nevertheless, regard values separately in this present chapter. This is partly because ordinary language usage makes a distinction between beliefs and behavior, and partly because empirical studies of other religious groups have shown the relationship between behavior and personal and social values to be, at best, ambiguous. Florence Kluckhohn and Fred Strodtbeck, in their crosscultural study of values, evolved a comprehensive definition:

> Value orientations are complex but definitely patterned (rank-ordered) principles, resulting from the transactional interplay of three analytically distinguishable elements of the evaluative process—the cognitive, the affective, and the directive elements—which give order and direction to the ever-flowing stream of human acts and thoughts as these relate to the solution of "common human problems [1961]."

This definition not only includes the cognitive aspect of beliefs within the area of values but also assumes that all men in all cultures face a series of common human problems which they must evaluate. Charles Morris, a philosopher who moved into empirical work with crosscultural values, notes that the three major usages of value all involve some form of the term "prefer." Value has been defined as the preferred, as a conception of the preferable, and as the preferable. He therefore concludes that "preferential behavior" defines the "value field (1956)."

The difficulty with such comprehensive definitions of value is simply that they fail to distinguish adequately between the preference for world peace, for instance, and the preference for chocolate ice cream. Most persons would call the former a major value, whether or not they shared it, and the latter a trivial value, yet both involve preferential behavior. It therefore seems preferable to limit the use of the designation "value" to those conceptions and behaviors that men or groups "choose and cherish." We developed this distinction to permit the value focus to center upon continuing, high-order preferences (Tapp, 1967b).

As a general introduction to the value concerns, thus conceived, of Unitarian Universalists, we may examine the responses to a broad question that was headed "For the social problems listed below, please indicate how important it is to you that liberal religion (in the local church or denomination) be involved in education and action." Nine areas were listed, and for each respondents were asked to check very important, somewhat important, or not important. These areas, listed in the rank order of responses, are shown in Table 4.1.

In terms of a distinction frequently made between personal morality and social morality, the first three problem areas are clearly social and the remainder, with the exception of organized crime, are more distinctly personal. This distinction has certain analogies with the criminologist's description of "crimes without victims." Gambling, alcoholism, or drug addiction may reflect undesirable behavior and undesirable habit formations, but, typically, the person involved brings direct harm to himself rather than to others. The social dimension of the seemingly personal issues is, of course, brought in when we look to the indirect effect upon others of an individual's undesirable habits, or when we recognize the social institutions which support and stimulate such habit formation (drug dealers, organized gambling, etc.). Recognizing these limitations, we shall distinguish between personal and social morality in our treatment. The usefulness of this distinction is further borne out by the fact that items of personal morality typically appear in Dimension 1 of Unitarian Universalist religiosity, whereas items of social morality form Dimension 2.

The posttraditionals ranked the nine areas of value concern in the same order as the total Unitarian Universalist population. Significantly, the right-wing Unitarian Universalists altered this rank ordering. Racial integration dropped to fourth place in their list, and problems of sexual morality were viewed as more important than problems of drug addiction.

TABLE 4.1
Social Problem Areas for Church Action, as Related to Self-Ascription

Item	Percent of total (Nwt)	Self-Ascription		
		Right %	Left %	L% minus R%
"For the social problems listed below, please indicate how important it is to you that liberal religion (in the local church or denomination) be involved in education and action." "Very important."				
1. Racial integration	70 (158,290)	49	75	26
2. Juvenile delinquency	68 (158,506)	71	65	−6
3. Poverty	61 (157,680)	50	64	14
4. Mental illness	57 (158,098)	49	58	9
5. Drug addiction	39 (158,060)	45	36	−9
6. Sexual morality	39 (157,694)	48	35	−13
7. Alcoholism	34 (157,875)	42	31	−11
8. Organized crime	32 (157,248)	37	29	−8
9. Gambling	15 (156,879)	25	11	−14

The posttraditional salience in assessing these problems is even more revealing than the significantly lower rank given to racial integration by the right-wing group. The posttraditionals were much more ready to regard integration and poverty as very important, and much less ready to so regard gambling, sexual morality, or alcoholism. In other words, there is a noticeable difference between left-wing and right-wing Unitarian Universalists in regard to the problems that they consider appropriate for church action. The posttraditionals are not only markedly more concerned with racial integration, but they are also relatively more concerned with areas of social ethics and relatively less concerned with areas of personal ethics.

THE BASIC VALUE SYSTEM

While there are certain merits in this distinction between personal and social ethics, and while any serious concern with values must necessarily be concerned with a large number of specific attitudes and values, we shall nevertheless postulate that each person has what may be termed a "basic value system." Values have a patterning, and, to the extent that this patterning is understandable, we may speak of the "integration" of values. From all that was known about the Unitarian Universalists, it was clear that values, both personal and social, would be an important part of their religiosity. Since it was known that many of them had come to this form of religion from some other kind of background, it seemed important to explore the relationship of the basic system of values and the new religious affiliation. Responses to the question designed for this purpose are shown in Table 4.2. When asked "How has your membership in a Unitarian Universalist Church affected your basic system of values?", 77% responded "Supported my previous value system." We will be exploring the developmental stages of value formation in Chapter 5, but it is important to note here that, as they see themselves, the Unitarian Universalists did not come to their new church and then find a new set of values, but, rather, came with a set of values, presumably joining because they found support for those values. This was more true for the posttraditionals than for the right wing. Only 7% of the UUs selected the alternative "My basic values are not closely related to my religion," thus confirming the assumption of the importance of values for this type of religiosity. Although the 14% response of the right wing to this alternative is markedly higher than the posttraditional response of 6%, it is

TABLE 4.2
Value Role of UU Church, as Related to Self-Ascription

Item	Percent of total (Nwt)	Self-Ascription		
		Right %	Left %	L% minus R%
"How has membership in a Unitarian Universalist church affected your basic system of values?"	(157,306)			
"Provided me with an essentially new value system"	12	12	11	−1
"Supported my previous value system"	77	70	78	8
"My basic values are not closely related to my religion"	7	14	6	−8
"Other"	4	4	5	1

probably a considerably lower response than would occur in mainstream religious group.

Personal Moral Values

We have been defining personal morality as sets of norms whose major operative impact is upon the self rather than upon some other person. Conversely, social morality would be sets of norms whose major impact and referent would be the other rather than the self. By way of illustration, norms regarding masturbation or marijuana would be personal, whereas norms regarding murder or racism would be social. Clearly, the traditional religions of the Western world have generated both personal and social norms in this sense. Behavior has been viewed as sinful when it either broke a norm or fell far short of such a norm. There is an abundance of clinical and empirical evidence indicating that the major meaning of sin for Western Christians has dealt with sexual matters. For this reason, a number of items on sexual values and morality were built into the questionnaire.

In examining the responses to these items, we shall be concerned to examine two different qualitative characteristics of group life as they are affected by self-ascription.

The first of these qualitative characteristics is the presence of consensus within a group upon some particular value. Consensus exists when some high percentage share the value. When consensus is absent, we may speak of polarization if the group preferences are divided between two opposing values, or of pluralization if several distinct value responses command shares of the group allegiance.

The second qualitative characteristic of group life is more complex, and is related to the locus of moral authority. Glock has suggested that there are four kinds of authority that operate within society, each having its own set of sanctions. The most obvious is legal authority, which is ultimately sanctioned by imprisonment—denying the law-breaker freedom of action. In any complex society, there are, additionally, a number of private associations which function as quasigovernmental, quasilegal bodies in relation to the enforcement of norms upon their members. The third type of authority is suprasocial, deriving its norms from some transcendental referent. This has been the usual form of religious authority. Insofar as the rewards or punishments that sanction the norms are not immediate but promised for the future, the authority is suprasocial. Finally, there is the authority "of the self as manifested in the individual sanctions." In this fourth type, the reward-punishment sanctions are less obvious, but no less real (Glock, 1960).

We shall use the term "privatization" to refer to the emergence of this fourth kind of authority system, wherein each individual is not only permitted but expected to make his own preferential choices in moral matters. Privatism is therefore the opposite of a moralistic position, where one individual attempts to impose his moral views upon others, whether through legal means, or through the quasilegal powers of formal, private associations, or through the suprasocial authority of religion. Nevertheless, there may exist within some group a consensus on some essentially privatistic moral position.

The questions on sexual morality, in order to be sensitive to this possibility of privatism, typically used the adjective "justifiable" to describe alternative moral positions. This seemed preferable to the more ambiguous term "moral," or to the term "permissible," which could either connote a *laissez-faire* attitude or convey too many confessional implications and bias the answers. In the final analysis, it seemed that persons would call a position justifiable if they felt that a reasonable case could be made for it. By then asking them to select the most justifiable position, their own orientations would become clear even if they happened to be highly privatistic. We shall regard consensus as present where more than 70% of a group or subgroup share a single response (or two responses that are conceptually close).

Divorce

Responses to the divorce question are shown in Table 4.3. The middle three items of this scale embody current divorce statutes. The "no valid grounds" extreme represented an absolutism that was unacceptable to Unitarian Universalists. The other extreme, that a marriage can be dissolved at the wish of either partner, was designed to be the most permissive alternative and apparently it functioned as this. If the justification of a divorce at the wish of either or both partners represents privatism, then it is clear that there is a privatistic consensus not only in the total sample but in all three of the self-ascription groups. The posttraditionals are clearly the most permissive on this issue. We will be examining the relationship between these attitudes on divorce and the respondents' actual marital status in Chapter 5 but it is worth noting here, since this is the one sexuality-value question for which we have information both on the value and on the behavior, that there is no significant difference in attitudes toward divorce between those who have been divorced and those who remain in their first marriage.

Nonmarital Sexual Behavior

Unitarian Universalists were asked to identify their own attitudes on sexual intercourse between unmarried persons with one of the five alternatives shown in Table 4.4, Item 1.

The responses of the total sample to this question are clearly pluralized, and it would be impossible to speak of any overall consensus. A majority of the right-wing group select the first two (moralistic) responses, while 65% of the posttraditionals opt for the last two (permissive) responses. While this is less than

TABLE 4.3
Grounds for Divorce, as Related to Self-Ascription

Item	Percent of total (Nwt)	Self-Ascription		
		Right %	Left %	L% minus R%
"What do you think should be grounds for divorce?"	(156,938)			
"If one partner to a marriage wishes a divorce, he or she should be able to obtain it without any legal obstacles"	18	9	22	13
"If the partners are incompatible and both wish to end the marriage, they should be able to do so"	67	62	68	6
"If the other partner has practiced mental or physical cruelty, a divorce should be granted"	9	14	8	−6
"Only if the other partner has deserted, is mentally ill, or has engaged in adultery or criminality should a divorce be granted"	5	14	3	−11
"There are no valid grounds for divorce"	1	1	less than .5	−1

consensus, there is clearly a direct correlation here between religious conservatism and value conservatism. In fact, the divergence based upon self-ascription is greater on this item than any of the other questions of sexual values. It will also be recalled that this item had the highest loading on the first factor of the factor analysis. We may therefore regard it as a particularly sensitive measure of the personal moral values of religious liberals.

Extramarital Heterosexual Behavior

Responses to a question on extramarital sexual intercourse are shown in Table 4.4 as Item 2. A clear pluralization is evident regarding the justifiability of such behavior, with equal percentages totally opposed to and favoring the most permissive option. Only within the right-wing group is there consensus, viewing extramarital sexuality as never justifiable. The posttraditionals' responses, as might now be expected, are more permissive with an almost-majority in the most permissive category. Partly as a result of the overall pluralization on this item, the differences between right-wing and left-wing responses are less than on the question of nonmarital sexuality.

TABLE 4.4
Nonmarital Sexual Permissiveness, as Related to Self-Ascription

| | Percent of total | Self-Ascription | | |
| | | Right | Left | L% minus |
Item	(Nwt)	%	%	R%
1. "Sexual intercourse between unmarried persons"	(157,279)			
"is never justifiable"	19	49	9	−40
"is justifiable for engaged couples"	6	7	5	−2
"is justifiable if there is mutual affection"	18	10	21	11
"should be left to free choice"	56	34	64	30
"should be encouraged"	1	less than .5	1	1
2. "Extramarital sexual intercourse"	(156,067)			
"is never justifiable"	43	70	32	−38
"is justifiable if marriage partner agrees"	19	10	22	12
"should be left to free choice"	39	21	46	25
"should be encouraged"	less than .5	less than .5	less than .5	less than .5

Contraception

Attitudes on contraception may not only involve personal moral values but may express certain social concerns and anxieties. To explore this, four questions were asked under the general heading "Do you approve or disapprove of making contraceptive information and devices or pills available to each of the following if they want them?" Respondents were then asked to use a four-point approve/disapprove scale regarding married persons, engaged couples, any adult, and any young person. Responses for the first three groups are summarized in Table 4.5, Items 1-3.

It should be noted that this table presents only the percentages who strongly approved the availability of contraception to each particular group as differentiated by self-ascription.

Previous studies have shown that permissiveness on contraception vary with the reference group, and these results confirm such a variance within the UU population. There was a clear consensus favoring the availability of contraception for those who are married and a majority of the denomination also strongly approved a similar availability for engaged couples or any adults. Even within marriage, however, it will be noted that the posttraditionals were more approving. The real differences emerge when we examine responses to the second and third reference groups, where the issue of nonmarital adult sexuality becomes involved. Here the differences in percentages were 38 and 34, respectively.

To point up the meanings of self-ascription, we have only discussed the "strongly approve" responses. Inclusion of the "approve" responses show majorities in all self-ascription groups approving contraception. For the total population, 100% approved for married persons, 86% for engaged couples, and 84% for any adults.

To complete this exploration of permissiveness, the fourth reference group was "any young person." This term seemed less ambiguous than reference to age or educational level, and the responses (shown in full as Item 4 of Table 4.5) support this assumption. By a considerably smaller majority, the UUs approve what would be, in effect, a universalization of contraception. There is almost a consensual approval (65%) by the posttraditionals, while the right-wing UUs disapprove by consensus (71%). The rather consistent differentiation between the right and left wings is more extreme on this item than on any other and clearly deserves to be labeled as the significant polarization.

TABLE 4.5

Permissiveness on Contraception, as Related to Self-Ascription

Item	Percent of total (Nwt)	Self-Ascription		
		Right %	Left %	L% minus R%
"Do you approve or disapprove of making contraceptive information and devices available to each of the following *if they want them?*" "Strongly approve" for:				
1. Married persons	92 (159,486)	80	96	16
2. Engaged couples	57 (157,623)	29	67	38
3. Any adult	51 (157,679)	27	61	34
4. Any young person:	(156,146)			
Strongly approve	27	13	33	20
Approve	28	16	32	16
Disapprove	29	36	26	−10
Strongly disapprove	16	35	10	−25

Perhaps the sharpest controversies in recent years with regard to sexual behavior have focused upon statutes regulating contraception and abortion. Various state laws have either restricted or prohibited information, prescription, or performance in these matters. In general, these state laws date back to the periods of effective Protestant control of legislatures. The opinion of most Protestant bodies has become increasingly permissive on these issues in the twentieth century, and Protestants have often supported secular attempts to liberalize such laws. Resolutions passed by various Unitarian and Universalist bodies over the years place these two denominations in the vanguard of this reform movement. The most open opposition to such reform has typically come from Roman Catholic forces.

The issues are complex, but most Protestants and many Catholics would probably now agree that the central matter is the relationship of parochial morality (moralism) to public policy. It is one thing for a religious group to urge, or even coerce its own membership to follow a particular moral policy, and quite another for a religious group to seek the translation of its own parochial morality into public policy by means of laws. This is one aspect of the process that we have been describing as privatism. The privatistic person may well choose certain courses of moral action for himself while, at the same time, being unwilling to legislate or even urge these upon his fellow citizens.

If we make certain assumptions, the data permit us to create a measure of privatism and examine the effect of self-ascription upon this measure. It seems reasonable to assume that the persons who approve the universalization of contraception as indicated on Table 4.5 would approve the removal of restrictive laws on contraception as a matter of public policy. It seems also reasonable to assume that the persons who regarded sexual intercourse between unmarried persons as "never justifiable" (Table 4.4) were reflecting their parochial as well as personal morality. For any group, the difference between these two percentages is the measure of sexual privatism, the unwillingness to translate personal or parochial morality into legislated morality. For the total group of Unitarian Universalists the difference is 46%. For the left-wing post-traditional group, it goes up to 56%. With the center group, it drops to 20%, and with the right-wing group, it falls to -20. This figure must be regarded as an extremely significant reversal and reflects the moralistic salience of the right-wing group on sexual morality.

Abortion

Movements to reform or remove abortion laws have typically been separated from movements to legalize contraception. Nevertheless, the two issues are logically correlated. Once we grant the right of persons to control their own reproduction, then abortion becomes the means of choice when contraception has been ignored or has failed. From a biological standpoint, it is hard to draw sharp lines between sperm or ovum, embryo, fetus, neonate, adult human, senile human, comatose human, and corpse. From a human standpoint, however, such distinctions have been vital and every society has made them on some theological or philosophical basis. This study has limited itself to exploring these values as they relate to the problems of contraception and abortion, although it would be reasonable to assume that a similarity of attitudes and values would have been found in regard to suicide and euthanasia.

Abortion attitudes were explored by a widely used list of bases which was headed: "Please indicate whether or not you think it should be possible for a pregnant woman to obtain a legal abortion under each of the following circumstances." Yes/No response was asked for each, and results are shown in Table 4.6. Within the total denomination, there is consensus that legalized abortion should be available under all of these circumstances except 2 (a married woman wants no more children) where the approval percentage drops to 62. Within the posttraditional group, there is consensus that abortion should be legalized under any and all of these circumstances. Within the right-wing group, however, the moralism already observed in the responses on contraception is maintained as a rather significant rejection of abortion in the case of the married woman wanting no more children (57%). It also be noted that only 53% of the right-wing group approve abortion when an unmarried mother does not want to marry the father (Circumstance 6).

We may generalize these attitudes toward abortion by noting that the total sample, as well as the three self-ascription groups, generally place the circumstances in the same rank order, and are less approving of abortion when basically psychological factors are involved (Circumstances 2 and 6). In those circumstances, the approval rate of the right-wing group drops more sharply.

This UU assessment of abortion circumstances also helps place the denomination within the broad American scene. Alice Rossi surveyed abortion attitudes using a national NORC sample in December, 1965, and the UU survey replicated her items to permit validation (this is a limited validation, since there has been a rapid liberalization on this issue which would have been operating during the 5-11-month interval between the NORC study and the UU data collection). The final column of Table 4.6 shows these national percentages. The rank orderings, it will be seen, are the same within both groups, but the all-U.S. magnitude of approval was sharply lower and the differentiation between the various bases is greater. The mean percentage of approval for all six was 39, whereas the UU mean was 84.

This data makes clear that any characterization of right-wing UUs as conservative makes sense only within denominational parameters since their mean approval percentage was 35 above the national figure. Within the national group (Rossi, 1967), men were found to be more liberal (also true for UUs), and liberalism increased with education (paralleled within the UUs). Since parochial education could operate as a confounding variable in any analysis of religious differences, Rossi argued that the meaningful comparison would be found within the group with some college. There she found mean approval percentages of 77 for Jews, 73 for agnostics, 51 for Protestants, and 31 for Catholics. Thus, the conservative UUs were only less liberal than Jews, while the overall denomination was more liberal on abortion than any of the major religious groups.

TABLE 4.6

Bases for Legalization of Abortion, as Related to Self-Ascription

Item	Percent of total (Nwt)	Self-Ascription Right %	Left %	L% minus R%	NORC %[a]
"A woman should be able to obtain a legal abortion:"					
1. "if there is a strong chance of serious defect in the baby"	97 (162,200)	96	98	2	55
2. "if the woman is married and does not want any more children"	62 (159,088)	43	71	28	15
3. "if the woman's own health is seriously endangered by the pregnancy"	99 (162,460)	98	100	2	71
4. "if the family has a very low income and cannot afford any more children"	76 (159,778)	62	82	20	21
5. "if the woman becomes pregnant as a result of rape"	97 (162,247)	98	98	0	56
6. "if the woman is not married and does not want to marry the man"	72 (158,840)	53	80	27	18
Mean % of approval	84	74	87	13	39

[a]From Rossi, 1966; N=1,482.

Homosexuality

A question was devised to explore Unitarian Universalist attitudes toward the encouragement or discouragement of homosexuality by law and/or education, and the results are shown in Table 4.7.

TABLE 4.7

Permissiveness on Homosexuality, as Related to Self-Ascription

Item	Percent of total (Nwt)	Self-Ascription		
		Right %	Left %	L% minus R%
"Homosexuality"	(157,206)			
"should be discouraged by law"	7	24	4	−20
"should be discouraged by education, not by law"	80	71	81	10
"should not be discouraged by law or education"	12	5	15	10
"should be encouraged"	less than .5	0	less than .5	less than .5

Homosexuality has become more problematic within American society as awareness of its prevalence has increased. This awareness has been coincident with an increasing privatization of sexual morality. Further compounding the issue have been discussions of possible genetic bases for homosexuality and psychiatric controversies regarding the alterability of homosexual preferences. To the extent that such inevitabilities or irreversibilities are believed to exist, the illegalization of homosexual behavior is rendered inhumane. It is clear that the overall UU consensus, as well as the consensus of each of the self-ascription groups, appears at the second alternative. As this option appeared on the questionnaire, the full wording was "Should be discouraged by education, not by law." Presumably, a full privatization regarding homosexuality would be the third alternative, which, on the questionnaire, was worded "should not be discouraged by law or education." It is worth noting that three times as many posttraditionals chose this alternative as did the right-wing UUs. It should also be noted that 24% of the right-wing group support laws against homosexuality. Thus it is clear that the general Unitarian Universalist permissiveness on sexual matters is more apparent within the structure of heterosexuality and marriage. This denominational group is less open to the possibilities of homosexuality, although no figures are available to indicate whether their restrictiveness is proportionately more or less than would be found in mainstream religious groups. It is also apparent that the pattern of posttraditional affinity with privatization continues to hold in this, as in other areas of sexual values.

Social Moral Values

In terms of the foregoing illustration of personal moral values of Unitarian Universalists by reference to the available data on their sexual values and attitudes, the general argument of this chapter should have been sustained that no sharp line can be drawn between personal morality and social morality. Our earlier contention was that social morality would be found in those sets of norms whose major impact and referent was the "other" rather than the "self." Thus social morality will try to change the other, on the justification that the other person is harming some third party or perhaps insufficiently promoting the good of some third party. Data on several issues were available to test this theoretical distinction with the Unitarian Universalists as well as to further our understanding of the meanings of self-ascription for them.

Viet Nam

When the questionnaire was designed and administered in 1966, the war in Viet Nam was a major issue but had not yet brought down a President, disrupted college campuses, or corroded the will and means to deal with major domestic problems in the United States. We may also recall that almost no Congressional voices had then been raised against this war, and that the general political climate was either diffident toward or supportive of American military aims in Southeast Asia. Whatever organized dissent existed among the adult population was largely confined to religious groups, and the Unitarian Universalist Association had passed several annual resolutions against the war.

A question was designed to explore attitudes within the denomination. Full wording of this question may be found in Appendix B, Question S-2. Five alternative policies were proposed, roughly ranging from "super-hawk" to "super-dove." Responses are shown in Table 4.8 In the political climate then existing, the first two alternatives could clearly be viewed as supporting U.S. policy whereas alternatives 3-5 were intended to represent a scale of increasing dissent from these policies. The fourth policy, of pullback to coastal enclaves, drew surprisingly little support from the UUs. The modal UU position, that the

TABLE 4.8
Alternatives Favored in Viet Nam, as Related to Self-Ascription

| Item | Percent of total (Nwt) | Self-Ascription | | |
		Right %	Left %	L% minus R%
Favored action in Viet Nam (1966)	(155,148)			
Military increase	9	17	7	−10
Military continue	32	50	25	−25
U.S. initiatives to end war	34	20	37	17
Pullback to coastal enclaves	4	4	4	0
Withdraw militarily	22	10	27	17

United States should take further initiatives to end the war, was as of that time clearly a doveish position, especially in view of the specific illustrations included such as a renewed bombing halt, or the encouragement of a coalition regime which would include the N. L. F. If this modal position, as well as alternatives 4 and 5, are viewed as doveish for 1966, then 60% of the UUs were doveish at that time. The percentage rose to 68 for the posttraditional group and dropped sharply to 34 within the right-wing group. Putting this in more extreme terms, 67% of the right-wing were hawks and 68% of the posttraditionals were doves, an exceedingly sharp polarization.

Shortly after the UU survey, NORC conducted a study of U.S. attitudes on Viet Nam (Verba, Brody, Parker, Nie, Polsby, Ekman & Black, 1967). While the items differed and direct comparisons are therefore not feasible, women were found to be more doveish, and religious affiliation, education, and political activism were discovered to have little effect on feelings about the war. If we continue to regard alternatives 3-5 as doveish, they appealed to 63% of the UU women as against 54% of the men, paralleling the NORC finding. Insofar, however, as the Self-Ascription Index differentiates types of religiousness within this group, there was a very strong religious effect. Education also had a differentiating effect within the UU group on this issue, as did membership in activist organizations.

Selective Conscientious Objection

There is considerable current discussion of the status of the conscientious objector. This issue has been especially important to Unitarian Universalists since they have, for several years, provided one of the highest proportionate numbers of conscientious objectors from among their young men of any of the non-peace churches. Matters of conscience have also been an pressing concern for UUs, since a large number of their young people were nontheistic and, therefore, ineligible for classification as conscientious objectors within the wording of the laws passed by the U.S. Congress.

The matter of selective conscientious objection is more controversial, and even at the time of this writing neither the U.S. Congress nor the courts have been willing to allow that an individual's conscience can be selective with regard to the wars that he is willing to fight. To be eligible for the status of conscientious objector, a man must establish that he is opposed to all wars. Thus, the issue of selective objection has appeared as a new social value within the general context of American life, stimulated by the ambiguities and protractedness of the conflict in Viet Nam. Most American and Canadian religious groups have, for many years, supported the general principle of conscientious objection, and supported their own young men who took such a position, but few have been willing to support young men who were selective rather than absolutist in their objection to war.

This is indeed ironic for religious groups, since the historic position of most Jewish and Christian bodies has not been pacifistic but, rather, within the general set of values from which the arguments for selective objection have emerged. That is to say, in theory the various churches have not automatically supported any and all wars that their nations have chosen to engage in but, rather, have felt compelled to argue that religious persons should only answer their country's call if the war is just. Most of the argumentation along these lines stems from St. Augustine in the fourth century, holding that a licit war must be defensive, hold a reasonable chance of victory, and be conducted by moral means. Pragmatically, this well-elaborated theory has never yet led any national church body to denounce the military endeavors of its own nation and call upon true believers to abstain, but the doctrine typically places on each church member the burden of making such an evaluation and acting upon it.

If this has been the dominant position held by theologians through the centuries, it is clear that laymen have not joined them in this view. The question devised to explore this moral value is shown as Item 1 in Table 4.9.

Thirteen percent of the UUs admitted that they had no position on this issue, and only 40% within the overall denomination were willing to support the eligibility of the selective objector for governmental recognition. While 45% of the posttraditionals would support such eligibility and 59% of the right-wing would deny it, these percentages fall considerably below the general doveishness and hawkishness of the two groups as seen by the responses on Viet Nam.

TABLE 4.9

Approval of Selective Conscientious Objection and Nonviolent Civil Disobedience, as Related to Self-Ascription

| | Percent of total | Self-Ascription | | |
| | | Right | Left | L% minus |
Item	(Nwt)	%	%	R%
1. "If a person of draft age is opposed to certain wars (such as Viet Nam) rather than to all wars, do you think he should or should not be eligible for classification as a conscientious objector?"				
"Should not be eligible"	46 (159,004)	59	42	−17
2. "Which of these statements comes closest to your feelings about nonviolent civil disobedience?"				
"I approve of civil disobedience when laws are unjust"	63 (155,277)	35	71	36

Nonviolent Civil Disobedience

By 1966, the Unitarian Universalist Association had presented awards to Martin Luther King and generally endorsed his efforts. Prior to this, the Beacon Press had published a number of works by and about Gandhi which no doubt contributed to this general support for nonviolent civil disobedience. During King's historic Selma march, about 40% of the Unitarian Universalist clergy and a large number of laymen found their way to Alabama to join him in that endeavor. Results on the item devised to explore this attitude throughout the denomination are shown in Item 2 of Table 4.9.

In interpreting these results, we must recall the context at the time of the survey. Almost the only recent uses of nonviolence had been in the cause of the American Negro. College students were only beginning to apply these techniques on the campus for broader purposes. Therefore, the phrase "when laws are unjust" was, in all probability, viewed by the respondents as referring to segregation laws. Thus, 63% of the overall denomination and 71% of the posttraditional group approved nonviolent civil disobedience under such circumstances. The expected polarization occurred on this item with 59% of the right-wing group disapproving civil disobedience under any circumstances.

It is instructive to compare these responses to the responses on selective conscientious objection. Both items, it may be assumed, evoke feelings about patriotism and law-abiding behavior. Probably, in terms of contemporary rhetoric, both items evoke certain anxieties about anarchy. Certainly, support of these two social values necessarily involves recognition of the sovereignty of the individual conscience which must decide whether a particular war or a particular law is just. Although UUs generally, and the posttraditionals especially, responded in the expected ways to these two items, nevertheless, the magnitude of their response was considerably greater in support of civil disobedience. Interpreting this, we would suggest that it is more useful to focus upon idealization of a community of moral consensus rather than upon the narrower issue of obedience or disobedience to law. After all, the question of selective conscientious objection actually asked whether it would be desirable to legalize such behavior. Even within that nonrevolutionary framework, it did not evoke majority UU support. By reference to the extent of the moral community, we are suggesting that this question raised the possibility of an individual setting himself against the consensual value of the total national community, whereas the issue of civil disobedience probably evoked the image of local or state customs or laws which were not in harmony with the national moral consensus and were, therefore, unjust. Thus, the UU could march in Selma, defying bad local law but feeling that he was doing so in the spirit of and with the support of good national law. But the same person was far less able to imagine himself rejecting the military necessities of a national consensus, even if it were legal to do so.

Sexism

It is easier to define sexism than to measure it with a questionnaire. To be a sexist is to hold that an individual's physiological maleness or femaleness makes a difference in situations where, in fact, it does not. One item in the questionnaire was designed to permit a partial and indirect approach to this attitude, and these recognized limitations necessitate the quotation marks in the heading of this section. The question used was: "If you were a member of the pulpit committee seeking a minister for your church, which of these statements would best describe how you would feel about a woman candidate?" Respondents were asked whether her sex would hamper, make little difference in, or improve her effectiveness. Of all UUs, 48% said hamper and 47% said make little difference. How should these responses be interpreted?

First of all, it must be recognized that the respondent is not being directly asked how he would vote but, rather, for his estimate of the receptivity of the members of his local church to the presence of a woman minister. Since it would be unreasonable to assume that every church in the sample would be equally prepared for the innovation that a female minister would represent, it is possible that the respondents are unbiased, accurate pulse-takers of their fellow members in this evenly divided response. It is also possible that, despite the reference of the question to third persons, the responses really reflect personal feelings. It is also possible that the "little difference" response stems from a kind of reflex liberalism which assumes that this is either the way the individual should answer or the way his fellow church members should feel. Item 1 of Table 4.10 presents the responses to this question as affected by self-ascription.

The posttraditionals are clearly less certain (44%) that a female minister would be less effective than are the members of the right-wing group (62%). From these results, we can reject the assumption that the rather evenly divided response of the whole population represented an unbiased estimate of the receptivity of 80 local churches, since it is unreasonable to assume that the different self-ascription types are proportionately represented in each of the 80 churches. The question, therefore, seems also to be exploring an attitude toward women ministers that is individually held, and that is correlated with the individual's theological position.

Now, let us suppose that the "little difference" response basically reflects a stereotyped, reflex liberalism. We would expect this to be most prevalent among the posttraditionals. Taking them as base, the response only diminishes by 30% when we shift to the right-wing group. The "hamper" response, however, which surely cannot reflect a stereotyped liberalism, undergoes a 41% shift as we move from the posttraditional to the right-wing group, implying that reflex liberalism is not a sufficient explanation for these responses.

The most reasonable interpretation, therefore, of this data is that it affords an indirect but nevertheless effective measure of sexism, and that sexism is less prevalent among the posttraditionals.

TABLE 4.10
Estimated Effectiveness of Women and Negro Ministers, as Related to Self-Ascription

Item	Percent of total (Nwt)	Self-Ascription		
		Right %	Left %	L% minus R%
1. Woman minister:	(159,020)			
"Her sex might hamper her effectiveness"	48	62	44	−18
"Her sex would make little difference in her effectiveness"	47	35	50	15
"Her sex might improve her effectiveness"	5	3	6	3
2. Negro minister:	(158,956)			
"His race might hamper his effectiveness"	26	48	21	−27
"His race would make little difference in his effectiveness"	63	47	67	20
"His race might improve his effectiveness"	11	5	13	8

Racism

The "woman minister" question that we have just discussed was repeated in the survey with the substitution "Negro minister," and the results are shown as Item 2 of Table 4.10. The overall denominational response is by no means evenly divided here, and 63% contend that race would make "little difference." This percentage increases to 67 within the posttraditional group.

The same chain of inferences that we made with regard to sexism should be valid with regard to this item as a measure of racism. Using the same analytical strategy and taking the posttraditional group as a base, the "stereotyped liberal" response only drops by 30% as we shift to the right-wing group, whereas the racist response (race would hamper effectiveness) increases by 129%.

The question on Negro ministers is, therefore, an indirect and effective, if partial, measure of racism, and shows that nonracism is closely correlated with posttraditionalism.

Further interesting comparisons emerge when the distributions on these sexism and racism items are compared. The ambivalence of the overall group on sexism is almost exactly replicated by the right-wing group's ambivalence on racism. And, somewhat ironically, the posttraditionals are nonracist in almost the same proportion that the right-wing UUs are sexist.

Self-Designation on Social Issues and Values

We will conclude this examination of the relationship of self-ascription to social morality by examining the self-designation of these respondents on these same six-point liberal/conservative spectrum that was used for theological issues and values. These figures are presented in Table 4.11.

TABLE 4.11
Social Values Self-Designation, as Related to Self-Ascription[a]

Own position on social issues	Self-Ascription			Percent of total
	Right	Center	Left	
Percentage who answered:				
Liberal	16	24	34	29
—	19	38	41	38
—	26	23	17	20
—	20	8	5	7
—	9	4	2	4
Conservative	10	3	1	2

[a]Nwt=156,380.

The several items on social values that we have been exploring have established the general validity of the Self-Ascription Index as a predictor of social liberalism and conservatism. The results shown in this table indicate that the designations of this index correlate quite closely with the social value self-designations "liberal" and "conservative." The responses in this table should be compared to the responses of Table 3.5 where theological self-designation was described. It will be seen that the most extreme liberal label is less acceptable to Unitarian Universalists with regard to their social values than it is to their theological values. Nevertheless, for either dimension of their religiosity, the liberal label is more acceptable than the conservative label. Recognizing the overall shift away from extreme liberalism as a social label, this common UU preference also holds for the right-wing group.

COMMUNITY AND POLITICAL INVOLVEMENT OF UNITARIAN UNIVERSALISTS

Up to this point we have been considering beliefs and attitudes of the Unitarian Universalists and, with the exception of the question on the frequency of prayer, not been discussing their reported behavior. The objection is often raised that surveys such as this study only what people say and not what they do. We have already raised the theoretical objection to this disjunction that saying is a form of doing. To gain a fuller understanding of Unitarian Universalist religiosity, the questionnaire did include items that reflected overt behavior more directly. One of the issues that has surfaced in religious studies of recent years is the question of church involvement as it is related to nonchurch involvement. Glock, for instance, has suggested on several occasions that these are inversely related, and that the church often functions as an organizational outlet for those who can't make it in secular organizations. The groundwork for a later discussion of this issue will be laid in this section.

Of equal interest is the political behavior of members of religious groups. Not only is this an additional indicator of external behavior, but it strengthens inferences we may want to make regarding the future behavior of persons based on their past behavior. In addition, such data will permit us to expand our understanding of the meanings of self-ascription.

Community Involvements

The final version of the questionnaire listed eight types of organization, and asked people to indicate whether or not they were members. These organizations are listed in Table 4.12. The question also included a "none" response, which 43% of the denomination checked. Many of the 57% who did indicate organizational memberships obviously belonged to more than one organization in the list. The question also included the category "other," and asked for marginal write-in. An examination of those responses revealed that the diversity was too great to necessitate the creation of additional categories beyond those shown in the table.

TABLE 4.12

Nonchurch Organizational Memberships as Percentage Belonging and as Variance from Chance, as Related to Self-Ascription

Organization	Percent belonging to organization			Variance from chance (%)			Nwt
	R	C	L	R	C	L	
NAACP	6	8	10	−4	−5	9	14,556
CORE or SNCC	2	3	5	−6	−7	13	6,524
ACLU	4	8	15	−7	−10	16	18,596
Memorial Society	7	13	18	−6	−5	11	24,163
Planned Parenthood	7	9	11	−3	−2	6	15,962
League of Women Voters	9	11	10	−1	2	−1	16,315
UN Association	6	9	8	−2	3	−1	12,693
SANE or UWF	3	5	6	−5	−2	7	8,000

The list that was used made no pretense of including all possible nonchurch organizations. With one exception, it concentrated upon action or reform organizations that reflected fairly clear value commitments. Membership in these organizations obviously reflects a great variety of levels, as well as kinds of commitment. In some cases, the organizations are primarily national, and membership reflects an exchange between annual dues and the receipt of information. In other cases, the organizations may be quite active on local levels, but the indication of membership may or may not indicate that the individual participates in such activity. It was known that not all of these organizations were real options for Canadian UUs, but attempts to develop a separate Canadian list proved fruitless. The inclusion of Memorial Societies in this list deserves explanation, since they may be unfamiliar to some readers and since they are clearly reform organizations on a different level than the others on the list. A Memorial Society is a local group committed to facilitating simple and low-cost funeral arrangements for its members. Many of the existing societies began in Unitarian Universalist Church basements and, as we shall be suggesting later, they may represent one of the significant contributions of liberal religion to American life.

These data have been arranged to facilitate understanding of the effect of self-ascription upon two aspects of nonchurch organizational membership. The first three columns of the table show the relative percentages of the three self-ascription groups that belong to each organization. This half of the table should thus be read as showing that 6% of the right-wing group belongs to the NAACP or Urban League, and that 10% of the posttraditional, left-wing group belongs to these organizations. The next three columns show the effect of self-ascription upon membership in each organization, expressed as the difference between the actual percentage belonging and the percentage that would have belonged by chance, that is, if self-ascription had not affected organizational membership.

Membership in the organizations of the first two rows represents a commitment to civil rights. The National Association for the Advancement of Colored People and the Urban League were paired together, as were the Congress on Racial Equality and the Student Non-Violent Coordinating Committee. In 1966, support of the first two organizations indicated a traditional liberal commitment to the achievement of integration by basically legal and educational means. Membership in CORE or SNCC (at that time) reflected the same basic values with the added commitment to the use of militant nonviolence as a tool of social change. The two less-militant organizations are older, more wide-spread, and better known, and it was not surprising therefore that more UUs belonged to them than to the more militant organizations. Membership in these organizations is closely related to self-ascription, with more of the posttraditionals belonging than of the right-wing group. This differentiation is further increased in the case of support of the more militant groups. Taking the posttraditionals as the base,

40% fewer right-wing UUs belonged to the NAACP or Urban League, while 60% fewer of the right-wing belonged to CORE or SNCC. The variances revealed the same picture. The posttraditionals are over-represented in civil rights organizations, especially in the more militant organizations.

The figures on membership in the American Civil Liberties Union further confirmed this differentiation, with 15% of the posttraditionals belonging as against 4% of the right-wing. Posttraditional over-representation, the pattern observed with civil rights, also obtains here. Memorial Society membership follows the same pattern, although this is probably to be explained in terms of the theological meanings of self-ascription rather than the social values that are involved. The Memorial Society may represent a rationalization and naturalization of death that does not accommodate well to the relativistically higher immortality belief of the right-wing. Planned Parenthood membership is similarly differentiated, although the extent of the differentiation is less than would have been expected in view of the contrasting attitudes on contraception of the right wing and the posttraditionals.

Only with League of Women Voters membership does the pattern attentuate. There is no significant ideological differentiation here (perhaps substantiating the League's contention that it is nonpartisan).

The final two organizational categories were intended to assess organizational commitments to peace in a similar way that the first two organizations assessed the commitment to civil rights. The United Nations Association is older and is more respectable, whereas the Committee for a Sane Nuclear Policy and the United World Federalists represent a more radical approach to the establishment of a peaceful world. As would have been predicted, the older organization has more members, but the differentiation on the basis of self-ascription holds for both kinds of organization. Comparing responses as we did for the civil rights organizations and taking the posttraditional membership percentages as a base, the right-wing membership in the UN Association drops off by only 25%, whereas the right-wing membership in SANE/UWF drops by 50%.

If we assume that these responses are a fair sample of the nonchurch organizational involvements of Unitarian Universalists, it is clear that the posttraditionals are more involved outside of their churches than are the individuals in the right wing, self-ascription group.

Political Involvements

Voting behavior, as well as political party preference and involvement, can further improve our understanding of Unitarian Universalist religiosity. The questionnaire provided information on party affiliation, voting during the last national election, and the political preference of the respondents' parents. For obvious reasons, we will discuss the U.S. and Canadian Unitarian Universalists separately.

U.S. Unitarian Universalists

The party affiliations listed by the U.S. respondents are shown in Table 4.13, as Item 1. The data shows that a substantial majority, 57% of the U.S. UUs, list themselves as Democrats. A polarization occurs, however, in terms of self-ascription. Two-thirds of the posttraditionals are Democrats and two-thirds of the right wing are Republicans. This is a dramatic differentiation, but it must be remembered that a number of regional and local factors may enter into party affiliation. In many New England areas, for instance, Protestantism and the Republican party have close affinities. Actual voting behavior is probably a better indicator of ideology, and we therefore turn to data on this.

TABLE 4.13
U.S. Political Behavior, as Related to Self-Ascription

Item	Percent of total (Nwt)	Right %	Left %	L% minus R%
			Self-Ascription	
1. Generally support Democratic Party	57 (143,016)	27	66	39
2. Voted for Johnson in 1964	74 (143,284)	53	79	26
3. Parents were Republican	48 (139,422)	67	41	26

Item 2 shows the 1964 voting of the Unitarian Universalists as related to self-ascription. These figures show that the posttraditionals, as well as the overall denomination, voted more heavily for Lyndon Johnson than did the general electorate. Nevertheless, it will be noted that the three-to-one ratio between the percentage of right-wing Republicans and left-wing Republicans was basically sustained in the Republican voting column. (Third party and nonvoting percentages for the three groups were, respectively, 8, 11, and 9.)

While Chapter 5 will be devoted to an exploration of the sources of self-ascription, it is appropriate to note here the responses to the question of parental politics reported as Item 3 of Table 4.13. These figures show that the parents of the posttraditionals were almost evenly split between Democrats and Republicans, whereas the parents of the right-wing were Republicans in approximately the same proportions as their children. When compared to the present affiliations of these respondents, it is clear that political shifting is more likely to occur among posttraditionals than among the right-wing UUs.

Canadian Unitarian Universalists

The party affiliations of the Canadian UUs are shown in Table 4.14, as Item 1. While a slight majority of the overall Canadian UU population belong to the New Democratic Party, this percentage increases to 57 with the posttraditionals. The sharpest differentiation among the Canadians on the basis of self-ascription occurs in Conservative Party membership, dropping from 16% in the right-wing group to 3% in the left-wing.

TABLE 4.14
Canadian Political Behavior, as Related to Self-Ascription[a]

Item	Percent of total (Nwt)	Self-Ascription		
		Right %	Left %	L% minus R%
1. Party generally supported:	(14,615)			
Conservative	4	16	3	−13
Liberal	34	51	32	−19
New Democratic	53	30	57	27
Social Credit	less than .5	0	less than .5	less than .5
Other	1	0	1	1
None	6	2	6	4
2. Vote in 1963 election:	(14,552)			
Conservative	36	50	32	−18
Liberal	50	25	55	30
New Democratic	less than .5	0	less than .5	less than .5
Social Credit	less than .5	0	less than .5	less than .5
Other	7	7	8	1
None	5	'18	5	−13
3. Parental politics:	(13,098)			
Conservative	26	21	25	4
Liberal	34	53	30	−23
New Democratic	11	0	13	13
Social Credit	less than .5	0	less than .5	less than .5
Other	5	0	6	6
None	8	14	9	−5
Politically divided	9	2	11	9

[a]Note: some Canadians indicated U.S. parties, thus all columns do not total 100%.

The last national Canadian election before the survey was in 1963, and UU voting in this election is shown as Item 2. This election was not as one-sided as the United States' election the following year, and the Canadian UUs followed this pattern. Fifty-five percent of the posttraditionals voted Liberal as against 25% of the right wing. There was a clear correlation between posttraditionality and voting Liberal in 1963.

As indicated in Item 3, the posttraditional Canadians come from family backgrounds more evenly distributed than the family backgrounds of the right-wing Canadians. The present affiliations of the latter group are almost identical to those of their parents. Thus, the posttraditional Canadian is more likely to have shifted politically.

SUMMARY

In surveying a number of value stances in this chapter, we found that both the personal and social values of the UUs are closely related to self-ascription, with the posttraditionals consistently holding to more liberal values, in the wider, nonparochial sense of that term.

The personal values discussed dealt with a number of attitudes regarding sexuality. All of these that had been included in the factor analysis (described in Chapter 2) loaded heavily on Dimension 1, the core religiosity dimension where we had located the belief and practice items analyzed in Chapter 3. That fact made it impossible to employ analytical strategies used or suggested for other groups. Glock, for instance, would no doubt regard these sexuality values as consequential, but in this case they are so highly correlated with belief and behavior that they are essentially interchangeable. In view of their conceptual and substantial distinctions from belief and (religious) behavior items, however, we resisted this semantic shrinkage and called attention instead to the breadth of this core religiosity, especially as it appears within the posttraditionals.

In analyzing the more social value items regarding war, demonstrations, and conscientious objection, we found similarly consistent relationships between posttraditionality and liberalism. The coherence of such values allowed fuller explication of Dimension 2 of UU religiosity—Social-Ethical Values.

Even further understanding of this second dimension emerged in the examination of community organizational involvements, where the posttraditionals were most multiply-committed, especially in more activist organizations. Noting that these involvements move into more overt behavior, we then examined the political stances of the U.S. and Canadian UUs, finding the now expected consistency between posttraditionality and liberalism.

In the course of these analyses, we found several instances of sharp polarization on the basis of self-ascription, shedding light on the generalization that had emerged from the factor analysis that, in terms of the overall denomination, personal and social values were related orthogonally rather than unidimensionally. We shall be returning to this issue in Chapter 8, where we will examine dimensionality more closely in terms of the different self-ascription subgroups. It is appropriate now, however, to turn from the meanings of self-ascription to some of its sources and determinants, and these will be the focus of Chapter 5.

Chapter 5

THE "WHY" OF UNITARIAN UNIVERSALIST RELIGIOSITY: THE SOURCES OF SELF-ASCRIPTION

Chapters 3 and 4 have described in some detail the meanings of Unitarian Universalist religiosity, focusing first upon the personal beliefs, values, and attitudes of the UU, and then centering upon his expectations regarding his local church and the larger denominational structure to which it belongs. This description of the way UUs are prepares us for some explanations of how they got that way.

Recognizing the diversities within this religious group, we have consistently used the Self-Ascription Index to differentiate UUs and to show the ways in which the right-wing, center, and left-wing subgroups resemble each other and differ on personal and institutional beliefs and values. In attempting now to explain UU religiosity, we shall not attempt anything as crude as searching for the cause of self-ascription. If the religious self-ascription of individuals, at least those found at the liberal end of the American religious spectrum, is the most useful and significant way of describing the meanings that religion has for them, we may take it as axiomatic that self-ascription is a multi-caused phenomenon. If we can even speak of it as caused, we must think of it as multi-caused and, probably, even as over-caused. With all of these qualifications in mind, the tables of this chapter shift to the format of treating self-ascription as a dependent variable and putting it in the rows, permitting us to see how it is affected when we put a variety of other conditions in the columns. Even when these conditions have clearly preceded the development of an individual's present self-ascription, as in the case of family religious background, we will move with extreme caution in regarding them as in any sense causal. Where we are examining the effects of other processes, such as education, which are clearly concomitant with the development of an individual's self-ascription, we will be less tempted to think of these in causal terms. Renouncing the misleading language of causation does not prevent us from using more interactional concepts such as association. If a particular kind of self-ascription is closely associated with some level of educational attainment, this is a fact well worth knowing since it will enable us to predict the values and behavior of other persons similarly exposed to this condition.

MAJOR DETERMINANTS OF SELF-ASCRIPTION

Age

It has been consistently found that conservatism on almost any measure increases with age. This generalization is confirmed with the Unitarian Universalists when we use the Self-Ascription Index as a measure of religious conservatism, as illustrated by the data shown in Table 5.1, Item 1. These figures show a consistent effect of age upon self-ascription. When we compare the two extreme age groups, this effect is more dramatic with the right-wing UUs, increasing by the factor of more than five, whereas the decrease in posttraditionality occurs only by a factor of one-half. Despite this age effect, it will be noted from the data in this table that a clear majority of UUs under 55 years of age are posttraditional in their religiosity.

Gender

The typical finding of greater conservatism among women is also borne out in the comparison of men and women on self-ascription, shown in Item 2 of Table 5.1. There is a greater differentiation on the basis of gender within the posttraditional group (63 and 52%) than within the right-wing group (8 and 11%).

Unitarian Universalist Longevity

One of the most central questions emerging from this kind of study has to do with whether church membership produces changes in people over a length of time. While recognizing that many other elements, such as age, are involved, it is important to know whether the long-term members of a religious group differ from the newcomers. A beginning answer to this question may be found in the data shown in Table 5.1 as Item 3. Since this survey only included adult members, we may assume that the born Unitarian Universalists have been exposed to the conditioning effects of this denomination longer than ten years,

TABLE 5.1

Age, Gender, and UU Longevity as Affecting Self-Ascription[a]

Self-ascription	1. Age (Nwt=159,686)				2. Gender (Nwt=159,262)		3. Years UU (Nwt=159,372)			
	Under 35	35-44	45-54	Over 54	Male	Female	0-2	3-10	11 or more	Born UU
(%) Right	4	7	10	22	8	11	5	5	13	31
(%) Left	68	65	54	37	63	52	63	65	52	31
Percent of total	*23*	*34*	*21*	*23*	*44*	*56*	*16*	*41*	*33*	*10*

[a] As noted in the text, this and most of the tables in this chapter treat self-ascription as a dependent variable, placing it in the rows of the table (and continuing to report only right and left percentages). This table should therefore be read: "Among UUs under 35 years of age, 4% are right on self-ascription and 68% are left (the remaining 28% being center). Among all UUs, 23% are under 35."

and, therefore, will reflect more fully whatever changes have occurred as a result of such exposure. As a matter of fact, in most cases the born UUs have probably been exposed to the values of Unitarian Universalism longer than the group in the third column of the table as well, those who have been members for eleven or more years. Building on this assumption, we can observe that posttraditionality decreases with length of membership and, conversely, that right-wing self-ascription, by a considerably larger factor, increases with prolonged membership. We should further note that a majority of all the converts in the first three columns are posttraditionals.

The combined effects of age and length of membership upon self-ascription may be seen in the data of Table 5.2 which shows the percentages of posttraditionality. The most striking shift revealed by this table is the sharp decrease in posttraditionality that occurs within the life-long UU group as a result of age, where 52% of those under 35 are posttraditional and only 15% of those over 54 are. Within the convert group represented by the first three columns of this table, no clear pattern is discernible, with the possible exception of the oldest age group where the percentage of posttraditionals drops from 48 for the newcomers to 40 for those who have been Unitarian Universalists for more than ten years.

TABLE 5.2
Percentage "Left" on Self-Ascription as Affected by Age and UU Longevity

Age	Years Unitarian Universalist				Nwt
	0-2	3-10	10 plus	Born	
Under 35	66	71	68	52	35,902
35-44	65	68	63	47	53,389
45-54	50	59	55	34	33,733
Over 54	48	48	40	15	35,348

Place of Residence

Where Unitarian Universalists live was found to have a strong effect upon their self-ascription, as indicated in the data shown in Table 5.3. This table makes clear that living outside of the urban-suburban areas makes a considerable difference in self-ascription. There is little difference between the urbanites and the suburbanites in terms of posttraditionality (61 and 59%, respectively) and only slightly greater difference in the percentage of right-wing UUs (7 and 10%). There is a sharp decrease in posttraditionality (to 45%) and an even greater increase in right-wing self-ascription (to 18%) among the UUs living in small towns (for all practical purposes, there are no rural members).

TABLE 5.3
Residence and Residential Mobility as Affecting Self-Ascription

Self-ascription	1. Place of residence (Nwt=159,092)			2. Years in present community (Nwt=158,528)		
	Urban	Suburban	Other	0-5	6-10	Over 10
Right(%)	7	10	18	4	7	15
Left(%)	61	59	45	65	63	50
Percent of total	*42*	*38*	*20*	*28*	*21*	*52*

THE MATCHED AND PREDICTIVE SUBSAMPLES

At this stage of our attempt to understand the sources of Unitarian Universalist self-ascription, it seems appropriate to introduce another analytic tool. While we will remain concerned with the necessity of explaining the Unitarian Universalists as they now exist, we will also want to infer trends within the group, and make certain extrapolations and predictions of the future of this group. If, for instance, age has a strong effect on UU ideology, and the overall age distribution of American society is shifting, we need some way to take this into account as a dynamic force affecting the future configurations of the group. Similarly, if there are internal forces within the group that will alter its future configurations, and these forces have an effect upon ideology, we will want to find some way of taking them into account. One way of doing this is to designate subgroups within which closer analyses can be made. In a technical sense, this is done by controlling certain variables, holding them constant and thus removing their effect.

We have already seen that age has a powerful effect upon self-ascription. Similarly, whether one is a convert or a born UU is a major determinant of self-ascription. We also have found that place of residence strongly affects self-ascription, and it is clear that the residential pattern of America is shifting from small towns into larger urban-suburban complexes. Given the dominance of converts within the denomination, we will designate those individuals who meet this criterion, who fall within the modal age bracket of 35-54 years, and who live in urban or suburban areas as a predictive subsample. Analyses of these persons will give us a clearer picture of the future patterns of Unitarian Universalism. Since we are also concerned with the differences between the newcomers and the born Unitarian Universalists, when we include those from the latter group who meet the age and residence criteria, we will refer to a matched subsample.

Retaining the weighting system used to analyze the total sample, the matched subsample constitutes 44% of the denomination. Converts account for 94% of the matched subsample (an increase of 4% compared to the overall denomination), and 49% of the matched subsample are male (an increase of 5%). Of the matched subsample converts, 49% are male, and of the born UUs, 45% are male.

ADDITIONAL SOURCES OF SELF-ASCRIPTION

Residential Mobility

Residential mobility is increasing in American life, and this seems likely to increase posttraditionality, as indicated by the data shown in Table 5.3, Item 2. There is a significant difference between the percentages of posttraditionals who have lived less than five years in their present communities and those who have lived more than ten years (65 and 40). Since a majority of present UUs are residentially stable, one may expect the larger demographic pattern to have a multiplier effect upon posttraditionality in the future.

Type of Church

Strictly speaking, we cannot treat the three types of Unitarian Universalist churches in the study (growth, ordinary, and fellowship) as sources of self-ascription. Nor, if we find that there are different proportions of the three self-ascription groups in different types of church can we assume that an individual's orientation (measured by self-ascription) determines the type of church that he joins. The ordinary Unitarian Universalist seldom has all three types of church equally available to him in geographical terms. Nevertheless, it is worth examining the relationship between self-ascription and the type of church in view of the widespread impression held by Unitarian Universalists that the fellowships represent a far-left fringe. The actual relationship is shown in Table 5.4. These data show that the fellowships contained the largest percentage of posttraditionals (67) and that the ordinary churches contained the smallest percentage (55). The differences in the percentages of right-wing and post-traditional UUs in these two types of church are even more striking (11 and 3, respectively). These differences are smoothed considerably if we look only at the predictive subsample, however, where 64% of ordinary church members are posttraditional, 65% of growth church members, and 69% of fellowship members. In other words, if we distinguish between the three types of church in order to predict some

TABLE 5.4
Type of Church as Affecting Self-Ascription

Self-ascription	Type of church (Nwt=160,800)		
	Growth	Ordinary	Fellowship
Right(%)	5	11	3
Left(%)	61	55	67
Percent of total	*6*	*84*	*10*

present event such as a denominational vote, the differences are marked, but if we control for age, convert status, and place of residence, the differences in posttraditionality are very minor. Assuming that the Unitarian Universalist movement continues on its present pattern of growth, it would appear that the three types of churches will converge ideologically.

Regionalism

In the discussion of the sampling procedure in Chapter 1, the creation of several hypothetical regions for analytic purposes was discussed. It will be recalled that both the Unitarians and the Universalists achieved their initial strength in New England. In the westward movement of the Unitarians in the nineteenth century, the then Western Conference (centering in Chicago) became the outpost for the more leftish theological tendencies. In subsequent years, Unitarian Universalists have commonly assumed that the churches of the Pacific slope were well to the left of the mainstream. Variations in the self-ascription within these several regions were shown in Table 1.7

On the basis of that limited regionalization of the denomination, it became clear that the New England churches are salient in their proportion of right-wing members and in their lack of posttraditional membership. It is also clear that for the regions defined, Canada and the Pacific Coast have the highest proportion of posttraditionality (70 and 71%, respectively). The Midwest region is lower in posttraditionality (65%), while in New England the percentage of posttraditionality drops to 27. The significance of the striking New England conservatism becomes greater when it is recalled that the denominational headquarters for the Unitarians as well as for the Universalists were in Boston, and the merged Unitarian Universalist Association has retained this locale. The preponderance of deliberative assemblies for the denomination as well as its predecessors have occurred in Boston. This, plus the fact that financial considerations make it predictable that local people will furnish a disproportionate share of committee personnel and that the headquarters' bureaucracy will be most exposed to local churches, suggests the considerable difficulties that the Unitarian Universalist movement has had in achieving a representative status.

OTHER SOURCES OF SELF-ASCRIPTION

In calling attention to differences in self-ascription that may be attributed to the convert status of Unitarian Universalists and to the peculiar role that regionalism has played in the development of this religious group, we were noting sources of self-ascription that were probably unique to Unitarian Universalism. We also discussed the role played by age, gender, and the place and stability of residence in order to describe the subsample that will be used throughout this chapter, even though these demographic determinants are present in all religious groups. Let us now consider the effects upon self-ascription of a series of other determinants which are common to all religious groups in order to discover their impact on the Unitarian Universalists.

Income

In describing the overall American population, social and political liberalism are inversely related to income. Since the Self-Ascription Index has been shown to be closely correlated with social and political liberalism among Unitarian Universalists, we would expect to find posttraditionality decreasing as we move up the income scale. The data, however, reveal no clear pattern, as indicated in Table 5.5, Item 1. If anything, the highest percentage (12) of right-wing UUs is found in the lowest income group. The highest percentage (62) of posttradition-ality is found in the middle income group (before-tax family income of $10,000 to $15,000), while the higher and lower income groups are approximately the same in their percentage of posttraditionality (57 and 55, respectively). Thus one major component of social class has essentially no discernible effect upon self-ascription.

Education

Education is also a measure of social class, and, as shown in the second item of Table 5.5, has a consistent and powerful effect upon self-ascription. The more education a Unitarian Universalist has, the more likely he is to be posttradition-al. If we contrast the two extreme groups in this table in terms of education, the decrease in right-wing membership in the higher education group is significantly stronger than the increase in posttraditionality. Another way of generalizing the data would be to note that the 58% of Unitarian Universalists who have some college or the bachelor's degree exhibit the same percentage of posttraditionality (57) as the overall denomination. Thus the college impact proves quite norma-tive for UU ideology.

It has usually been found that the educational level of parents has an effect upon the values of an individual. Information was available regarding the educational attainment of the respondents' fathers, shown as Item 3 of Table 5.5. This was found to have no effect upon self-ascription.

Despite this seeming absence of relationship between the educational level of the family (as measured by the father's education) in the subsequent self-ascrip-tion of Unitarian Universalists, there may be forces operative here that deserve further attention. For one thing, educational level is a useful reflection of social class, and we need to understand the relationship of social class to self-ascrip-tion. We must also raise questions about possible relationships of class mobility to self-ascription. Mobility is the dynamic aspect of the class structure within any society. Given our data, we can derive a useful measure of class mobility by comparing the highest educational level attained by respondents with that attained by their fathers. Within the total denomination, 3% have less education than their fathers, 50% have the same, and 48% have more. While the group of downwardly mobile UUs is almost too small for analysis, valid comparisons are quite feasible betwen the stable UUs and the upwardly mobile UUs.

In a classical historical analysis of the role of denominations in the development of American religion, H. Richard Niebuhr depicted the denomination as basically a class-related institution (1929). Thus, an individual shifting within the class structure would typically be accompanied by a shifting within the denominational structures. The preponderance of converts (90%) among Unitarian Universalists permits an ideal test of this theory. If the theory is valid, and if educational mobility is sufficient measure of class mobility, we should find a larger percentage of upwardly mobile persons among ex-Catholic and ex-fundamentalist UUs, since those religious groupings within the American context are more typically lower class, and we should expect a lower percentage of upwardly mobile persons from ex-liberal Protestant backgrounds, since the liberal Protestants have typically been upper class. We will perform this analysis separately for the men and women since the research design did not permit the matching of husbands and wives where both were members. As there may be a gender-related pattern in which one gender characteristically determines denominational affiliation, this separate analysis of men and women will minimize the confounding effect of such a possible pattern. The percentages of upwardly mobile persons coming from different family religious backgrounds is shown in Table 5.6. The mean percentages for all converts were 54 for men and 43 for women. Using a variance of 5% from these means as a criterion, a striking confirmation of the general hypothesis appears within both genders. Among the ex-fundamentalists, the upwardly mobile men are overrepresented by 10% and the women by 11%. Within the ex-Catholic group, the respective percentages of overrepresentation are 13 and 11. In further confirmation of the hypothesis, among ex-liberal Protestants, the underrepresentation among men is 8%, and among women, 5%. It is worth noting that these underrepresentations drop even more sharply within the group whose family background was Unitarian Universalist (24 and 10, respectively). The overrepresentation of upwardly mobile men and women among the UUs whose family background was mixed Catholic/non-Catholic may probably also be taken as further confirmation. The very significant overrepresentation of upward mobility among both men and women from Conservative or Orthodox Jewish backgrounds is more difficult to explain. It will be noted that the representation of upward mobility among both the male and female UUs from Reform Jewish backgrounds does not vary significantly from the means. On present evidence, the explanation for this differentiation among ex-Jews who are now Unitarian Universalists would seem to be that Reform Judaism is close enough to Unitarian Universalism (as already indicated by the religious distance

TABLE 5.5

Income, Education, and Father's Education as Affecting Self-Ascription

Self-ascription	1. Family income (Nwt=154,797)			2. Education (Nwt=158,519)				3. Father's education (Nwt=154,442)	
	Under 10,000	10,000-15,000	Over 15,000	High school or less	Some college	College degree	Graduate degree	High school or less	Some college
Right(%)	12	7	10	14	10	9	8	10	10
Left(%)	55	62	57	49	57	57	62	58	57
Percent of total	*37*	*33*	*30*	*16*	*23*	*35*	*26*	*60*	*40*

TABLE 5.6

Educational Mobility of Men and Women Related to Family Religious Background[a]

Percent with more education than fathers'	Family religion										
	UU	Liberal Protestant	Fundamentalist Protestant	Liturgical Protestant	Catholic	Reform Jewish	Conservative/ Orthodox Jewish	Catholic/ non-Catholic	Jewish/ non-Jewish	Other religion	No religion
Men	30	46	64	52	67	57	74	61	54	56	58
Women	33	38	54	40	54	40	60	52	42	47	38

[a]Nwt=144,196.

114

data of Table 3.6) that conversion is not characteristically associated with upward mobility. Or it may be that the educational level of Reform Jews is such that upward mobility is less characteristic of that religious group, and, therefore, less characteristic of those who convert from it. The only item in Table 5.6 not readily explicable in terms of the relationship between American denominations and the American class structure is the minimally significant underrepresentation of upwardly mobile women among the UUs with a nonreligious family background.

Class Mobility and Self-Ascription

One of the strongest sources of posttraditionality is conversion. It will be recalled from Table 5.1 that only 31% of the born UU group were posttraditional, whereas 60% of the convert group were designated left by the Self-Ascription Index. Using our measure of educational mobility as a reflection of class mobility, we are now ready to ask whether class mobility has an overall effect on self-ascription, and, more specifically, whether differences in class mobility will help explain the sharp ideological differences between the born and the convert groups. For this analysis, we will use the matched subsample in order to control several demographic variables. The relationships of mobility and self-ascription are shown in Table 5.7.

TABLE 5.7
Educational Mobility as Affecting Self-Ascription, in Matched Subsample[a]

| Self-ascription | Own/Father's education | | | | | |
| | Less | | Same | | More | |
	Convert	Born	Convert	Born	Convert	Born
Right(%)	4	19	7	13	6	20
Left(%)	55	68	62	43	67	56

[a]Nwt=68,882.

Since only 2% of the matched subsample were downwardly mobile (the "Less" columns), we shall not view those percentages as reliable for comparative purposes but, rather, will concentrate upon the stable persons ("Same" columns) and the upwardly mobile ("More" columns).

Within the matched subsample, 47% of the born UUs were posttraditional and 64% of the converts were. While this is a considerably smaller gap than within the total denomination, it is a substantial differential and should be kept in mind. The data in the study clearly show that self-ascription is related to class mobility. The differential between the convert and born groups of nonmobile UUs is 19%, whereas the gap is reduced to 9% among upwardly mobile UUs.

Not only may this convergence be observed, but there is also a significant increase in posttraditionality as a result of upward mobility. Within the convert group, this increase is 5%, and within the born UU group it is 13%.

Forms of Employment and Self-Ascription

In determining class status, the type of employer and the nature of employment are often components of an index. Granting the limitation in class breadth of the Unitarian Universalists, it seems worthwhile to examine the possible effect that these variables may have on self-ascription.

Each respondent was asked to indicate the type of employer for the main earner of the family. This information, as it affects self-ascription, is shown in Table 5.8. As compared to the overall American population, it is clear that relatively large percentages of UUs are employed by the government or non-profit organizations. A comparatively large percentage are self-employed, and a small percentage are employed by private enterprise.

TABLE 5.8
Type of Employer of Main Earner as Affecting Self-Ascription[a]

	Type of employer				
Self-ascription	Private enterprise	Non-profit	Government	Self-employed	Non-employed
Right(%)	9	9	6	11	26
Left(%)	57	61	61	59	35
Percent of total	*44*	*14*	*26*	*13*	*3*

[a]Nwt=153,040.

Among those employed, the smallest percentage of posttraditionality is found among those working in the private sector (for simplicity at this point we shall not distinguish between persons directly engaged in different types of employment and their spouses). Those in government employ or working for nonprofit institutions are more likely to be posttraditional (61 as against 57%). This difference is statistically significant but not large. Posttraditionality within the self-employed group is 59%. At the other end of the ideological spectrum, the government employees are least likely (6%) to be in the right-wing group, while self-employed persons are most likely (11%). Although only 3% of the UUs are unemployed, it is worth noting that posttraditionality is least (35%) within this group and the largest proportion (26%) of this group is right wing. If we use a 5% variation from the mean as a criterion, we can conclude that the type of employer does not affect self-ascription.

In addition to the type of employer, we have information on the respondent's occupation. One item asked for the occupation of the main earner in the family.

Since our concern here is with the more direct effect that occupation may have on self-ascription rather than with its familial impact, we shall assume that in most cases the main family earners are male and examine these effects among men in the predictive subsample. The information is shown in Table 5.9.

Within this subsample, 6% of the men were right-wing and 68% were posttraditional. Continuing to use the 5% variation criterion and, for statistical reasons, disregarding the 1% of the subsample engaged in manual or service work, the only reportable variation in self-ascription as a result of type of employment occurs with the men engaged in sales or clerical work, whose posttraditionality is 10% below the mean. Insofar as the Self-Ascription Index also reflects a salient political and social liberalism, it would appear that the only type of employment where work norms transcend personal and religious norms in their press for conformity is in the sales and clerical kind of employment. With this one exception, we may conclude that an individual's type of employment has no demonstrable effect upon his self-ascription.

Occupational information was asked, as an additional item, in the event that the respondent was the second earner in a family. Among these second earners, 95% were women. Table 5.10 presents the effect of the type of employment of the second earners on their self-ascription. Since 5% of the persons on this table are male, and since we will be discussing the effect of type of employment upon self-ascription, we may note here the general finding that males are more posttraditional, and then further note that 32% of the second-earning men are students, and 37% of them are professionals, distributed evenly between the teaching, science/engineering, and "other" categories. Insofar as most of these types of employment are associated with posttraditionality, the presence of the few men does not seriously contaminate the findings. Within the total denomination, 52% of the posttraditionals are women. In this tabulation, 52% of the second earners are posttraditional. We will regard these as essentially identical groups, and use a variance of 5% from the latter figure as the criterion of significance.

On this basis, the UU who, as second earner, is employed as a teacher, as an "other" professional, or as a student is most likely to be posttraditional. While the professionals employed in science or engineering are statistically underrepresented in posttraditionality, it will be noted that only 1% of the second earners are so employed. The right-wing respondents represent 11% of the persons in this table, and the only significant variations from this appear in two occupational categories containing only 1% of the second earners. We therefore conclude that the type of employment of the second earners is not significantly associated with right-wing self-ascription, but is significantly associated with posttraditionality in the case of teachers, other professionals, and students who, together, comprise 23% of the second earners.

TABLE 5.9

Occupation of Main Earner as Affecting Self-Ascription Men in Predictive Subsample[a]

	Main earner's occupation							
Self-ascription	Manual	Trade	Sales	Manager	Professional: teacher	Professional: scientist	Other professional	Student
Right(%)	2	8	5	6	5	4	7	0
Left(%)	90	70	58	64	70	71	69	less than .5
Percent of total	*1*	*5*	*7*	*18*	*10*	*31*	*29*	*less than .5*

[a] N_{wt}=32,039.

TABLE 5.10

Second Earner's Occupation as Affecting Self-Ascription[a]

	Second earner's occupation								
Self-ascription	Housewife	Manual	Trade	Salesman	Manager	Professional: teacher	Professional: scientist	Other professional	Student
Right(%)	12	15	17	9	11	8	17	9	5
Left(%)	50	49	50	57	54	59	40	58	70
Percent of total	*66*	*1*	*1*	*6*	*2*	*10*	*1*	*8*	*5*

[a] N_{wt}=93,056.

Regional Variations in Employment

Although we have found only slight relationships between types of employer or employment and self-ascription, mention should be made of the few regional variations from the denominational pattern that obtain. In type of employer, 7% more of the Canadians were employed by government. Among New Englanders, 7% more were employed by private enterprise and 13% less were in government employ. In terms of type of employment, the only significant variations occurred with the New Englanders. Within these churches were 6% more skilled tradesmen, 8% more managers or owners, 7% fewer scientists or engineers, and 6% fewer "other" professionals.

THE FAMILY PATTERN AND SELF-ASCRIPTION

We have already shown that posttraditionality is associated with upward educational mobility. Thus, it is more likely to occur when a break with the class pattern of the family occurs. Insofar as the once-married, nuclear family represents a traditional pattern in Western culture, and parenthood represents a traditional concomitant of the family role, the possible effects that these have upon self-ascription must be examined.

The Marital Pattern

Table 5.11 presents the relationship between marital status and self-ascription. In terms of what has been said, we would expect posttraditionality to be more prevalent among persons who deviate from the traditional family pattern.

TABLE 5.11
Marital Status as Affecting Self-ascription[a]

Self-ascription	Marital status				
	Single	Married	Remarried	Divorced	Widowed
Right(%)	17	10	4	6	19
Left(%)	51	57	65	68	37
Percent of total	9	73	8	5	5

[a]Nwt=159,267.

Since the data does not permit us to establish the priority in time of a divorce or of posttraditionality, we shall not suggest that either causes the other, but it may be that some common personality structure is associated with both. The data of this table suggest that those persons who had gone through the processes of divorce are also more likely to be posttraditional. Among those who have remarried, 65% are posttraditional, while the percentage increases to 68 among those who have not remarried. If, however, we approach these data assuming that married persons in an unbroken nuclear family establish some kind of traditional norm, then we must note that 57% of them are posttraditional, the same incidence of posttraditionality that occurs within the total denomination. It will also be noted that single persons are significantly more right-wing and significantly less posttraditional (+7 and −16%, respectively). Conceptually, this would indicate that single persons are even more traditional than those who marry. In the case of the widowed persons in this table, the low posttraditionality and high right-wing orientation may partially be a function of age.

Certain regional variations in the marital patterns of Unitarian Universalists should be noted. The Canadians are significantly more once-married (80%). Of the Pacific Coast UUs, only 60% are once-married, 15% have divorced and remarried, and 11% are presently divorced or separated without remarriage. While these variations might seem partially to explain the higher posttraditionality of the Pacific Coast UUs, that thesis would require a conservatism among the Canadians which is, in fact, not present.

The Effect of Children

Table 5.12 shows the relationship between parenthood and self-ascription. Table 5.11 revealed that only 51% of the 9% of the UUs who had never married were posttraditional. The data here suggest that an additional 9% of the UUs are married and childless, and are no more likely to be posttraditional than the single persons. The same tendency is present at the other end of the ideological spectrum, with significantly more nonparents and single persons likely to be right-wing.

TABLE 5.12
Parenthood and Church School Parenthood as Affecting Self-Ascription

Self-ascription	1. Children (Nwt=160,800)		2. Church school children (Nwt=160,800)	
	None	Some	None	Some
Right(%)	15	9	13	9
Left(%)	51	58	52	59
Percent of total	*18*	*82*	*28*	*72*

The Effect of Church School Parenthood

Not only are 82% of the Unitarian Universalists the parents of children, as just indicated, but 72% of them have children presently in the church school. Item 2 of Table 5.12 shows the effect that this has on self-ascription. While those without children in the church school are slightly more likely to be right-wing in their self-ascription, they are significantly less likely to be posttraditional.

We would suggest that the posttraditionalizing effect of children upon parents, whether in or out of church school, is best explained in terms of the close association of posttraditionality with younger persons. Parenthood thus exposes individuals to the transmission belt of posttraditionality in a way that is denied to childless persons.

Religious Background

As already indicated, information on the religious backgrounds of Unitarian Universalists included data on their "family religion during childhood" as well as on their "religious preference before joining a Unitarian Universalist church." In examining the effects of religious background upon self-ascription, we shall need to consider both of these kinds of information in view of the fact that many of the Unitarian Universalist converts did not come directly to their present affiliation from their childhood religion but, rather, had some intermediate preference or affiliation. Table 5.13 displays the relationships between self-ascription and the family religions and prior religions of the UUs.

Looking first at the effects of family religion upon self-ascription, we are reminded that the born Unitarian Universalists, when compared to the total denomination, are 20% higher in right-wing self-ascription and 25% lower in posttraditionality. From this data, we learn also that those from Jewish backgrounds are significantly less right-wing and very significantly more posttraditional (31% more, for instance, in the case of those from Reform Jewish background). We also note that those from Catholic background, while only slightly more posttraditional, are significantly less likely to become right-wing UUs. If we focus upon the men and women in the predictive subsample, thus controlling the effects of extremes in age and place of residence, we probably obtain an even clearer picture of the effects of religious background upon present converts. Women of liberal Protestant background are 9% lower in posttraditionality. Ex-fundamentalist women are 5% higher. Ex-liturgical Protestant men are 5% lower in posttraditionality. The ex-Catholic men and women move in different directions, the men being 7% higher and the women 5% lower in posttraditionality than the mean for the subsample. The ex-Jews in the subsample continue to be significantly higher in posttraditionality, with no differences between men and women in this regard. Finally, we must note that the men coming from no religious background are 31% higher in posttraditionality.

When we turn to the effects upon self-ascription of the immediately prior religious preference, as shown in Item 2 of Table 5.13, many stronger relationships appear. These effects are much harder to interpret since they are com-

TABLE 5.13

Family Religious Background and Prior Religion as Affecting Self-Ascription

1. Family religion (Nwt=146,084)

Self-ascription	UU	Liberal Protestant	Fundamentalist Protestant	Liturgical Protestant	Catholic	Reform Jewish	Conservative/ Orthodox Jewish	Catholic/ non-Catholic	Jewish/ non-Jewish	Other	No religion
Right(%)	30	10	9	8	4	3	1	7	0	7	10
Left(%)	32	54	60	56	61	86	83	58	78	60	57

2. Previous religion (Nwt=157,611)

Self-ascription	UU	Liberal Protestant	Fundamentalist Protestant	Liturgical Protestant	Catholic	Reform Jewish	Conservative/ Orthodox Jewish	Catholic/ non-Catholic	Jewish/ non-Jewish	Other	No religion
Right(%)	31	11	15	10	5	1	1	a	a	5	3
Left(%)	31	50	48	51	52	87	86	a	a	67	76

[a]Not applicable on this item.

122

pounded by the effects of earlier religious shifting from family backgrounds (compare to Table 1.5 where the paths of conversion were described). We can begin to understand some of the shifts as we compare differences in the percentages of present UUs who were raised in particular religious groups with those percentages who were in those groups prior to becoming Unitarian Universalists. While only 3% of the UUs were raised in families with no religious affiliation, 28% of the converts describe themselves as unaffiliated prior to joining a Unitarian Universalist church. The other group showing an increase is the liberal Protestant categorization listed as the prior religion of 37% of the UUs, but as the family religion of only 30%. In the case of all other religious backgrounds, the percentage growing up in the religion is higher than the percentage remaining in the religion until the shift to a UU church.

The data permit us to explore some questions regarding the relationship of the old to the new. Assuming that individuals retain something of their past when they undergo religious conversion, the significant question will really be whether they retain it as a good memory or as a bad one. In the case of those who have converted to Unitarian Universalism, the new represents a general shift to the left for those persons whose old had been some Christian religious grouping. Let us also make another, more hypothetical, assumption that there is sufficient consistency in the path of religious shifting (at least for persons from the educational and class background of the UUs), to support the hypothesis that any intermediate religious affiliation also represented a leftward shift for the individual involved. In other words, if the UU convert grew up in a Lutheran ("liturgical Protestant") home, he would have been very unlikely to have shifted to a fundamentalist group and much more likely to have shifted to a liberal Protestant group along the road to his present Unitarian Universalist affiliation.

With these assumptions in mind, let us examine the data regarding UUs from fundamentalist, liturgical Protestant, and Catholic backgrounds. In all three cases, a significant amount of intermediate conversion had occurred, as indicated by the smaller percentages in the bottom row of the second item. On the assumption that these intermediate conversions were typically leftward movements, we would expect that persons who had not made such intermediate conversions but had come directly into UU churches would not typically have moved as far to the left in their religious ideology. Such a prediction would be confirmed if the percentage of posttraditionality was higher within the larger group born into one of these denominations than in the smaller group who came from that denomination directly to a UU church. In all three cases, the data confirmed this prediction. Only 48% of those coming directly from fundamentalism are posttraditional, as against 60% of those who were born fundamentalists. Within the group coming from liturgical Protestant churches, the percentages are 51 and 56. For those from Catholic background, the percentages are 52 and 61. This generalization is further confirmed by those from these religious backgrounds if we examine their prevalence at the other end of the UU spectrum. Of the fundamentalists who moved directly to a UU church, 15% are right wing, whereas only 9% of the larger group who were born fundamentalists have become right-wing UUs.

Using the 5% variation from the mean as a criterion of significance, no pattern is discernible among UUs who have converted from liberal Protestant churches. Since we have already shown that the liberal Protestant churches serve as an intermediate conversion step for many UUs, this might be expected. Of all the converts to Unitarian Universalism who were raised as liberal Protestants, 54% are now posttraditional. That only 50% of those who were affiliated with a liberal Protestant church prior to their conversion have become posttraditional UUs clearly reflects the presence in this larger group of a number of ex-fundamentalists, ex-Lutherans, and the like, who, while having moved leftward from their own family religion, nevertheless were still, at the point of conversion, somewhat more conservative than were their fellow liberal Protestants who subsequently moved with them into UU churches.

In the case of those who have converted from some form of Judaism to Unitarian Universalism, there are different forces at work. The historic patterns of Judaism, especially its Reform version, make it difficult to speak of conversion to Unitarian Universalism as an inherently leftward shift. While most religious Jews would no doubt regard such persons as having defected from Judaism, it is nevertheless clear that, from the standpoint of their own overwhelmingly posttraditional self-ascription, they have not become Christians. Thus we would not have expected to find any significant differences in self-ascription between those who came directly or indirectly from Judaism to Unitarian Universalism.

Finally, we must examine the persons in the last columns of these two tables. Only 3% of the UUs were raised in families with no religious affiliation, whereas 31% describe this as their religious status prior to joining a UU church. Only with these persons is the likelihood of posttraditionality lower for those beginning here as compared to those who moved here as an intermediate position (57% as compared to 76%). In all probability, this seeming reversal is explainable in terms of the disparity in size of the groups reflected on the two tables and by the inference that those who made the shift to a "no religion" orientation and then subsequently decided to join a Unitarian Universalist church would be most likely to find affinities with the posttraditional tendencies within that church.

LIFECYCLE STAGES IN RELATION TO SELF-ASCRIPTION

Previous studies of human development have been almost unanimous in holding adolescence to be the period of religious change. Most studies of conversion have focused upon persons moving from a less intense to a more intense form of religiosity, in the conventional sense of that word. Since such a large percentage of the UUs are converts, it seemed fruitful to ascertain the effect of the lifecycle upon their religious development. While their religious backgrounds were more or less representative of the American population, and while their shift to Unitarian Universalism represented a movement away from traditional religiosity, the conversion nevertheless might have been accompanied by an intensity similar to that of the convert to a more traditional religion.

For the sake of clarity, let us review this three-step process which we are about to relate to stages of the lifecycle by moving backward from the present situation of the UU convert. He now has a present affiliation (UU) and a present ideological orientation (self-ascription). We have been assuming that this actual denominational affiliation was preceded by an earlier religious identification with certain liberal ideas and values. That identification is the middle step in the full conversion process which culminates in affiliation. The first step, rendering the middle step possible, must have been an alienation or disenchantment with some earlier set of religious ideas and values. The analysis here proceeds in terms of this disenchantment/identification/affiliation process.

Disenchantment

To discover the stage of alienation or disenchantment, respondents were asked "During which of the following stages of life did your previous religion cease to be meaningful for you?" These responses, as cumulative percentages, are shown as item 1 (Disenchantment) of Table 5.14. By the end of high school, 44% had ceased to find meaning in their former religion, and by the end of college and/or before marriage, 76% reported this alienation.

The relationship of the disenchantment stage to subsequent UU self-ascription was examined within the predictive subsample to minimize confounding effects of college-attendance patterns within different age-cohorts. These percentages are shown in the two self-ascription columns. There is a very clear relationship between the earlyness of disenchantment and posttraditionality. This could, of course, indicate that posttraditionalizing is an ongoing process within individuals and the sooner it begins, the further it progresses as of some later age. The effects of age that we examined at the beginning of this chapter, however, would not lend much support to such an interpretation. It seems more likely that the data reflect that early emphasis within the psychology of religion of the centrality of religious turmoil during adolescence, except that these posttraditionals experienced the turmoil in negative form, as a deconversion.

Mobility and Disenchantment

We have already established the close relationship between upward educational mobility and self-ascription. Since educational attainment differentials

TABLE 5.14

Disenchantment and Identification as Affected by Lifecycle Stages, Cumulative Percentages of Total Sample, Right and Left Self-Ascription Groups within Predictive Subsample, and Upward Educationally Mobile Men and Women

| | 1. Disenchantment (Nwt=121,793)[a] | | | | | 2. Identification (Nwt=157,577) | | | | |
| | | Self-Ascription | | More education than father | | | Self-Ascription | | More education than father | |
Lifecycle stage	All	Right	Left	Men	Women	All	Right	Left	Men	Women
Grade school	12	6	15	13	9	7	15	7	6	5
High school	44	25	48	49	38	26	41	28	23	22
College or before marriage	76	64	81	86	73	55	59	59	59	52
Early marriage	87	83	90	92	87	70	75	73	73	69
Early parenthood	92	90	95	95	94	87	85	89	88	88
Early maturity	100	100	100	100	100	100	100	100	100	100

[a] Excludes born UUs and respondents indicating no previous religion.

may represent a major alienating force in relation to the family and its religious affiliation, the relation of mobility to disenchantment has been shown, for men and women separately, in the two "More education than father" columns of item 1 of Table 5.14. By the end of high school, 49% of the upwardly mobile men had experienced disenchantment, as against 38% of the women. This is very similar to the gender differentiation found within the posttraditional group as a whole. Nevertheless, the upwardly mobile women experience a considerably earlier disenchantment than those UUs who have moved into right-wing self-ascription. Thus, upward mobility, early disenchantment, and subsequent post-traditionality are strongly related.

Identification

We would not be justified in assuming that a new set of commitments is automatically the concomitant or even the result of alienation. Even for those persons who shift to a new value structure, there may well be an intermediary anomic period. Therefore, a second question was devised to provide estimates of this time gap. In the case of the Unitarian Universalists, it was clear that many of these converts had come to their present set of value identifications long before they actually affiliated with a UU church. The comparison of the life stage of disenchantment with the stage of affiliation would therefore have been mislead-ing. To overcome this, respondents were asked "During which of the following stages of life did the values of liberal religion first become personally meaningful for you?" It was felt that this phrasing would permit a more accurate designa-tion of the point of new value commitments. Responses are shown as item 2 (Identification) of Table 5.14. Comparison of this data with the information on disenchantment makes clear that the assumptions underlying these two ques-tions were correct. Whereas 44% of the UU converts were alienated from their previous religion by the end of high school, only 26% of the Unitarian Uni-versalists identified with the basic values of liberal religion as personally mean-ingful for them at that life stage. It should also be noted that the identification information reflects responses from the total denomination, on the assumption that even nonconverts went through a stage of life in which they personally appropriated the values of their family religion. Even if one assumes that the individual raised as a Unitarian Universalist would have been more likely to interiorize these values at an earlier age, the differences between the stage of disenchantment and the stage of commitment are striking. While the stages of the lifecycle used to elicit these responses do not represent equal blocks of time, we might still generalize that the disenchantment process essentially seems to occur one stage prior to an identification with liberal values.

Inspection of the effects of the stage of disenchantment upon subsequent self-ascription suggested that early disenchantment is more likely to produce posttraditionality. The data on the stages of identification suggest what might appear to be an opposite trend, in which posttraditionality is more likely to result from the commitment to liberal values at a later stage of the lifecycle. Taken together, these two trends suggest that posttraditionality is the result of relatively early disenchantment and relatively late commitment to liberalism. In the production of right-wing Unitarian Universalists, these data also suggest a combined effect of the stage of disenchantment and the stage of identification. The later the stage of disenchantment, and the sooner the stage of commitment, the more likely the result will be right-wing self-ascription.

Mobility and Identification

Patterns of upwardly mobile men and women are shown in the last two columns of item 2 of Table 5.14. The gender differentiation only appears at the college/before marriage stage, and is never as pronounced as it had been with disenchantment. In other words, these UU women resemble the right-wing subgroup pattern of relatively later disenchantment and relatively earlier identification.

In summarizing these findings, we can conclude that the college experience has been crucial in the production of UU religiosity. Even as the college is the major facilitator of mobility within the American context, it has been for the UUs also the facilitator of both disenchantment and identification. For 32%, this was the stage of disenchantment, and for 29% it was also the time of identification.

UNITARIAN UNIVERSALISM AS A SOURCE OF SELF-ASCRIPTION

In Chapters 3 and 4, we examined many aspects of Unitarian Universalist religiosity in relation to self-ascription, and found that self-ascription was a consistent and useful way of describing variations within this denomination. In the present chapter, we have explored the sources of UU self-ascription, exploring ways in which various background determinants might explain the variations in self-ascription. While we found that a few of these considerations had negligible impact, the overall effect of the considerations of this chapter has surely been to underscore the initial expectations that we would find self-ascription to be not only multiply-caused, but also over-caused. Before we accept this less-than-tidy conceptual conclusion, however, we need to examine one more possibility. Doing so, we will turn our attention away from the demographic data or the data on the backgrounds of Unitarian Universalists and focus directly upon the religious movement itself. Is it possible that the explanation of self-ascription lies in the impact of Unitarian Universalism? Putting this another way, is this kind of religiosity in any sense contagious, leading to variations in pattern based on length of exposure to the UU climate?

At the beginning of this chapter, in examining the effect of "Unitarian Universalist longevity" in Table 5.1, it appeared that right-wing propensities increased with length of membership, and posttraditionality decreased. Let us now examine this generalization more critically in terms of the predictive subsample. In this way, we are narrowing our focus to those converts between 35 and 55 years of age who live in urban-suburban areas. We will further control our focus by looking at the men and the women in this subsample separately. These data are presented in Table 5.15.

TABLE 5.15
UU Longevity as Affecting Self-Ascription, Men and Women in Predictive Subsample

Self-ascription	Years UU		
	0-2	3-10	11 or more
Men (Nwt=32,547)			
Right(%)	5	5	5
Left(%)	65	68	69
Percent of total	*15*	*51*	*35*
Women (Nwt=32,427)			
Right(%)	7	6	8
Left(%)	58	63	57
Percent of total	*15*	*49*	*37*

Of the men in the subsample, 6% are right wing and 68% are posttraditional. For the women, the respective percentages are 10 and 60. Inspection of the effects of longevity on these means shows that the largest variation, in either the right-wing or posttraditional group, is only 4%. If there is any discernible pattern, it is the slight tendency toward polarization among the men, but the shifts are not statistically dramatic.

We must thus conclude that this continental denomination does not, as a whole, generate religio-ideological changes within its members which cannot be explained in terms of nonreligious determinants. This is not quite the same thing as concluding that religion makes no difference in the lives of individuals. We shall, in fact, be examining this more closely in Chapter 8 where we explore the milieu of the local church. But it does mean that whatever changes occur within Unitarian Universalists do not occur consistently across the denomination as a whole.

SUMMARY

We have, in this chapter, examined rather extensively a number of possible sources or determinants of UU self-ascription. In summarizing these analyses, we will concentrate upon posttraditionalism, since this is so clearly the dominant position within this denomination and especially among those converts who (so uniquely) dominate the denomination. Almost without exception, the determinants of posttraditionality are inversely related to the right-wing position more common to those born UUs who have opened the doors of "the stepfathers' house" to the newcomers.

Let us first review the relatively dynamic sources of posttraditionality, those determinants reflecting changing patterns within American society itself. To the extent that these patterns persist, they will thus have a multiplier effect upon leftness of self-ascription. These sources include population shifting toward megalopolis and the concomitant residential mobility. This, plus other factors, point toward an increasing religious mobility which is related in partial ways to increases of posttraditionality. Not only do ex-fundamentalists and ex-Jews typically become left-wing UUs, but also those who come to this denomination as a third affiliation.

The most important source of all is the increasing proportion of young persons who have some kind of college experience. Not only does this college experience itself increase posttraditionality, but it also facilitates class mobility which compounds the effect. For the present UUs, college was the scene of their break with their religious pasts and their identification with liberal religious values. This alienating effect of the colleges is no doubt far from uniform and very likely becomes much weaker in community colleges and junior colleges, but we would still conjecture that it will remain the major source of posttraditionality.

Somewhat more static sources of posttraditionalism are parenthood and maleness. It seems doubtful that either of these characteristics will undergo rapid changes in the larger culture, and there is no reason to expect any significant shift in the male/female proportions within this denomination.

Since posttraditionality was found to be age-related, it might seem that we should add youthfulness to this listing of static determinants. Yet it is not at all clear that any individual UU will move to the right as he grows older. There may well be a cohort effect here that physical age alone cannot account for, and those forces moving any particular age-cohort of UUs to some proportion of posttraditionality may indeed have more lasting effects. Without a series of longitudinal studies, there is no way of knowing.

A final determinant of posttraditionality, quite unique to this denomination for the historic reasons noted, is living outside New England. If the former growth rate is ever reachieved and the denomination assumes a more equalized national distribution, this might become a dynamic source.

In concluding this inventory of sources and determinants, we must note that the length of actual membership (longevity of UU affiliation) has no major effect on posttraditionality. This somewhat surprising finding deserves fuller analysis, and we will return to this problem in Chapter 8. We can also note that family income, type of employer, and occupation have little clear effect on posttraditionality.

Chapter 6

THE SUNDAY THING—
TOGETHERNESS IN RELIGIOSITY

The examination of the meanings and sources of Unitarian Universalist religiosity in Chapters 3-5 prepares us to explore some of the shared institutional values that generate and sustain the commitment of Unitarian Universalists to their local congregations. We will also assess some of their attitudes toward their continental denomination.

We will continue to use the Self-Ascription Index as a way of describing UU similarities and differences. The findings reported in the previous chapters have shown the usefulness of this index in predicting beliefs and values, and it therefore seems worthwhile to discover whether it is an equally useful predictor of institutional values.

THE CHURCH—ACTUAL AND IDEAL

In the discussion of religious behavior in Chapter 3, we showed that the most important function or purpose of religion for UUs, regardless of their ideological self-ascription, was intellectual stimulation. This was followed by the expressed desire for personal reflection, and by a desire for experiences of fellowship. The more traditional connotations of worship were of less importance. It seems fair to assume that an individual's description of the functions of religion reflects some blend of what he is presently experiencing and what he would like to be experiencing. To elicit these two aspects of "getting" and "wanting" separately, a list of eight institutional emphases of local churches was developed and individuals were asked to assess the relative importance that each of these should have and were then asked, using the same list, to describe the relative importance that each emphasis now had. The denomination as a whole ranked the desired functions in the following order:

1. Religious education
2. Ministerial leadership
3. Fellowship among members
4. Public worship
5. Social action
6. Lay leadership
7. Adult programs
8. Personal development

This ranking is based upon the percentage delineating each emphasis as very important. This descriptive rank ordering of present church emphases was essentially shared by both the posttraditional and the right-wing groups.

When the Unitarian Universalists turn from description to desire, ranking the same eight emphases as they should be rather than as they now are, important alterations occur and very important differences between the self-ascription groups appear. The rank ordering of emphases within the denomination for the future church is:

1. Religious education
2. Ministerial leadership
3. Personal development
4. Fellowship among members
5. Social action
6. Adult programs
7. Public worship
8. Lay leadership

The distribution of "very important" responses, as affected by self-ascription, is shown in Table 6.1. Clearly, religious education, for the UUs, is and should be the most important emphasis of the local church. Similarly, the UUs as a whole are agreed upon the importance of ministerial leadership. It is equally clear that they feel considerably slighted in the emphasis placed upon personal development in the local church. And it is quite clear that they collectively feel that worship is being overemphasized.

If we examine the contrast between the posttraditionals and the right wing, the disparities between the ideal and the actual are underscored. Both groups share the commitment to religious education, but differ sharply on public worship, social action, personal development, and ministerial leadership. Worship ranks third for the right wing and eighth for the posttraditionals, while social action is third for the latter group and drops to eighth place within the right wing. Personal development is second for the posttraditionals and only fifth for the right wing. Ministerial leadership, second for the right wing, drops to fifth for the posttraditionals.

TABLE 6.1

Desired Church Emphases, as Related to Self-Ascription

Item	Percent of total (Nwt)	Self-Ascription		
		Right %	Left %	L% minus R%
"... what you feel your local church's emphases should be." "Very important."				
1. Religious education	70 (159,196)	77	67	−10
2. Ministerial leadership	56 (158,493)	71	50	−21
3. Personal development	53 (158,223)	45	55	10
4. Fellowship among members	51 (159,419)	49	52	3
5. Social action	48 (158,180)	26	54	28
6. Adult programs	42 (158,968)	31	45	14
7. Public worship	36 (158,114)	69	25	−44
8. Lay leadership	33 (158,281)	30	34	4

Once we move beyond the total consensus on the paramount importance of religious education, therefore, it is apparent that there are considerable differences within this denomination regarding the appropriate emphases for local churches, and that these differences vary considerably in terms of self-ascription or theological orientation. In Chapter 7 we will be examining this more closely as we develop a Church Satisfaction Index. At this point, it is sufficient to note that institutional expectations are closely related to theological orientation.

THE CHURCH AS EDUCATOR

In view of the consensus just shown on the importance of religious education, we will next examine the responses UUs gave to items dealing with emphases in the religious education curriculum of their church. To ascertain this, a list of eight emphases was used. The questionnaire first asked respondents to evaluate each emphasis on an approve/disapprove basis for the church school curriculum, and then asked them to evaluate the same list in respect to adult education programs. In the design stage of this research, it had been assumed that there would be considerable differences in what the adult UUs wanted for themselves and in what they wanted for their children. Using the "strongly approve" response to each emphasis as the basis for ranking, the rather surprising fact emerged that there was no difference at all in the emphases that these adult UUs want for themselves and those that they want for their children. Table 6.2 shows the "strongly approve" responses for each emphasis, listing them in the descending order of approval which held for both child and adult curricula. This ranking is:

1. More stress on social problems of modern world
2. More stress on religious implications of science and modern knowledge
3. More stress on personal psychological development
4. More stress on creative and artistic activities
5. More stress on Unitarian Universalist past and present
6. More stress on non-Western religions
7. More stress on Judeo-Christian traditions
8. More stress on the Bible

Clearly the emphasis here is upon the contemporary world rather than historical religious materials, whether Western or non-Western. Even the particular historical traditions of the denomination receive a relatively low ranking. Social problems and the religious applications of science and knowledge are clearly primary.

In assessing the importance of these responses, it must be remembered that they reflect desired changes rather than an absolute set of curricular priorities. In other words, the responses are conditioned by the impressions that Unitarian Universalists have of their present local educational program. Since the curricular materials available to them from the denominational publisher (Beacon Press) include a number of text books on biblical materials, Jesus, and non-Western religious traditions, it would be a mistake to interpret the ranking above as an indication that Unitarian Universalists do not feel such materials are relevant to the curriculum. Unless we make the somewhat doubtful assumption that an increased stress in one area must necessarily lead to a decreased stress in another, it seems more realistic to interpret this ranking as a measure of satisfaction and dissatisfaction with the emphases listed.

Contrasting the posttraditionals and the right wing, the most significant disagreement relates to the Bible. The posttraditionals are least desirous of expanding this emphasis, while it is of first importance for the right wing in relation to their children. For the posttraditionals, the most neglected emphasis is on social problems, whereas the right-wing group puts this in fifth place. The posttraditionals are also more concerned with personal psychological development and with creative and artistic activity.

TABLE 6.2

Desired Religious Education Emphases, as Related to Self-Ascription

Item	Percent of total (Nwt)	Right %	Left %	L% minus R%
		Self-Ascription		
"If changes in emphasis were made in our *church school* curriculum?" "Strongly approve more emphasis on:"				
1. Social problems of the modern world	41 (154,309)	17	49	32
2. Religious implications of science and modern knowledge	35 (153,983)	20	39	19
3. Personal psychological development	34 (153,262)	15	39	24
4. Creative and artistic activities	26 (153,645)	11	31	20
5. UU past and present	22 (153,392)	26	22	−4
6. Non-Western religions	10 (150,999)	5	11	6
7. Judeo-Christian tradition	10 (151,661)	23	6	−17
8. Bible	8 (151,702)	33	3	−30

THE CHRISTIAN LABEL

We have already noted, in our discussion of the Self-Ascription Index, that 57% of the Unitarian Universalists did not view their personal religion as Christian. In view of the fact that this designation has not only been used to refer specifically to a religious tradition in the Western world but is also generally used as synonymous with good, decent, or normal, it was surprising to find so many of the UUs unwilling to employ it as a descriptive of their own religion. It seems likely that their answers, in the context of a questionnaire designed to study their particular kind of religiosity, display a reflective self-analysis rather than the more offhand general usage.

Since this study was concerned with religion in both personal and institutional manifestations, respondents were further asked "Do you define your local church as 'Christian?' " The responses to this item are shown in Table 6.3, Item 1, where it will be seen that 60% replied negatively. A considerable polarization on this issue exists between the self-ascription groups. Ninety percent of the posttraditionals responded negatively while 82% of the right-wing UUs responded affirmatively.

The question of religious label was explored even further by the item "Would you say that others in your community generally regard your local church as 'Christian?' " Response is shown as Item 2 of Table 6.3. Unitarian Universalists as a whole answered this query negatively in almost the same ways that they labeled their local church or their personal religion (56, 60, and 57%, respectively).

TABLE 6.3
Christian Designation of Local Church, as Related to Self-Ascription

Item	Percent of total (Nwt)	Self-Ascription		
		Right %	Left %	L% minus R%
1. "Do you define your local church as 'Christian?' "				
"No"	60 (157,840)	18	90	78
2. "Would you say that others in your community generally regard your local church as 'Christian?' "				
"No"	56 (153,519)	45	60	15

Viewed together, the responses to these three probes of the labeling problem led us to explore the relationship between the way a Unitarian Universalist views himself, views his fellow church members, and feels that they are viewed by outsiders. Within the right-wing group, Christian by definition, 82% feel that this designation characterizes also their fellow church members. Similarly, 90% of the posttraditionals have the same feeling of consensus within their local church. Both groups, however, feel misunderstood by the wider community of non-UUs. Again, the perceived disparities are quite parallel, with 27% of the right wing feeling that their local church is incorrectly perceived as non-Christian, and 30% of the posttraditionals feeling that their local church is incorrectly perceived as Christian. To the extent that we are correct in urging the importance of religious self-designation, there clearly exists a considerable degree of what might be called "image anxiety" as the UUs move about within their communities.

It should be noted here that in many New England areas, for historical reasons, the Unitarian and Universalist churches have been members of local and state federations of Protestant churches. From time to time, the legitimacy of their presence has been questioned by more conservative Protestants, leading in some cases to expulsion. In most other parts of the country, the Unitarians and Universalists have regarded themselves and have been regarded by their more orthodox neighbors as outside the cooperative structures of Christian organization. As an illustration of this, the Universalist Church of America applied, in 1947, for membership in the Federal Council of Churches (now called the National Council of Churches). This application was turned down on the grounds that the Universalists did not regard Jesus as "Lord and Savior." The American Unitarian Association never submitted a formal application for membership in the Federal Council.

DEALING WITH CONTROVERSIAL SOCIAL ISSUES

The decade of the 1960s was characterized by an increasing polarization within religious institutions with regard to social issues. Ministers, priests, nuns, and rabbis were marching more frequently in behalf of social causes, and congregations were rejecting such behavior more frequently and penalizing those involved in it. In more conservative churches, congregations were telling their ministers to stick to religion and leave the social issues alone. While that particular slogan would have little validity in most Unitarian Universalist churches, it nevertheless seemed unlikely that these churches would be immune from the general climate of polarization. To uncover this, respondents were given a list of seven ways in which churches have dealt with controversial social issues and asked, in each case, to indicate their approval or disapproval. The "strongly approve" responses, and their relation to self-ascription, are shown in Table 6.4. For the purposes of our exposition here of the institutional style of the UUs, we list these seven ways of dealing with controversy in the rank order of the "strongly approve" responses by the overall denomination:

1. Discussion meetings
2. Sermons
3. Public stands by minister
4. Participation in demonstrations by members
5. Public stands by congregation
6. Participation in demonstrations by minister
7. Public stands by a committee

Unitarian Universalist literature has stressed the tradition of the free pulpit, and this rank ordering would seem to support the reality of the tradition. Clearly, these congregations will support their ministers in controversial sermons or public stands and, to a somewhat lesser degree, even in participation in demonstrations. The bottom ranking accorded to "public stands by a committee" probably reflects the anxiety that churches have that the whole will be represented by a part. It may also reflect the sophistication nurtured by experience in liberal organizations regarding the ease with which a small group can commandeer a platform.

TABLE 6.4

Approval of Methods of Dealing with Controversial Issues, as Related to Self-Ascription

Item	Percent of total (Nwt)	Self-Ascription		
		Right %	Left %	L% minus R%
"Strongly approve"				
1. Discussion meetings	69 (159,751)	46	75	29
2. Sermons	51 (152,298)	32	56	24
3. Public stands by minister	33 (157,556)	15	39	24
4. Participation in demonstrations by members	28 (157,126)	7	36	29
5. Public stands by congregation	28 (157,561)	10	34	24
6. Participation in demonstrations by minister	23 (157,441)	7	29	22
7. Public stands by a committee	21 (157,344)	8	26	18

If we analyze the full responses not in terms of approval but, rather, in terms of the extent of disapproval, even the least popular measure (public stands by a committee) was disapproved by only 33% of the UUs. Only 1% disapproved discussion meetings and only 7% disapproved sermons on controversial issues. Generalizing, controversial social issues are no longer a controversial issue for Unitarian Universalists.

There are certain contrasts between the posttraditionals and the right wing which should be observed. The rank ordering of the posttraditionals is identical to that already given for the overall denomination. The right-wing group differs slightly from this rank ordering, being less approving of participation in demonstrations, either by the minister or by church members, and by being somewhat more approving of public stands by a committee. If, however, we compare these two groups in terms of the differentials between the percentages strongly approving each particular item, the differential is least on the matter of public stands by a committee. It will also be seen from the actual responses that the posttraditionals were much more likely to move to the extreme of "strong approval," whereas the right wing consistently took the less intensive "approve." Finally, we may note that the only instances of a majority of any group disapproving a particular way of handling controversial issues occurs with the right wing in regard to demonstrations, whether by minister or members.

HOW STRONG A FOUNDATION?

Many factors must enter into any estimate of the strength of the local church. Budget, membership, church school membership, ministerial stability, and financial support of the denomination, are among the objective factors that are involved. Any full estimation must also incorporate subjective factors such as morale, denominational commitment, and the feeling of the worthwhileness of the enterprise.

To the questionnaire item asking respondents to describe the strength of their local church, 14% answered "very strong;" 42%, "strong;" 34%, "average;" 10%, "weak;" and 1%, "very weak." Since one objective measure of church strength had been used in the stratification of the sample, namely the identification of "growth" churches as those showing the highest mean percentage growth in the preceding five years, a preliminary validation of this subjective estimate of church strength was possible. Table 6.5 shows the relationship of the strength estimates to the types of churches in the sample. Growth church members are far more likely to describe their own churches as strong (79%) than are members of ordinary churches (56%) or fellowships (33%). It should also be noted from this table that the fellowship members are most likely to describe their local situation as weak.

TABLE 6.5
Church Strength Estimates Reflect Church Type[a]

"Would you describe your local church as strong, average, or weak?"	Type		
	Growth	Ordinary	Fell
Very strong	24	14	4
Strong	55	42	29
Average	18	34	43
Weak	2	9	22
Very weak	less than .5	1	3

[a]Nwt=161,042.

Further insight into the meanings of local church strength comes from responses to a subjective estimate of relative class status. When asked to describe the "social status" of other members of their local church, 4% of the UUs responded "lower;" 81%, "about the same;" and 15%, "higher." Table 6.6 shows the effects of these estimates upon the estimates of local church strength. Data in this table suggest that UUs are inclined to view their local church as stronger to the extent that it contains relatively more members of higher social status than themselves. This is an interesting finding, but it must be stated cautiously in view of the relatively small percentage (15) of UUs who saw most of their fellow church members as having a higher social status.

TABLE 6.6
Local Church Strength as Affected by Imputed Relative Class Status[a]

	Social status: other/own		
Local church strength	Lower	Same	Higher
Very strong	14	13	17
Strong	35	42	43
Average	33	34	31
Weak	16	9	9
Very weak	2	1	1

[a]Nwt=162,159.

Activity and Commitment

We have noted that the available measure of church activity was a self-estimate and described the difficulty of using any other measure with this religious group. Assuming the general validity of such a measure, let us explore several patterns found with other religious groups in terms of their applicability to Unitarian Universalists. It has been found, rather consistently, that the Protestant churches in America evoke peak commitments from women, from older persons, and from non-urban dwellers.

While the UU respondents under 35 years of age reported slightly less activity, there was little differentiation elsewhere within the age brackets. Nor did age analysis come to the support of a rather widespread UU assumption that high church activity is closely related to the child-rearing years. If anything, those under 35 are probably the most likely group to have children in the church school, and they report lower activity than all older groups. Similarly, Unitarian Universalists increase their church activity as they grow older.

Analysis by gender revealed no important differences (i.e., 2% or less) between Unitarian Universalist men and women in the degree of their self-reported church activity. Differences in place of residence, similarly, were not related to church activity. Among urban dwellers, 58% report themselves as very or moderately active, whereas 63% of the suburbanites use these designations. This percentage rose only to 64 among the small-town UUs.

A somewhat paradoxical aspect of church activity appears when we look at the effect of type of church upon activity, as shown in Table 6.7. These data show that patterns of church activity are inversely related to the organizational needs of that group. The fellowships are the smallest groups and, therefore, presumably make the greatest demands upon individual members if any kind of program is to be carried on. This explains the fact that 68% of the fellowship members indicate that they are very or moderately active. At the other extreme, the growth churches, by their very success, apparently permit a somewhat more passive style of belonging, with only 54% of their members describing themselves as very or moderately active. The ordinary church percentage for these categories falls between these two extremes with 61%.

TABLE 6.7
Growth Church Members Less Active[a]

Church activity	Type		
	Growth	Ordinary	Fell
Very active	15	21	28
Moderately active	39	40	40
Slightly active	34	29	26
Inactive	12	10	6

[a]Nwt=165,193.

These understandings permit assessment of a very prevalent self-conception found among Unitarian Universalists—that the problem of their particular denomination is that it is a "way station" for persons on the move from some kind of religious affiliation to no religious affiliation. While a full examination of this generalization would require intensive study of the turnover patterns of local churches, it may be inferred from the data in Table 6.8 that the generalization may be untrue. The stereotype is usually developed along the following lines: Converts come to UU churches with high enthusiasm, are immediately swept into organizational activity beyond their expectations, eventually become burned out, and then retreat. For this to be an accurate characterization of the religious lifecycle of the typical Unitarian Universalist, we would expect to find a high level of church activity reported in the early years of membership and then a sharp drop-off after several years. The data suggest that, in fact, the reverse is the case. The levels of reported church activity increase with years of membership rather than decrease, and those who have remained in the denomination all their lives report the highest levels of church activity. At this point, however, we should regard this finding as only an indirect rejection of the generalization, since it is possible that those persons who reached an early peak of church activity have already dropped out of these churches, and therefore are not reflected in the questionnaire study. Nevertheless, the relatively low level reported by the new members suggests rejection of the generalization.

TABLE 6.8
Church Activity Increases with UU Longevity[a]

Church activity	Years UU			
	0-2	3-10	11+	Born
Very active	10	20	28	29
Moderately active	40	40	39	39
Slightly active	39	31	24	24
Inactive	11	9	10	8

[a]Nwt=165,341.

Previous research with other religious groups has repeatedly shown curvilinear patterns of participation in respect to age, with the lowest levels of participation and religiosity occurring during the middle of the lifecycle. Church activity has also usually been stronger among women than among men. The UUs clearly depart from both of these patterns.

Many sociologists of religion have inferred from such patterns a deprivation-theory of religion. Quite apart from the ambiguities in defining such a concept, it is evident from the UU data just discussed, and from the examination of the effects of education, income, and social mobility in Chapter 5, that UU religiosity and activity do not increase with social deprivation. If anything, this particular form of religiosity is more directly related to social success.

THE ROLES OF THE MINISTER

The central importance of ministerial leadership in the church conceptions of Unitarian Universalists has already been observed. We have also noted the considerable range of freedom accorded to the minister in the expression of controversial ideas in discussions and sermons. At this point, we will turn in more detail to the particular roles played by the minister in UU churches.

The Minister—Actual and Ideal

Unitarian Universalists were asked to evaluate the skills and preparation of their present minister in five areas, rating him in each one from very strong to very weak. On the basis of the "very strong" evaluations, the following rank ordering appeared:

1. Preaching
2. Social action
3. Dealings with people
4. Religious education
5. Counseling

Examination of the percentages showed that there was basically little difference between the self-ascription groups in their evaluation of their present ministers. The posttraditionals placed social action 1 percentage point higher than preaching, but this was not a significant differentiation. Within the right-wing group, 43% saw their minister as very strong on preaching and only 36% saw him as very strong on social action. In view of the lower esteem that social action holds for the right wing, this evaluation may be more a rejection of the minister's skills in these areas rather than a judgment that these skills were actually lower. Apart from these differences noted, self-ascription made little difference in estimates of present ministerial skills. It should further be noted that in all five areas a majority of the overall denomination, as well as of each self-ascription group, viewed the ministers as very strong or strong. Insofar as the five areas reflect the major skills that the Unitarian Universalist minister in general is expected to have, it is clear that the parishioners regard their ministers as well prepared for their professional roles.

Noteworthy ideological differentiations appeared in a second question worded "If you were on a pulpit committee to select a new minister, how important would his skills in each of the following areas be for you?" The responses on this question ranged from "very important" to "not important." The rank ordering of these skills desired in the future minister, based upon the "very important" response as shown in Table 6.9, was:

1. Dealings with people
2. Preaching
3. Counseling
4. Religious education
5. Social action

Not only is this a very different ordering than occurred with the evaluation of present ministers, but the differentiation in the magnitude by which each skill is viewed as "very important" is dramatically wider (even taking into consideration that this was a three-point scale). "Dealings with people," the paramount skill, was deemed very important by 84%, whereas "social action," the least important skill, was only deemed very important by 45% of the overall denomination. It should also be noted that only negligible percentages of the self-ascription groups or the overall denomination were willing to call any of these skill areas "not important," with the single exception of the right-wing group where 22% felt this for "social action."

The most dramatic ideological differentiation occurred with regard to social action. Within the posttraditional group, 50% regarded it as very important, while only 23% of the right wing deemed it so. In the case of preaching, this situation was reversed, with 87% of the right wing deeming it very important and only 70% of the posttraditionals. A similar decrease appeared in religious education, with 67% of the right wing viewing it as a very important ministerial skill, as against 58% of the posttraditionals.

On the surface, some of these findings appear to contradict other institutional values that have been reported. How, for instance, can we reconcile the consistent high place given by the Unitarian Universalists to religious education with the fact that only 58% of them view it as a very important ministerial skill? The answer probably lies in the fact that many of these churches employ full-time or part-time directors for their religious education program and do not see this as a major area of direct ministerial supervision. It may also partly stem from the presence of a large number of professional educators within the Unitarian Universalist parishes. Insofar as these persons come forward to staff the church schools, religious education ceases to be a deficit area where the minister is expected to fill the void.

We would suggest that a similar interpretation may be placed upon the relatively low concern for a minister's skills in social action. In view of the Unitarian Universalist commitment to social action on the part of the local church, and to the relatively high consensus that we have already discussed on a variety of social values, this is probably not viewed as a deficit area.

The most dramatic shift between what the parishioners are getting and what the parishioners want occurs in the skill areas of "dealings with people" and "counseling." These can probably be viewed as complementary or even overlapping skills, and it is clear that there are significant unmet needs here. It is also clear that the felt needs in these areas are quite unrelated to any differences in self-ascription.

The Minister as Source of Help

We will be exploring the meanings of ministerial satisfaction as measured by the combination of these responses regarding present ministers and their successors in Chapter 7. At this point, however, it is important to understand more fully the counseling-helping role of the minister. Since marriage has been a form of human association very closely linked with religion, we will first examine sources of help in marital crises.

Marital Crises

Respondents were asked "If your marriage ran into serious difficulties, what would be the likelihood of your turning to the following sources of help?" Seven sources were listed, and responses on each ranged from very likely to very

unlikely. The rank ordering within the overall denomination, based upon the "very likely" response, was:
1. Marriage or family counselor (36%)
2. Psychotherapist or psychiatrist (26%)
3. Minister (24%)
4. Family (19%)
5. Friends (14%)
6. Lawyer (8%)
7. Other physician (8%) (In the questionnaire, this followed psychotherapist or psychiatrist)

Responses for the first five sources of help, as related to self-ascription, are given in Table 6.10, Item 1. The posttraditionals parallel the denominational ordering but differ sharply from the right wing in being less likely to turn to the minister or family and somewhat more likely to seek help from psychotherapy. This relatively low placement for the minister is consonant with the low priority for counseling skills discussed in the previous section. It should also be clear that major qualifications are being added to the ministerial leadership which we found to be so important to the traditional UUs. Counseling, marital or other, is not a major component.

Reliance upon the family as a source of help also appeared far less likely for the posttraditionals. This may simply reflect their higher residential mobility which has physically separated the generations within families.

TABLE 6.9
Desired Ministerial Skills, as Related to Self-Ascription

Item	Percent of total (Nwt)	Self-Ascription		
		Right %	Left %	L% minus R%
"Very important"				
1. Dealings with people	84 (160,062)	88	83	−5
2. Preaching	74 (159,710)	87	70	−17
3. Religious education	58 (159,299)	67	54	−13
4. Counseling	58 (159,289)	61	56	−5
5. Social action	45 (158,928)	23	50	27

Emotional Crises.

The same help sources were listed in a second question headed "If you faced a serious personal emotional problem, what would be the likelihood of your turning to the following sources of help?" The "very likely" percentages appear in this case as Item 2 of Table 6.10. Again the posttraditionals parallel the total sample. In terms of overall denominational pattern, the marriage/family counselor drops in ranking, as would be expected (in fact, drops to sixth place—between other physician and lawyer). The minister drops to fourth place. If this is explained in terms of emotional problems being more serious than marital

TABLE 6.10

Sources of Help in Marital and Emotional Difficulties, as Related to Self-Ascription

Item	Percent of total (Nwt)	Self-Ascription		
		Right %	Left %	L% minus R%
1. If "marriage ran into serious difficulties, . . . very likely" to turn to:				
Marriage or family counselor	36 (152,298)	36	36	0
Psychotherapist or psychiatrist	26 (151,286)	20	29	9
Minister	24 (151,128)	33	21	−12
Family	19 (150,999)	32	15	−17
Friends	14 (151,661)	15	14	−1
2. With "personal emotional problem, . . . very likely" to turn to:				
Marriage or family counselor	11 (157,840)	11	11	0
Psychotherapist or psychiatrist	36 (156,194)	27	40	13
Minister	19 (156,256)	28	17	−11
Family	31 (157,561)	41	26	−15
Friends	24 (154,309)	15	24	9

problems, the UUs may here regard their clergy as less well trained. The 36% who would seek psychotherapeutic help here, however, would appear to parallel the 36% who would turn to a marriage counselor with a marriage problem. This line of explanation seems further weakened by the increased role that friends would be asked to play in emotional crises. We must therefore again conclude that UUs do not place heavy reliance upon their ministers as a counseling resource.

Some explanation is also required for the apparently greater turning to the family (31 as compared to 19%) in the event of emotional crises. The referent here has probably shifted. In marital crises, family would obviously refer to children or parents, whereas spouse would be included in the case of a personal emotional crisis. The similar differential between the self-ascription groups with both types of crisis supports this inference.

The ideological distinctiveness of posttraditionality persists in regard to sources of help. Ministers are less important, and psychotherapists more important. This would have been expected on the basis of a number of other attitudinal indicators. A new element appears here, however. Not only are the posttraditionals more open to psychotherapeutic professionalism in both types of crisis, but they are more open to help from their friends with their personal problems (a percentage differential of 9). These same posttraditionals, it will be recalled, placed great emphasis on psychological materials in church curricula. For this reason it would be a mistake to interpret reliance upon psychotherapy as simply a substitute for the right-wing reliance upon the family. Posttraditionality seems to be related to a different set of diagnostic canons. In this sense it marks a break with traditional individualism. If friends are viewed as sources of help, they are also being seen as part of the diagnostic scene within the culture. By inference, the larger assumption supporting such attitudes appears to be a wider estimate of human changeability, drawing upon psychological vistas and institutionalized within churches as a result of posttraditionality.

THE ROLE OF THE UNITARIAN UNIVERSALIST ASSOCIATION AS A DENOMINATION

The development of the denomination as a national institutional pattern has been a peculiar American phenomenon. In many ways, the denomination may be viewed as the American adaptation of the European pattern of state churches to the context of religious pluralism. This is too broad a generalization, however, and must be qualified if it is to fit a number of American denominations, including the Unitarian Universalist Association. While the state church pattern was associated with the mainstream of the Protestant Reformation, there developed from what has been termed the "left wing" of the sixteenth century reformation a fierce tradition of local congregational autonomy. Elements of this may be found in the Baptist, Congregational, Quaker, Brethren, Mennonite, Disciples groups as well as the Unitarians and Universalists. Within this left-wing tradition, super-organizations on a district or national level existed by the sufferance or the free agreement of autonomous local congregations. This situation is commonly labeled "congregational polity." From this perspective, the denomination must be viewed as a service organization rather than an initiatory one, existing to meet needs that are generated on the local level or that have achieved some relatively high level of consensus among the participating local congregations. Thus, there is a built-in tension between the autonomous claims of the local congregation and the desire for the efficiency of a "clear national voice" which often emerges in competition with the more centralized patterns of other denominations.

This tension is further compounded when the tradition of congregational polity evolves to its own logical conclusion, namely the tradition of individual polity. By the end of nineteenth century, both the Unitarian and Universalist denominations had come to recognize that they had no coercive powers over the free congregations within their membership and also had no coercive powers over the free individuals within those free congregations. Once each individual is accorded the right to determine his own religious and social values, however, the possibilities of any kind of collective action are sharply limited. There is a real sense in which the denomination within the left-wing Protestant tradition can speak only for itself and not for its member churches, and certainly not for the individual members of those churches. Our discussion of the denominational role will first look at the more traditionally religious face of the Unitarian Universalist Association and then examine the aspect of social values in change.

The Religious Thrust of the Denomination

In recent years, a number of secular magazines have carried an advertisement by the Unitarian Universalist Laymen's League headed "Are You a Unitarian Universalist Without Knowing It?" Different formats of the ad then suggested that if you were tired of being asked to believe things that you no longer believed, or of having your children exposed to superstitions, or of belonging to a church which did not stand clearly for social values, that you might more appropriately consider a Unitarian Universalist church. A coupon was enclosed with the ad, and respondents were furnished with pamphlets and placed in touch with their local Unitarian Universalist group. From all reports, this ad has been highly successful in discovering new members.

Several years ago, this advertisement was criticized by a leading Protestant journal as being even more parochial and patronizing of other religious groups than "the literature of the Knights of Columbus." The charge led to considerable internal discussion within the denomination regarding the advertisements, but their use has been continued. In many ways, this situation is paradigmatic of the problems of a denomination comprised of free churches. Clearly such an adver-tisement makes a much stronger appeal to a posttraditionally religious person than to a traditionally religious one. Since individual Unitarians, and, presum-ably, their churches as well, range widely on such a left-to-right spectrum, the success of this kind of advertising campaign can only serve to strengthen the posttraditional group. In a technical sense, the Laymen's League is an autono-mous institution and does not directly reflect the activities of the Unitarian Universalist Association. Nevertheless, especially in the absence of any alterna-tive advertisement on the part of the denomination itself, it does represent a kind of national outreach that is ideologically selective.

It will be recalled that the question on desirable denominational directions was deemed of sufficient importance to build it into the Self-Ascription Index. That question asked present Unitarian Universalists where they wished the denomination to be at the end of a decade, and presented them with four alternatives. Two of these would have moved (or kept?) the denomination within a Protestant, or at least Christian, framework. The other two would have kept (or moved?) the denomination in the sphere of a universalistic or humanis-tic religiousness that, in the context of the alternatives of the question, was clearly post-Christian.

Only 11% of the respondents wished the denomination to be within a Christian framework at the end of the decade, while 89% chose the more radical alternatives. By most criteria, this is a clear consensus, but the lingering policy question remains regarding the relationship between free individuals, free local churches, and a representative national denomination. In interpreting the de-nominational responses by means of the Self-Ascription Index, it will be remem-bered that all of the left, posttraditional group chose this more-than-Christian direction.

The Denominational Thrust on Social Values and Actions

While the commitment of the Unitarian Universalists to individual freedom of belief has consistently vitiated any attempts to promote a denominational "creed," even if clear consensus was found, this has not been the case with a wide range of social issues. A major feature of the annual meetings of the denomination is the discussion and voting on resolutions dealing with social problems. In the narrowest sense, the delegates to an annual assembly who vote for a particular resolution vote only in the name of that assembly. Their actions do not bind individual churches or members or even subsequent assemblies. In a larger sense, however, the passage of such resolutions furnishes historians with a good estimate of the general tenor of values within a representative group.

This study attempted to probe the actual feelings of the individual Unitarian Universalists on a number of social issues by a question headed "Our denomina-tion now operates in a number of areas of social controversy. Do you approve or disapprove of including each of the following in planning denominational activities for the next five years?" Seven areas were listed, and the rank ordering based upon the "strongly approve" responses was as follows:

1. Civil liberties
2. Civil rights (race relations)
3. Peace activities
4. Service committee work at home
5. Service committee work abroad
6. Legislative activity (U.N. and Washington offices)
7. Church-state relations

The rank orderings of the posttraditional group were essentially parallel to those of the overall denomination. Within the right wing, however, some significant modifications occurred. For the more conservative UU, service committee work at home was in first place and civil liberties dropped to fifth. Service committee work abroad was third, and civil rights dropped to fourth. On all seven kinds of social activity, the absolute percentage of strong approval by the posttraditionals was higher than the same response of the right-wing group.

This difference between the groups in rank ordering becomes clearer when we examine the actual differentials on items shown in Table 6.11. The right-wing UUs drop legislative activity to the bottom of their list of priorities. Taken by

TABLE 6.11

Future Denominational Social Action Areas, as Related to Self-Ascription

Item	Percent of total (Nwt)	Self-Ascription		
		Right %	Left %	L% minus R%
"Strongly approve"				
1. Civil liberties	47 (156,000)	18	58	40
2. Civil rights (race relations)	47 (157,043)	20	54	34
3. Peace activities	42 (156,727)	28	47	19
4. Service committee work at home	38 (156,546)	30	39	9
5. Service committee work abroad	32 (156,385)	25	34	9
6. Legislative activity (U.N. and Washington offices)	30 (155,154)	12	35	23
7. Church-state relations	28 (154,227)	15	33	18

itself, this might have been interpreted as a rejection of church intervention into government, a position typically held by political and religious conservatives. The position is often argued in terms of "the separation of church and state." In view of the similarly low priority accorded by the right wing to "church-state relations," however, that interpretation would appear doubtful since "church-state relations" was assumed to cover the separation issue.

The percentage differentials are lowest in approving activities by the denominational Service Committee, the most acceptable form of action to the right wing. Peace activity, it may be noted, remained in third place with the traditionals. In 1966, peace activities were not heavily favored by mainstream Protestant laymen. Somewhat surprisingly, the greatest differential emerged regarding civil liberties, indicating that the traditionalist UU commitment to freedom may be more intrachurch than societal.

In the format of the questionnnaire, the "civil liberties" area followed immediately after "civil rights (race relations)," but there may still have been some item ambiguity for some respondents, confounding these two. We are therefore presenting the full differentiation by self-ascription of the civil rights item, which clearly dealt with race, in Table 6.12. These responses show an even more dramatic polarization between the right wing and the posttraditionals than was found regarding social action within the local church. Only 20% of the right wing strongly approve denominational action on race, as contrasted to 54% of the posttraditionals. This is confirmed by the disapproval figures where 30% of the right wing would not endorse denominational action in this area. In terms of all that has been said about the peculiar nature of the denomination in relation to the autonomy of local congregations and individuals, we feel that these responses should be interpreted not simply in terms of social conservatism but also in terms of an ecclesiastical traditionalism. The right-wing Unitarian Universalist is hesitant to have his denomination move into areas of social concern, even where he personally would endorse those areas, or where he would be willing to have his local church become involved.

TABLE 6.12
Approval of Denominational Civil Rights Actions, as Related to Self-Ascription

| | Percent of total (Nwt) | Self-Ascription | | |
Item		Right %	Left %	L% minus R%
"Civil rights (race relations)."	(157,043)			
Strongly approve	47	20	54	34
Approve	44	50	41	−9
Disapprove	7	20	4	−16
Strongly disapprove	2	10	1	−9

The Issue of Consensus

The meanings of this feeling regarding the limited role of a denomination were further explored by three items following a general statement: "By resolutions and reports, the Unitarian Universalist Association stimulates discussion and moves toward some consensus. How do you feel about such efforts toward consensus and common public statement in the following areas?" Responses ranged from strongly approve to strongly disapprove. Ranking the three areas of consensus in the order of the "strongly approve" response for the overall denomination, the listing is:

1. Consensus on social issues
2. Consensus on denominational goals
3. Consensus on theological issues

Responses for these three areas, as affected by self-ascription, are shown in Table 6.13. A close comparison of the data suggests that there are several crosscurrents at work. If we were to rank the three areas of consensus approval either in terms of "least disapprobation" or of the combination of "strongly approve" and "approve" responses, we would put consensus on denominational goals in first place. Indeed, for the right-wing group, it is in first place regardless of the criterion chosen to perform the rank ordering. What therefore emerges from close inspection of all responses is the saliency with which the posttraditionals strongly approve the development of a consensus on social issues. It may also be observed that the posttraditionals are somewhat salient in their disapproval of any consensus on theological issues.

TABLE 6.13

Movement Toward Denominational Consensus on Social Issues, Goals, and Theological Issues, as Related to Self-Ascription

Item	Percent of total (Nwt)	Self-Ascription		
		Right %	Left %	L% minus R%
"By resolutions and reports, the Unitarian Universalist Association stimulates discussion and moves toward some consensus. How do you feel about such efforts toward consensus and common public statement?" "Strongly approve."				
1. On social issues	30 (155,028)	13	34	21
2. On denominational goals	27 (154,176)	21	29	8
3. On theological issues	17 (153,647)	16	18	2

We would suggest that the clue to interpreting these somewhat puzzling results is to be found in the general history of the Unitarian and Universalist movements and in a number of incorrect generalizations upon which the respondents were operating. In both Unitarian and Universalist history, the use of denominational consensus on theological issues has typically been a device by the more conservative to exclude the more liberal members. Insofar as the more left-wing members operate within the assumption that this is still the likely outcome of any consensus on theological issues, their responses make sense. Since their theological position had become the majority position as of the time of this survey, however, it will be interesting to see if their reticence on this issue remains, indicating that it was a matter of principle, or if they become much more willing to approve consensus on theological issues, indicating the reticence to have been more pragmatic.

The antipathy of the right wing to consensus on social issues may simply reflect the more conservative role that this group sees for the denomination, or it may reflect a disaffection of this group from the denominational pattern of recent years wherein social issues have become very important in the stance and operations of the Unitarian Universalist Association.

Apart from the differences reflecting the varied ideological positions among the Unitarian Universalists, it is quite clear that they are rather united in their willingness to develop and promote a consensus on "denominational goals," although this willingness might become attenuated if these goals became at all specific in regard to either theological positions or social positions.

The Effects of Merger

As we have already indicated, the Unitarian Universalist Association was created in 1961, although cooperation between Unitarians and Universalists on specific levels had been in operation for some years. Each of the former denominations had national organizations as well as intermediate organizations. In the case of the Unitarians, the intermediate organizations tended to be regional and multistate. While they had considerable autonomy, they were also rather closely linked to the American Unitarian Association which, in relation to the size of its constituency, was one of the wealthy and strongly bureaucratized denominations in American church life.

The basic strength of the Universalists, on the other hand, was not in the Universalist Church of America but, rather, in the intermediate "state conventions," several of which held larger portfolios than the national organization. The state conventions had a tradition of considerable autonomy, and in terms of their ecclesiastical and social stances, were generally more conservative than the Universalist Church of America.

As might have been expected, the merger plan that was adopted for these two denominations attempted a structural compromise on the intermediate level, calling for the creation of 24 districts and an intermediate bureaucracy some-what between the two prior bureaucracies in size. Although outsiders would have found it difficult to discover major ideological differences between Unitari-ans and Universalists, there were nevertheless somewhat intense local rivalries in some cities, and there was a general pattern of distance between the intermediate organizations of the two denominations.

Since the survey took place four years after the formal merger vote, an attempt was made to discover the success of the new intermediate organizational structure in relating individual Unitarian Universalists more closely to their new denomination. The question designed to explore this was headed "The Unitarian Universalist merger of 1961 led to the creation of twenty-three districts, each staffed by a district executive. In the case of your church, how has this affected your relationship to the continental denominational movement?" The responses to this question, as affected by self-ascription, are shown as Item 1 of Table 6.14. The most striking fact is that 70% of the respondents indicated that they did not know. This lack of awareness of the effects of merger was significantly related to self-ascription with 73% of the posttraditionals signifying that they did not know, as against 58% of the right wing.

Since these "don't know" responses were the highest on the questionnaire, and since the assessments and attitudes explored by this (and the next) item were so denomination-specific, they were both examined in relation to the length of membership. Those who had been UUs less than three years over-whelmingly answered "don't know" (93 and 91%); for 3- to 10-year members, 75 and 70%; 11 or more years, 59 and 54%; and lifelong UUs, 51% on both items. In view of this confounding element, we shall, in this case, characterize enthusi-asm for the new district organization by the ratio of the "more closely" to the "about the same" responses. For the overall denomination, this is .56. The posttraditionals are even more enthusiastic, with a ratio of .63, while the right-wing is least enthusiastic, with .46.

Prior to the merger, members of Unitarian and Universalist churches in the same city or area would have had no direct organizational contact with each other. Merger would have put such churches within the same district organiza-tion and, therefore, in direct contact. To assess the efficacy of this process, respondents were asked "How has the creation of districts affected the relation-ship of your local church to other liberal churches in your area?" Responses to this question, as affected by self-ascription, are shown in Item 2 of Table 6.14. Almost as large a percentage (66) indicated that they did not know on this question as had similarly signified on the question concerning postmerger rela-tionships to the denomination, and a similar pattern differentiated the right wing (56% "don't know") and the posttraditionals (68%). Interpreting the specific responses to this question by the same reasoning used in examining the prior question, the ratio of enthusiasm within the overall denomination is .65 rising to .72 for the posttraditionals, and falling all the way to .50 for the right wing.

TABLE 6.14

Effects of Merger and Districting on Local Church and Interchurch Relationships,
as Related to Self-Ascription

Item	Percent of total (Nwt)	Self-Ascription		
		Right %	Left %	L% minus R%
1. "The Unitarian Universalist merger of 1961 led to the creation of twenty-three districts, each staffed by a district executive. In the case of your church, how has this affected your relationship to the continental denominational movement?"	(159,042)			
"Related us more closely to the denomination"	10	12	10	−2
"About the same"	18	26	16	−10
"Weakened our relationship with the denomination"	1	4	1	−3
"Don't know"	70	58	73	15
2. "How has the creation of districts affected the relationship of your local church to other liberal churches in your area?"	(158,998)			
"Strengthened our ties"	13	14	13	−1
"About the same"	20	28	18	−10
"Weakened our ties"	1	3	1	−2
"Other"	1	less than .5	1	1
"Don't know"	66	56	68	12

The Role of the Fellowship Group

Certain things have already been said about the fellowship groups which have played such an important role in the development of modern Unitarian Universalists. These lay-led groups have served several functions. In many cases, they provided a focal point for a nucleus of religious liberals to gather, to affiliate with the denomination, to attract others who were religiously like-minded, and eventually to grow into a church, complete with building and professional ministerial leadership. Whereas the more traditional Protestant churches have typically expanded by the use of a "mission church," with a subsidized professional ministry from the outset, the Unitarians and, to a much lesser extent, the Universalists were able, by the fellowship movement, to generate new congregations with considerably less capital expenditure from headquarters or neighboring churches. At one point, denominational planners argued that any city of 100,000 population was large enough to sustain a liberal church. If it contained a university (and this would be true for most such cities), the chances of success would be even higher. The rapid growth of fellowships occurred as such potential cities were saturated, and many of these fellowship groups did indeed grow into conventional churches.

In other cases, the fellowship began as a spin-off from some established Unitarian or Universalist church, often as the result of the suburbanization of groups of members. The current denominational literature encourages this process, arguing from past examples that this fission process has led to a net gain in membership and financial strength for both the old group and the new group.

A third role for the fellowship has been to provide some kind of spiritual community for a small group of religious liberals where there was no realistic likelihood of expanding into a church-sized unit. Many such fellowships have survived through several decades.

Finally, there are a few cases where a fellowship has grown large enough to acquire buildings and property and has consciously chosen to sustain itself on a lay-led basis and not call a professional minister. In some places, these groups have hired professional staff to direct their religious education, but have chosen to reserve the pulpit for a succession of laymen.

Given these differing roles that the fellowship movement has played, and granting that denominational awareness of the full panoply of meanings might be limited, a question was devised to explore some of these aspects. Respondents were asked "How do you feel about the Unitarian Universalist fellowships?" Their responses, as affected by self-ascription, are shown in Table 6.15.

TABLE 6.15

Significance of Fellowships, as Related to Self-Ascription

Item	Percent of total (Nwt)	Self-Ascription		
		Right %	Left %	L% minus R%
"How do you feel about the Unitarian Universalist fellowships?"	(157,177)			
"They are most useful as they develop into churches"	55	58	53	−5
"They will help us develop a religious organization that no longer needs to depend upon professional ministers"	13	4	16	12
"Don't know"	32	38	32	−6

SUMMARY

The institutional expectations and fulfillments of the UUs have been discussed in this chapter. The views that they hold of their local churches and their denomination are basically consonant with their more personal religious identity and behavior that was described in Chapter 3. Given the high desire for intellectual stimulation, it is not surprising that religious education is regarded as the most important emphasis.

This seeming consensus, however, was found to mask the persisting disagreements between right-wing and posttraditional UUs. The former see education as involving more Biblical and traditional materials, while the latter regard education as a means of exploring social problems and personal development. The same cleavage appears in regard to local church and ministerial functions, where it emerges as worship versus social action.

Important differentiations also occur in relation to whether the local church is or is not Christian and how it is viewed, in terms of such labeling, by non-UU neighbors. The right-wing UUs prefer the Christian label, whereas the posttraditionals eschew it. The depth of this issue may be seen in the fact that almost one-third of each group feels that their non-UU neighbors misperceive the actual nature of their local church.

UUs have generally come to accept the involvement of their churches and ministers in controversial issues, although there is an ideological differentiation here, and taking part in demonstrations was (in 1966) least acceptable.

UU participation in local church activities was found to increase with length of membership, and there is little difference between the participation levels of men and women. These findings, it was noted, vary from typical U.S. denominational patterns.

While there is a basic satisfaction with the overall professional training and skills of their present ministers, it is significant that UUs, regardless of ideology, desired greater skills in "dealing with people." As would be expected, the posttraditionals would emphasize social action skills in a future minister, a low-priority item for the right wing.

In respect to their continental denomination, it is clear that an overwhelming majority wish the Unitarian Universalist Association to continue its movement away from its Christian origins and toward a distinctive new religious orientation. There is overall approval of the denomination's involvement in social action, and considerable willingness for the emergence of continental consensus on goals, ideology, and social values. This, most probably, should be understood in the light of the long-standing primacy given by UUs to individual freedom, rather than to any shift in the balancing of individual and collective prerogatives.

The positive attitudes toward the development of lay-led fellowship groups are somewhat harder to interpret. Within a more traditional religious group, these attitudes would indicate anti-clericalism. Among UUs, they probably reflect an appreciation of the numerical expansion role that the fellowships have played, along with an acceptance of lay involvement in all aspects of church life, including worship and preaching.

Chapter 7

RELIGIOUS SATISFACTION, RELIGIOUS REFERENCE, AND SELF-ASCRIPTION

In our discussions of the meanings and sources of the self-ascription of Unitarian Universalists, we explored the data from a number of perspectives. At times we focused upon the belief-value patterns within individuals. At other times we explored the ways in which individual UUs assess their local churches, their own ministers, and their denomination. At the beginning of Chapter 6, we discussed the relationships between wanting and getting in their institutional setting. It was noted there that the questionnaire was designed to explore a number of religious values in terms of how well they were presently being met, and how the respondents felt that they should be met. The analyses there permitted us to examine a number of church functions in terms of present emphases and desired emphases. Using a similar contrast between the actual and the ideal, we explored overall assessment of ministerial preparation and skills. We also examined the ways in which Unitarian Universalists viewed themselves in reference to their ministers, their local church boards, and their denomination in terms of theological values and also in terms of social values.

In this chapter we shall attempt a more sophisticated analysis of this data taking account of the wanting/getting, actual/ideal polarities within individuals as they are related to local churches and ministers. We will also explore the polarities in religious self-reference, as these were expressed theologically and socially.

Describing this another way, we will develop a number of relative measures as they are used referentially by Unitarian Universalists, and attempt to understand their meanings. As an example, consider the outlook of an individual with reference to religious education. We need to know his relative satisfaction with the functioning of the local church in this area. We can describe him as "satisfied" with this particular church function if it is either very important to him and also very important within the local church, or if it is unimportant to him and also unimportant within the local church. This relative satisfaction level is obviously quite independent of the preference that an individual has for religious education. Nevertheless, his religious satisfaction is an important part of his religiosity. It must be explored in ideological terms.

SATISFACTION WITH THE FUNCTIONS OF THE LOCAL CHURCH

In this section we will examine the eight functions of the local church that were evaluated by the questionnaire. It will be recalled from the opening section of Chapter 6 that individuals were asked to evaluate each of these eight functions in terms of the operation of their present church and then in terms of their place in an ideal church. The data on the ideal church responses were presented in Table 6.1.

In terms of his response to the paired now/future assessment of a church function, each individual was given a "church satisfaction" category ("score"). The response scale was "very important," "somewhat important," "not important," and "can't decide." Individuals who did not respond to both items of the pair or who could not decide on either of the items were excluded from the scoring. Persons who gave the same response to the now/future questions were categorized "same." Persons indicating that the item was more important in the future than at present were categorized "more," and those indicating that the item was more important in the present than in the future were categorized "less."

To illustrate the development of these church satisfaction categorizations by the combination of responses to this paired set of questions, Table 7.1 presents the distribution, as affected by self-ascription. The percentages in the second row, headed "want same," are the percentages of persons in the various self-ascription subgroups who are essentially satisfied with what they are finding in their local churches.

To summarize the data on these eight functions and at the same time show some of the ways in which their assessment is affected by self-ascription, the functions have been ranked in descending order of the percentages of satisfied ("want same") persons within the overall denomination. This ranking is pre-

TABLE 7.1
Church Satisfaction Regarding Worship as Affected by Self-Ascription[a]

Church satisfaction: worship	Self-Ascription			Percent of total
	Right	Center	Left	
Percentage categorized:				
Want more	25	14	8	12
Want same	65	67	61	63
Want less	10	19	30	24

[a]Nwt=146,319.

sented in Table 7.2. It will be seen from this table that religious education is the church function with which Unitarian Universalists are most satisfied. The first two data columns of this table show the respective percentages for the "right" and "left" subgroups as designated by the Self-Ascription Index (for simplicity of presentation, the "center" subgroup has been omitted from this table). This rank order also provides a measure of the controversiality of the separate functions, with religious education being least controversial and personal development being most controversial. It will be seen that the satisfaction percentages within the posttraditional group are consistently lower, but that the only differences in rank ordering occur with regard to the slightly higher order of satisfaction that the right wing has with worship and the slightly higher order of satisfaction than the posttraditionals find with ministerial leadership.

The value of this measure of satisfaction with church functions is that it not only permits us to rank the functions in terms of satisfaction levels but also to describe the relative amounts and directions of dissatisfaction. In the case of

TABLE 7.2
Satisfaction with Church Functions as Affected by Self-Ascription

Church function	Percent satisfied		Percent of dissatisfied who want more	
	Right	Left	Right	Left
Religious education	70	67	68	55
Ministerial leadership	64	63	69	54
Worship	65	61	71	21
Lay leadership	64	62	46	55
Fellowship	63	56	59	65
Adult programs	60	56	60	69
Social action	52	49	38	71
Personal development	53	46	85	91

religious education, for instance, 70% of the right-wing subgroup are satisfied, leaving the remaining 30% dissatisfied with this function. We would expect the dissatisfied group to be divided, some wanting more and some wanting less religious education. Since the actual percentages of those categorized in either direction will be a function of the total percentage of the subgroup who are dissatisfied, these percentages will not permit us to make direct comparisons between functions. To facilitate such comparison, the percentages have therefore been converted into the percentages of the dissatisfied members of that sub-group who want more religious education than they are getting. Thus the third and fourth columns of Table 7.2 should be read as indicating that, of the 30% of the right-wing Unitarian Universalists who are dissatisfied with religious education, 68% want more. Similarly, of the 33% of the posttraditionals who are dissatisfied, 55% want more religious education.

Let us now turn to the separate functions, bearing in mind that we are dealing with relativistic judgments based upon the reference points of separate local churches. Thus, variations in the percentages of dissatisfied persons who want more represent a complex relationship between a somewhat "absolute" prefer-ence for the function and a clearly "situational" assessment of the function within the individual's local church.

Religious Education

In terms of the question just indicated, the finding that 13% more of the dissatisfied right-wing Unitarian Universalists want more of religious education is the combination of the already established high preference of this group for religious education and the also established relationship between posttraditional-ity and higher estimates of church strength which may also be an indication that the churches of the posttraditionals are more likely to have strong religious education programs in being.

Ministerial Leadership

There is again a differential on this function, 15% less of the dissatisfied posttraditionals wanting more leadership from their ministers. We must interpret this as the combination of relatively stronger ministerial leadership in the churches of the posttraditionals combined with their stronger preference for lay as distinct from ministerial leadership.

Worship

While most of the Unitarian Universalists, regardless of ideology, are highly satisfied with worship within their local churches, the differences between the directions preferred by the right-wing and the posttraditional groups are suffi-ciently strong to regard these data as further confirming a denominational polarization in this regard. Where 71% of the dissatisfied right-wing want more worship, only 21% of the dissatisfied posttraditionals would move toward the increase of this function. On this function, we must reiterate the general interpretive question sounded above. The high level of satisfaction with the worship function in local churches must not be interpreted as a generalized judgment that worship is presently prevalent or salient. In fact, the ideological differentiation suggests just the reverse. The churches of the posttraditionals are most likely to have a sufficiently low level of worship to meet their satisfactions.

Lay Leadership

A very mild polarization between the self-ascription subgroups may be observed by comparing the direction of responses within the dissatisfied members of those two groups. A majority of the posttraditionals want more (55%) while a majority of the right wing want less (54%).

Fellowship

While there is a difference in the intensity of subgroup responses on this church function, it would not appear to be a major differentiation related to self-ascription. This differentiation, and the differentiation regarding personal development, are the smallest for any of the functions.

Adult Programs

Again the differentiation is slight (9%), with more of the dissatisfied posttraditionals wanting an increase in the function.

Social Action

Along with worship, social action must be seen as the most differentiating church function. Not only do a clear majority of the dissatisfied posttraditionals want more (71%), but a clear majority of the dissatisfied right wing want less (62%). The meaning of this differential of 33% is underscored when we note that almost half of the Unitarian Universalists are dissatisfied with this function in their local churches.

Personal Development

The placement of personal development at the bottom of the list indicates that it is the church function evoking least satisfaction among UUs. In that sense, it could perhaps be described as controversial or more correctly as problematic. Strikingly beyond controversy, however, is the direction that the dissatisfied UUs would move, quite regardless of their ideological differences. They are overwhelmingly in favor of more emphasis on personal development.

SATISFACTION WITH THE SKILLS AND TRAINING OF THE MINISTER

The development of measures of satisfaction of Unitarian Universalists with their minister proceeded along essentially the same lines as the development of the church satisfaction scores. In this case, however, the original pair of questions had employed different response categories. The present minister had been evaluated on a five-point scale from "very strong" to "very weak." In assessing the skills of a future minister, respondents were asked to rate each skill "very important," "somewhat important," or "not important." The data that we are about to discuss will not reflect the members of fellowships since they had no present ministers to evaluate. The ministerial satisfaction category "want same" was given to respondents who used either of the "strong" evaluations for their present ministers and rated that particular function "very important" in the future, or who viewed their present minister as "average" and rated the function "somewhat important" for the future, or who applied either of the "weak" assessments to their present ministers and saw the function as "not important" for the future. The "want more" categorization was applied to those who saw the function as "very important" in the future and rated their present minister "average" or less, and to those who saw the function as "somewhat important" in the future and used either of the "weak" ratings for their present ministers. Conversely, the "want less" categorization was given to those who saw the function as "not important" in the future and rated their present ministers as "average" or above and to those who saw the function as "somewhat important" in the future and applied either of the "strong" assessments to their present ministers.

Table 7.3 presents the results of this categorization with the paired items relating to the social action skills of the minister as these relate to the respondents' self-ascription. Data on the skills of the ideal, future minister was shown in Table 6.2.

The interpretation of Unitarian Universalist satisfaction with ministerial skills proceeds along the same lines as the interpretation of satisfaction with church

TABLE 7.3

Ministerial Satisfaction Regarding Social Action as Affected by Self-Ascription[a]

Minister satisfaction: social action	Self-Ascription			Percent of total
	Right	Center	Left	
Percentage categorized:				
Want more	6	9	14	11
Want same	35	48	51	49
Want less	59	43	36	40

[a]Nwt=125,036; fellowship members not included.

function. Table 7.4 presents data on the five ministerial skills, arranged in descending order of the overall denominational percentages of satisfaction. In interpreting this table, we must reiterate the general caution already sounded with regard to the complexity of judgments that are reflected. Ministerial satisfaction is a relativistic measure of the disparity between what individuals would like and what they are getting, stated in reference to their present ministers. Thus a high level of satisfaction does not necessarily reflect a high estimate of the importance of a particular skill, but only the consonance between the ideal and the actual. With this caution in mind, let us turn to an interpretation of the data regarding the separate skills.

TABLE 7.4
Satisfaction with Ministerial Skills as Affected by Self-Ascription

Ministerial skills	Percent satisfied		Percent of dissatisfied who want more	
	Right	Left	Right	Left
Preaching	70	62	71	49
Religious education	57	53	56	40
Dealings with people	56	58	86	76
Counseling	51	53	63	60
Social action	35	51	8	28

Preaching

To some extent, the right-wing UUs are more satisfied with the preaching competence of their present ministers than are the posttraditionals. Among those within each self-ascription subgroup who are dissatisfied, a significantly larger percentage of the right wing would want more competence in preaching.

Religious Education

There is only slight differentiation in the satisfaction levels with ministerial skills in religious education. As already noted, the concern for the minister's competence in this area is to some extent a function of the size and budget of a local church, in that stronger churches are more likely to have additional professional staff handling the church school program. Insofar as posttraditionality is more closely associated with membership in a strong church, the difference in intensity and direction regarding this skill within the dissatisfied right-wing subgroup and the dissatisfied posttraditional subgroup may reflect this situation in individual churches as well as reflecting an absolute judgment on the importance of religious education as a ministerial skill.

Dealings with People

There is no significant differentiation as a result of self-ascription in regard to satisfaction with this ministerial skill. To some extent, the dissatisfied right-wing UUs would, with greater intensity, want more of this in the minister, but the consensus within the dissatisfied UUs regarding the need for more skill in this area is only slightly affected by self-ascription.

Counseling

Although almost half of both the right wing and the posttraditionals are dissatisfied with their minister's skills in counseling, and although clear majorities of those dissatisfied within either group would want the minister to have more skill in this area, there is no significant differentiation on the basis of self-ascription in these levels of satisfaction.

Social Action

As already noted in examining social action as a church function, there is a marked polarization among Unitarian Universalists in regard to this as a ministerial skill. This is especially clear within the right-wing subgroup where 65% are dissatisfied with their minister's skills in social action and only 8% of this group would want him to have more skill. While a lower percentage of the posttraditionals are dissatisfied (49%), only 28% of that group would want the minister to have more skill in this regard. While this is a significant differentiation related to self-ascription, it is equally clear that ministerial social action is a controversial function within the Unitarian Universalist denomination.

THEOLOGICAL CONSONANCE WITH MINISTER, BOARD, AND DENOMINATION

As we have already noted, the questionnaire asked respondents to characterize their own position on "theological issues and values" along a six-point spectrum whose extremes were labeled "liberal" and "conservative." The distribution of these responses, as related to self-ascription, was reported in Table 3.5. Using the same spectrum, respondents were then asked to make a theological designation for their minister, their local church board, and the denomination. Granting the inherent subjectivity of such a designation, we may nevertheless assume with this population a high level of connotative consistency in applying this labeling to self or others. Therefore, it seems feasible to explore the consonances between such designations for the self in reference to the minister and to levels of the religious institutional structure. In categorizing the relationship of self-designation to other-designation, respondents who marked the same point on the spectra of both scales were categorized as "same." A disparity of one point on the six-point spectrum led to categorization as "more conservative" or "more liberal," depending on the designation of the self-point, and a disparity of two or more spectrum-points resulted in a categorization as "much more conservative" or "much more liberal." This categorization of theological self-designation with reference to the individual's theological designation of his minister, as related to self-ascription, is shown in Table 7.5. Similar categorizations were developed in reference to church board and denomination, and the data on all three levels may be summarized and compared by procedures parallel to those that we have just used in discussing church and ministerial satisfaction. Table 7.6 presents these data. For the overall denomination, the level of consonance, theologically, is highest between individuals and their ministers, and lowest between individuals and their designation of the theological position of the denomination. While a similar ordering of the levels of consonance appears in both the right-wing group and the posttraditional groups, it is clear that markedly more of the posttraditional group (61% as against 45%) feel themselves to be theologically consonant with their ministers. It is also clear from this table that the direction as well as the intensity of dissonance is closely related to self-ascription. Of the 55% of the right-wing UUs who designated dissonance from their ministers, only 13% designate themselves as more liberal. Within the posttraditional group, only 39% are designationally dissonant, theologically, and 61% of these regard themselves as more liberal than their ministers.

TABLE 7.5
Theological Comparison of Self to Minister[a]

Theological comparison: self-minister	Self-Ascription			Percent of total
	Right	Center	Left	
Percentage categorized:				
Much more conservative	24	9	3	7
More conservative	24	19	12	16
Same	45	56	61	58
More liberal	6	11	17	14
Much more liberal	2	17	7	6

[a]Nwt=117,241; respondents from fellowships excluded.

Considerably less consonance appears with the other institutional references. Less than half of either the right wing or the posttraditionals designate themselves as consonant, theologically, with their local church boards. Among those who differ in these comparative designations, 61% of the right wing feel themselves to be more conservative than the local board, whereas 86% of the posttraditionals feel themselves to be more liberal. This absence of consonance increases, almost to a point that would justify using a stronger term such as alienation, when the self-designations are compared to the designations of the denomination. In this case, only 40% of either self-ascription group use conso-nant designations. Of the remaining right-wing UUs, 78% feel themselves to be more conservative than the Unitarian Universalist Association, whereas 83% of the dissonant posttraditionals feel themselves to be more liberal than the UUA.

Clearly, these findings reveal a strong awareness of theological differences. These are, to be sure, subjective estimates. But it is precisely on the basis of such feelings and estimates that people develop their sense of institutional morale and relatedness. If these perceptions are incorrect, they can be altered by more adequate communication. If, however, they are in some objective sense correct, then the Unitarian Universalist Association is clearly a religious institution comprising persons of very wide theological diversity.

TABLE 7.6

Referential Theological Consonance as Affected by Self-Ascription

Self in reference to:	Percent consonant		Percent dissonant and more liberal	
	Right	Left	Right	Left
Minister	45	61	13	61
Local church board	46	44	39	86
Denomination	40	40	22	83

SOCIAL VALUE CONSONANCE WITH MINISTER, CHURCH BOARD, AND DENOMINATION

Unitarian Universalists in the survey were also asked to characterize their own position on "social issues and values," using the same six-point spectrum used for theological self-designation. These responses, as related to self-ascription, were shown in Table 4.11.

Using the same statistical procedures that have just been described for the referential comparisons of theological self-designation, the comparable designa-tions on social issues and values were categorized. Results of this categorization for the comparison between self and minister are presented in Table. 7.7. Using the same procedures described in connection with the analysis of theological consonance on the three referential levels, comparative categorizations were developed which are summarized in Table 7.8.

From these data it is clear that Unitarian Universalists feel far less consonance on social values in reference to their religious institution than is the case with their theological values. Almost half (47%) of the overall denomination designate their social values as consonant with those of their ministers. Nevertheless, in the right-wing subgroup, this percentage of consonance drops to 35. Of the 65% of the right-wing who feel social values dissonant in reference to their ministers, 92% designate themselves as more conservative. Of the considerably smaller group of posttraditionals who experience dissonance with their ministers on social values (51%), 30% describe this dissonance as the result of their being more liberal than their ministers.

TABLE 7.7
Social Value Comparison of Self to Minister[a]

Social ethic comparison: self–minister	Self-Ascription			Percent of total
	Right	Center	Left	
Percentage categorized:				
Much more conservative	35	16	11	15
More conservative	25	30	25	27
Same	35	45	49	47
More liberal	4	6	10	8
Much more liberal	1	2	5	4

[a]Nwt=115,962; respondents from fellowships excluded.

Equally interesting are the referential consonances experienced in relation to the local church board and to the denomination. The patterns in both cases move in the same direction and are essentially parallel to the patterns found with regard to theological consonance. In regard to social values, approximately six out of ten Unitarian Universalists describe their own positions as dissonant from the positions of their local church boards and their denomination. Large percentages of the right-wing UUs who are dissonant in social values describe themselves as referentially more conservative (68% in reference to the local church board and 71% in reference to the denomination). This pattern is reversed for the dissonant posttraditionals, where 70% describe themselves as more liberal than their local church boards and 62% feel that they are more liberal than the Unitarian Universalist Association.

Our earlier comments on the institutional implications of theological dissonance are even more pertinent to the dissonance on social values that we have

TABLE 7.8
Referential Social Value Consonance as Affected by Self-Ascription

Self in reference to:	Percent consonant		Percent dissonant and more liberal	
	Right	Left	Right	Left
Minister	35	49	8	30
Local church board	40	40	32	70
Denomination	38	42	29	62

just described, given the variation that exists in relation to basic ideological diversity. Unless this variation can be attributed to misperceptions which are correctable, the Unitarian Universalist Association must be described as an institution whose members perceive considerable theological pluralism and an even greater pluralism in regard to social issues and values.

INDIVIDUAL CONSONANCE ON THEOLOGICAL AND SOCIAL VALUES

We are now in a position to examine the relative valences of the designations "liberal" and "conservative" as they are used in self-designation by the Unitarian Universalists. We have already seen that most of the UUs are quite willing to use the general adjective liberal to describe themselves, whether they are referring to their theological values or their social values. Which of these aspects of his religiosity—the theological or the social—does the Unitarian Universalist tend to designate as more liberal, and how is this affected by self-ascription? This question can be answered from the data presented in Table 7.9 which shows the results of a categorization of the comparison of social self-designations with theological self-designations.

TABLE 7.9

Comparison of Individual Social to Theological Positions in Terms of Relative Liberal/Conservative Self-Ratings[a]

Own social ethic compared to theology	Self-Ascription			Percent of total
	Right	Center	Left	
Percentage categorized:				
Much more conservative	8	10	12	11
More conservative	21	25	32	29
Same	51	50	49	50
More liberal	16	12	6	8
Much more liberal	4	3	2	2

[a]Nwt=142,797.

Basically, these figures show that essentially half of all Unitarian Universalists, regardless of ideology, use the designation liberal with the same connotation whether they are referring to themselves theologically or in terms of their social values. Within the other half of the right wing of UUs, 59% describe their social values as more conservative than their theological values. Within the half of the posttraditionals who do not use the same, consonant, theological/liberal self-designation, 86% refer to their social values as more conservative than their theological values. Once again, the note of caution must be sounded that the data in this table as we have just been interpreting it is relativistic data. That is to say, the posttraditionals as a group are much more likely to use the adjective liberal in describing themselves, whether theologically or socially, and the point of the data we have just been discussing is the relative intensity of the adjective when applied to both dimensions of religiosity at the same time.

SUMMARY

In this chapter we have been looking at the institutional experiences of the UUs in terms of the feelings of satisfaction and consonance that the individual member expresses in relation to his church and its leadership.

We found additional evidence of the polarization that had already appeared regarding the appropriate emphases of worship and social action. The right wing is dissatisfied with worship (there is too little) and with social action (there is too much). Among posttraditionals there is a similar dissatisfaction, but with a reversed diagnosis. In terms of the contrasts found between the two UU ideological wings, this is a polarization. In view of the far greater proportional strength of the posttraditionals, this is less a polarization than an indication of major institutional dysfunctioning, a domination by a minority.

Widespread feelings of dissonance were also apparent in relation to local church governing boards and the denomination, with the right wing feeling that these bodies were too liberal and the posttraditionals feeling that they were not liberal enough. This held whether they were thinking of theological or social stances. If the two wings were of equal strength, the dissonance could simply symbolize some basic correctness of a centristic institutional stance. But they are not equal in size, and that line of reasoning also fails to take into account the fact that UUs in both wings share a quite common feeling of greater consonance with their ministers. Whatever alienation exists here is therefore fairly selective. Were it only related to the denomination, it might either be lessened by a changed denominational stance or explained in terms of distance and lack of information and corrected by more adequate communication. Because the sense of dissonance only lessens slightly in reference to the local church board, however, it is more difficult to postulate distance or lack of information and the alienation would appear to reflect a more pervasive kind of institutional distrust which is not carried over into assessments of persons (the ministers).

This chapter has also made clear the positive valence of the adjective liberal for almost all of the UUs. By this label they describe themselves theologically and, with somewhat lessened intensity, socially.

Chapter 8

THE INTEGRATIVE ROLE OF RELIGION

The preceding chapters, with their arrays of statistical material, have attempted to give a comprehensive picture of the religiosity of modern Unitarian Universalists. Attention has been paid to the sources as well as the implications of this religiosity. There is a sense in which the present study could end at this point, holding that such analytic descriptive information added something to our knowledge of human behavior and, therefore, was not without intrinsic interest. Considerable scholarly attention has been devoted in the past to far smaller and far less influential religious groups.

Nevertheless, it seems worthwhile to consider our information on this kind of religiosity from yet another angle, and one which has far wider human implications. To what extent does religion play an integrative role in human life? The very term we have chosen to explore in this chapter is more characteristic of sermons and theologians than it is of the behavioral sciences. We would suggest, however, that there are many points of contact. To integrate is to give some kind of unity or wholeness to that which had been fragmented. In early Greek thought, this was the role given to man's powers of reason. Much of medieval theology based itself on these rationalistic assumptions. When the theologians thought that they were forced to go "beyond reason," they typically did so with deep apologies. While a number of anti-rationalistic chords were sounded by Luther and Calvin during the sixteenth-century Protestant Reformation, their

173

followers quickly reverted to the more ecumenical trust in the reasonableness of nature, if not God or man.

Even if the origins of modern science are still debatable, there can be little doubt that a reliance upon the lawfulness of nature which correlated with the rationality of man was central in traditions otherwise as disparate as Catholicism, Puritanism, and Deism. One of the commonest slogans of the nineteeenth-century idealist philosophers was the stress upon "internal coherence" and "external consistency."

We have surveyed these cultural currents both to set the course for our own analytic strategy in this chapter and to place certain current behavioral science theories in a wider context. The gestalt psychologists a long time ago were arguing for the organizing power of mind, the tendency in us to search for "closures" in our problems. Festinger's work (1957) on "cognitive dissonance" has stimulated wide discussion of this issue among psychologists, and a recent survey of this research may be found in Abelson, Aronson, McGuire, Newcomb, Rosenberg, and Tannenbaum (1968). The general position taken is that an awareness of dissonance in cognitive structures produces a kind of discomfort and moves individuals to reduce the pain of the dissonance. We should bear in mind that the psychological connotations of "cognitive" are considerably larger than those used by modern philosophers, and extend into realms of beliefs and values, rather than being restricted to propositions of "knowledge." We shall preserve this larger focus in exploring matters of consistency and congruence in religiosity among the Unitarian Universalists. This is certainly not the place to argue whether the majority of UUs are correct in their disbelief in human immortality, or whether their commitment to human brotherhood in any sense partakes of truth. We have simply treated all of these aspects of their religiosity as cognitive in a psychological rather than a philosophical sense. Certainly they are high-level values for those individuals who hold them, more central to their existence than clusters of attitudes would be, and, presumably, more stable.

We shall therefore assume that men's religiosity is very directly involved in, and measurable by, their values regarding themselves and nature, as well as their assessments of the behavior of themselves and others. We shall further assume that religiosity always has some kind of communal impulse, pressing persons toward others holding similar values. Whatever institutions create and maintain such values, and provide communal participation with them, we shall regard functionally as "churches."

Our explorations of the integrative functions of religion and churches will proceed in two phases. First we will look at the overall Unitarian Universalist denomination in terms of differentials of integration within the right- and left-wing self-ascription groups, and, then, since we have data from the members of 80 local churches, we will explore the milieux of these local churches in terms of integrative effects upon the members.

COMMUNITY INTEGRATION WITHIN A RELIGION

If we are correct in our delineation of the religious group or church as the institutionalization of centrally-held values, then we may expect individual members to experience cognitive dissonances when they perceive sharp value differences within their own group. This will be truer if these value differences are closely associated with subgroups within the religious group. If, for instance, the young members of a church all hold one value and the older members hold its opposite, the dissonance that each subgroup will experience is disintegrative in a double sense. It not only reflects opposing value commitments but also reflects an age-polarization within the community. Much of the current rhetoric regarding a generation gap points, within the larger society, to this kind of double awareness of community nonintegration. Most studies of groups of Americans have shown that there are indeed generation gaps in regard to values, along with gender and class gaps. We shall examine these three gaps within the Unitarian Universalist population in terms of the effect of religious ideology upon the gaps. We shall do this by contrasting the right-wing and left-wing self-ascription groups. Those who have examined closely the tabular data of the preceding chapters will recall that the "center" self-ascription group was consistently found to occupy a center position in relation to values, beliefs, and attitudes. Therefore, for simplicity, we will here bypass that group and contrast the more extreme groups. Readers will also recall the peculiar contextual connotations of describing a UU as right wing. While he may occupy such a position within his own denominational group, he is still probably well to the left of the American center.

The broad hypothesis that we shall test is that within any religious group, the left-wing ideology will be more effective in closing extraneous gaps of age, gender, and class than is the right-wing ideology. We will select items reflecting the eight dimensions of Unitarian Universalist religiosity that were developed in Chapter 2, in most cases selecting the item that loaded the factor most heavily and, therefore, presumably, is most representative of that dimension. We shall then determine the effects that age, gender, and class have upon these items within the right-wing and left-wing Unitarian Universalist groups. Again using gamma as the measure of association, our hypothesis regarding the gap-closing function of left-wing theology will be confirmed if the distribution of values within that group is less closely associated with the known gap-producing variables of age, gender, and class. Such a nonassociation would be reflected in a low value for gamma, indicating that the various value positions are independent of any effect from the demographic factor.

Age

Table 8.1 presents the results of this form of analysis for age. This table makes strikingly clear that the age effect is less operative on all eight religiosity dimensions within the posttraditional, left, UU subgroup than within the right-wing group. This is summarized in the contrasting means of absolute gamma—.19 for the right UUs and .11 for the left. Using more general terminology, there is far less of a generation gap on the Unitarian Universalist left than on the right.

TABLE 8.1

Age Gaps on Eight Dimensions of UU Religiosity: Age Effect, Measured by Gamma, for Right and Left Self-Ascription Subgroups

		Self-Ascription
Dimension[a]	Right	Left
1. Personal beliefs, styles, and values (23)	−.36	−.19
2. Social-ethical values (28)	.02	.00
3. Church sociality values and participation (29)	−.24	−.10
4. Psychological development values (31)	.18	.11
5. Aesthetic-reflective-worship values (8)	−.11	−.08
6. Educational function of the church (30)	−.11	−.06
7. The church as source of personal friendships (45)	.33	.17
8. Intrasectarian affirmations (44)	−.17	−.12
Mean of absolute gamma	.19	.11

[a]Dimensions represented in this table by highest-loading items from factor analysis. Identifications in parentheses are for item numbers of Table 2.6.

An age gap is most noticeable, for both UU subgroups, on Dimensions 1, 7, and 3. Perhaps some reference to percentages here will help remind us that we are speaking of generation gaps within self-ascription subgroups on various dimensions in citing these gamma values. The differences between the subgroups, as we have already shown, are considerable. The item reflecting Dimension 1, sexual intercourse between unmarried persons, had 49% of the right wing responding "never permissible" and only 9% of the left wing made this response. Within the right wing, 22% of the youngest age group responded "never," along with 64% of the oldest age group. Within the posttraditionals, these percentages were 6 and 19, respectively.

One of the most interesting results shown on Table 8.1 is the absence of generation gap, within the self-ascription subgroups, on Dimension 2, relating to church social action. This item was most representative of a whole range of social values. While twice as many posttraditionals as right-wingers deem church social action "very important," this is not a function of age within either group.

Gender

Table 8.2 contains the results of a similar analysis to determine the presence of a gender gap—the extent to which dimensional differences are a function of being male or female. On Dimensions 1,3,5, and 6, the gender gap is more marked within the right wing. The overall dimensional picture, reflected in the mean of absolute gamma, shows that there is a slightly wider gender gap within the right-wing subgroup.

TABLE 8.2

Gender Gaps on Eight Dimensions of UU Religiosity: Gender Effect, Measured by Gamma, for Right and Left Self-Ascription Subgroups

	Self-Ascription	
Dimension[a]	Right	Left
1. Personal beliefs, styles, and values (23)	−.20	−.05
2. Social-ethical values (28)	−.20	−.25
3. Church sociality values and participation (29)	−.22	−.15
4. Psychological development values (31)	−.06	−.17
5. Aesthetic-reflective-worship values (8)	−.36	−.25
6. Educational function of the church (30)	−.32	−.21
7. The church as source of personal friendships (45)	.11	.14
8. Intrasectarian affirmations (44)	.04	.08
Mean of absolute gamma	.19	.16

[a]Dimensions represented in this table by highest-loading items from factor analysis. Identification in parentheses are for item numbers of Table 2.6.

The differentiation within groups was most marked on Dimension 1. The right-wing "never" percentages were 40 for men and 55 for women; within the posttraditional group the corresponding percentages were 6 and 12. It may be noted that Dimensions 2-6, were categorized from "important" to "unimportant." Thus the negative sign of gamma on these dimensions indicates that the UU women were more likely to give more importance to each of these items (since women were in the second column used in computing gamma).

Class

The most dramatic gap-closing produced by different UU ideologies occurs with reference to social class insofar as this can be measured by educational attainment. These figures are shown in Table 8.3. Only on Dimension 4 is there a lesser gap within the right-wing group.

This finding, which further confirms the gap-closing role of posttraditional religious ideology, may be less capable of generalization to other religious groups than our findings with regard to age and gender. The UUs are such an atypical population in their educational attainment levels that some caution needs to be exercised in any extrapolation.

Nevertheless, the overall pattern clearly shows that the left-wing religious subgroup (within this generally left-wing religious denomination) suffers far fewer divisions that are related to age, gender, or social class.

TABLE 8.3

Class Gaps on Eight Dimensions of UU Religiosity: Educational Attainment Effect, Measured by Gamma, for Right and Left Self-Ascription Subgroups

	Self-Ascription	
Dimension[a]	Right	Left
1. Personal beliefs, styles, and values (23)	.18	−.00
2. Social-ethical values (28)	.10	.05
3. Church sociality values and participation (29)	.10	.02
4. Psychological development values (31)	.01	.08
5. Aesthetic-reflective-worship values (8)	.10	.02
6. Educational function of the church (30)	.03	.00
7. The church as source of personal friendships (45)	−.12	−.07
8. Intrasectarian affirmations (44)	−.17	.00
Mean of absolute gamma	.10	.03

[a]Dimensions represented in this table by highest-loading items from factor analysis. Identifications in parentheses are for item numbers of Table 2.6.

DIMENSIONAL INTEGRATION WITHIN THE DENOMINATION

In terms of the reduction of dissonance, or the movement toward congruence model that we have introduced in this chapter, we should be able to make some estimate of the vitality of any religious group (and perhaps even of its viability) in terms of the relative absence of dissonance within its dimensions. Assuming that this kind of internal congruence or coherence is the essence of religiosity, it may also provide a measure of the morale of any religious group. To set the stage for such an examination of the Unitarian Universalists, representative items from each of the eight dimensions were intercorrelated. Results of this analysis are shown in Table 8.4.

As indicated in footnote *a*, we have reverted to the use of the Self-Ascription Index to reflect Dimension 1. This index and its meanings and sources are more familiar to readers as well as being more conventionally "religious" in content. To some extent, this matrix may be compared to the Protestant and Catholic dimensional matrices developed by Stark and Glock (1968) or to the matrix of UU associations developed with some parallelism (Table 2.6). However, it must be stressed that this present matrix is based upon dimensions which were initially described by the empirical technique of factor analysis rather than upon an intuitive basis. For this reason, we start out with the knowledge that the

TABLE 8.4

UU Religiosity Dimensional Associations, Measured by Gamma

Dimension[a]	\multicolumn{8}{c}{Dimension}							
	1	2	3	4	5	6	7	8
1. Personal beliefs, styles, and values	1.00	-.27	-.03	-.08	.15	.19	.01	-.16
2. Social-ethical values (28)		1.00	.19	.12	.12	.04	-.09	.05
3. Church sociality values and participation (29)			1.00	.34	.16	.28	-.31	.04
4. Psychological development values (31)				1.00	.14	.28	-.09	.04
5. Aesthetic-reflective-worship values (8)					1.00	.24	-.14	-.02
6. Educational function of the church (30)						1.00	-.07	.04
7. The church as source of personal friendships (45)							1.00	-.02
8. Intrasectarian affirmations (44)								1.00

[a]Dimensions represented in this table by highest-loading items from factor analysis. Identifications in parentheses refer to item numbers of Table 2.6. For Dimension 1, the Self-Ascription Index has been used. It is based upon items 35 and 10, which were second and sixth respectively, in loading Dimension 1.

179

dimensions are maximally uncorrelated. Factors are, in other words, an artifact of factor analysis. Many other assumptions enter into this process, of course. We are assuming in our matrix that a high-loading individual item may be taken as representative of that factor. Beyond the items most clearly related to the first general factor, the sequence in which subsequent factors is extracted is directly related to the proportion of items with this quality within the group of variables being factored. This latter point must be borne in mind in understanding Table 8.4; where, for instance, Dimensions 3 and 4 are less strongly associated with Dimension 1 than are Dimensions 5 and 6. If we bear in mind the real function of a factor analysis—reducing some large number of variables to a smaller number of uncorrelated factors—then the information in the matrix of Table 8.4 will be seen as a partial undoing of the factor analysis, or, more accurately, as a simplified statistical check on the actual uncorrelation of the discovered factors and a way for reasonably straightforward subgroup comparisons.

Dimensions 1 and 2, as represented here, show some relationship as indicated in the gamma value of $-.27$. Similarly, there is some relationship within the overall denomination on Dimensions 3 and 4 and between 3 and 7. It is harder to make any assessment from such data regarding the relative unidimensionality of the Unitarian Universalist religiosity. What this kind of data can do is provide the basis for a general model which can then be used in the analysis of subgroups to explore patterns of variance. In effect, we will be treating congruence and dissonance as related to known patternings of association rather than to some hypothesized unidimensionality.

INDIVIDUAL INTEGRATION AND THE LOCAL CHURCH MILIEU

It is now clear that different forms of Unitarian Universalist religiosity have very different effects upon the members of this denomination with regard to the gaps in community occasioned by age, gender, and class. We were able to establish this by looking at each of the dimensions of UU religiosity as they were affected by these demographic variables. Let us shift our focus now from the denomination as an institution and its membership as a population to a focus upon the eighty local churches comprising the sample and upon the individual members of those churches. The size of the overall sample as well as the number of churches represented makes this statistically feasible.

Up to this point, our delineation of "Unitarian Universalist religiosity" has treated this as a quality distributed throughout the population of the United States and Canada. The fact is, of course, that individual UUs perceive UU religiosity within a local church which they have chosen to join. They may at times think of this kind of religiosity as more than local, but it seems reasonable to assume that the primary embodiment and mediation of UU religiosity is the local church. While each of these 1100 local churches, represented by our

80-group sample, shares a common characteristic of affiliation with the Unitarian Universalist Association, we must also assume that each is unique in a number of ways. Similarly, each individual member shares the common characteristic of denominational affiliation but is unique in the structuring of his own religiosity. Using the eight-dimensional model of UU religiosity, we might characterize the idiosyncratic patternings of each individual in terms of the interrelations of these dimensions. We can then ask whether there is any relationship between the milieu (context, climate) of a local church and the dimensionality patternings of its members. Applying the concept of cognitive consistency, we can describe the level of individual integration of the dimensions of religiosity in terms of the quantitative correlations of dimensions.

Let us, therefore, examine the hypothesis that the nature of the local church milieu has some consistent relationship to the dimensionality-patternings of the individual members of that church. To make the test of this hypothesis more strenuous, we shall use several criteria to differentiate church milieus. The three milieu criteria that we have selected are: the Self-Ascription Index, an item on the importance of racial integration as an education and action goal of local church and denomination, and an item on the importance of psychological materials in the curriculum of adult religious education. These three milieu criteria characterize UU religiosity and private morality, public morality, and institutional religious expectation regarding secular knowledge. They also reflect Dimensions 1, 2, and 4 of the religiosity model. These three criteria have the further merit of differentiating value orientations within the broad American population and not simply within the Unitarian Universalist minority. We can place a liberal-left designation on a response direction of each of these criteria with some confidence that we are using these labels in a semantically unexceptionable way. The three criteria are described in footnote *b* of Table 8.5, and the particular responses designated liberal-left are indicated. While the Self-Ascription Index might not be directly useful with a non-UU population, many of the items of personal morality that we have shown to be closely correlated with this index would be moral issues for the larger American population, and the particular responses correlated with leftness on Self-Ascription would generally be termed liberal-left by this larger population.

Using these criteria, the churches in the sample were categorized and ranked in terms of their approximation to four ideal types of church milieu: least deviant from the overall sample distribution, homogeneously liberal-left, homogeneously conservative-right, and heterogeneous. The results of this categorization are shown in table 8.5. The procedure was to select the ten churches with the least mean deviation from the criterion response distribution of the overall sample as "Least Deviant" (Table 8.5, "LD" on Table 8.6). The twenty churches with the greatest mean deviation on each milieu criterion were dichotomized on a left/nonleft basis ("Left" and "Right" on Table 8.5, "L" and "R" on Table

TABLE 8.5

Most Representative Churches in Four Milieux as Selected on Three Milieu Criteria[a]

	Milieu											
	Milieu criterion[b]											
	Left			Least Deviant			Heterogeneous			Right		
Rank	S-A	Race	Psychology	S-A	Race	Psychology	S-A	Race	Psychology	S-A	Race	Psychology
1	29	29	70	38	11	97	44	44	71	45	47	93
2	10	74	86	26	19	42	48	95	65	47	49	45
3	103	103	92	9	5	55	41	35	58	49	86	99
4	106	56	106	56	107	57	7	28	74	35	78	10
5	43	93	103	54	30	5	53	32	56	99	46	82
6	31	97	32	42	3	21	2	13	31	30	96	105
7	86	59	78	21	79	8	24	10	52	46	84	95
8	89	2	87	98	27	11	92	38	17	32	98	101
9	c	70	41	5	7	6	14	72	9	84	83	84
10	c	c	13	52	22	14	c	85	68	33	99	100

[a] Code numbers are for 110 groups in initial sample. Growth churches (stratum 1) coded 1-10; ordinary churches (stratum 2) coded 11-59; lay-led fellowships (stratum 3) coded 60-110.

[b] The three milieu criteria used in Tables 8.5 and 8.6 were responses to:

S-A: The Self-Ascription index described in Table 1.6. The "left" category of the index was used for "left" criterion characterization.

Race: "For the social problems listed below, please indicate how important it is to you that liberal religion (in the local church or denomination) be involved in education and action":

Racial integration

Very important	69.7%	L
Somewhat important	24.7	
Not important	5.6	
	100.0%	

182

Psychology: "Would you approve or disapprove if each of the following changes of emphasis were made in our adult program materials?" (Distributions for seven additional emphases not shown.)

More stress on personal psychological development

Strongly approve	36.7%	L
Approve	51.8	
Disapprove	10.6	
Strongly disapprove	.8	
	99.9%	

"L" indicates category used to determine "Left" rankings among most deviant churches.

[c] No churches in these ranks for designated responses within twenty most deviant churches.

183

8.6) in terms of the frequency of the response designated "L." The limitation imposed on this dichotomization was that churches were not to be designated "L" unless their response frequency on the designated category exceeded that of the overall sample and, conversely, were not designated "R" unless their response frequency fell below that of the overall sample. This limitation occurred within the group of churches designated as having a "Left" milieu by the first and second milieu criteria. The selection of churches for the Heterogeneous milieu category ("H" on Table 8.6) was a ranking based on equal distribution of responses. The flatter the distribution curve, the more heterogeneous or pluralistic the church on that milieu criterion. In those few cases where churches had already been given another milieu designation, they were not included a second time in the Heterogeneous milieu.

The relationship of these four milieux can be visualized in Figure 1. A histogram for the psychological milieu criterion is shown as 1a. The eighty churches have been theoretically placed on a left/right continuum in terms of this criterion in 1b. The ten Most Left and ten Most Right churches will obviously be at the extremes of this continuum. The ten Least Deviant churches can be imagined to cluster about a point on the continuum analogous to the median of the frequency polygon smoothed into a curve. The ten Most Heterogeneous will be located somewhere between the Least Deviant church and the noneskewed extreme. Assuming that there is some variation in the response patterns, the Left, Right, and Least Deviant groups will be discrete. Depending on the shape of the curve (skewness and kurtosis), the Heterogeneous group might overlap the Left or Right and/or the Least Deviant group. As indicated, we have omitted such overlapping cases.

Using this characterization of different types of local church milieu, we can

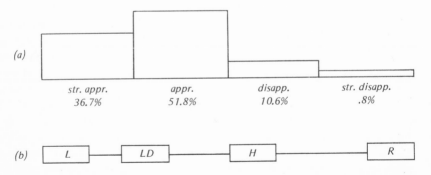

Figure 1. *Schematic designation of four milieux by milieu criterion. (a) Sample distribution on milieu criterion item 3: more stress on personal psychological development in adult program materials (N = 12,146). (b) Schematic location of church milieux (Left, Least Deviant, Heterogeneous, Right) using "strongly approve" response as index of "leftness" (N = 80).*

now refine and test our hypothesis. To what extent does the milieu of a local group, in this case a church, affect the individual members? More specifically, to what extent does the nature and quality of a milieu, characterized by one level of behaving, affect patterns within individuals at other levels of their personality? Is homogeneity within a group on some political value associated in any meaningful way with homogeneity at a religious level? If so, does the quality of that homogeneity (its leftness or rightness) make any difference, or is there simply a consistent process operative whereby individuals resemble their local groups more than they resemble some larger population, whether this process is a result of socialization or of self-selection? If the two levels of personality being examined (in this case the religious, on the one hand, and political-moral-psychologistic on the other) are sufficiently different, the discovery of patterns that are related to the quality of homogeneity (and not simply the quantity) will suggest that some kind of socialization is operative.

Let us look, therefore, at the integration of UU religiosity within the several different milieux. We shall hypothesize that greater integration of dimensionality will be found within the Left churches. Alternative hypotheses would be that the integration of religious dimensionality is not affected by the milieu of the local church or that it is directly related to the degree of homogeneity in local church milieu, whether the homogeneity is of a right- or left-wing quality.

In order to test the main hypothesis, gamma was computed, within each church, for the association between Dimension 1, represented by the Self-Ascription Index, and the other seven dimensions of UU religiosity (represented by the same most-characteristic items used in Tables 8.1-8.3). The mean value of gamma was computed for the churches of each of the four milieux on each of the three milieu criteria. These are reported in Table 8.6. Actual church by church values for gamma in each of the four milieux as defined by the three milieu criteria, are given in Appendix D, Tables 1-4.

In terms of the hypothesis, the strongest associations should be found within the homogeneous left churches, and the lowest associations with the homogeneous right groups (predicted rankings 1 and 4). The least deviant and most heterogeneous churches will be predicted as ranking 2 and 3, depending upon the skewness of the distribution on the milieu criterion, as discussed in connection with Figure 1. These predicted rankings are shown on Table 8.6. The arithmetic sums of actual gamma were used in computing the means, since a reversal of the direction of association within an individual church in comparison to its own group was held to be significant; whereas in ranking the mean gammas, absolute values were used since the focus at that point was upon the intensity of association rather than its directionality.

Let us now test our original hypothesis on the rankings shown in the lower half of Table 8.6, assuming that a "1" there represents the church-milieu with the highest congruence between any two dimensions and a "4" reflects the

TABLE 8.6

The Effect of Milieu on Religiosity Dimensional Associations[a]

Association[b]	Milieu criterion[a]											
	Self-Ascription				Racial integration				Psychological development			
	L	LD	H	R	L	LD	H	R	L	LD	H	R
Self-Ascription and:												
Dim. 2	-0.13	-0.21	-0.28	-0.43	-0.09	-0.15	-0.16	-0.52	-0.19	-0.15	-0.21	-0.17
Dim. 3	-0.08	0.06	-0.00	0.01	-0.14	-0.04	-0.04	0.07	-0.08	-0.01	-0.03	-0.01
Dim. 4	-0.08	-0.02	-0.12	-0.11	0.13	0.03	-0.02	-0.08	-0.01	-0.00	0.08	-0.02
Dim. 5	0.13	0.21	0.15	0.09	0.18	0.00	0.05	-0.03	0.06	0.12	0.08	0.10
Dim. 6	0.31	0.15	0.14	0.10	-0.03	0.12	0.17	0.22	0.27	0.09	0.05	-0.02
Dim. 7	0.38	0.00	-0.03	0.01	0.13	0.09	0.12	0.07	0.19	0.11	0.02	0.01
Dim. 8	-0.22	-0.16	-0.10	-0.22	-0.35	-0.18	-0.11	-0.28	-0.17	-0.23	-0.01	-0.31

TABLE 8.6 (continued)

The Effect of Milieu on Religiosity Dimensional Associations

Association[c]	Predicting ranking of associations				Actual ranking of associations			
	1	2	3	4	1	2	3	4
Self-Ascription and:								
Dim. 2	4	3	2	1	2	4	1	3
Dim. 3	1	4	3	2	1	3	2	4
Dim. 4	1	3	4	2	3	4	1	2
Dim. 5	1	4	2	3	4	1	3	2
Dim. 6	4	3	2	1	1	2	3	4
Dim. 7	1	3	2	4	1	2	3	4
Dim. 8	1	3	4	2	3	2	4	1

[a] Cf. Table 8.5 for description.

[b] Mean of actual gamma shown here. Cf. Appendix D, Tables 1-4.

[c] Ranking based upon absolute values of mean gamma.

187

lowest congruence (or the most dissonance). Insofar as it would have been arbitrary to settle for any single criterion in characterizing Right or Left milieux, we have used three which give us a slightly different group of churches in each case. If we find similar patterns in the groups regardless of the selection criterion, we can have more confidence in the results.

The simplest way of summarizing these rankings is to add them. That milieu with the lowest total presumably is the milieu with the greatest congruence between dimensions in its membership. On this basis, the Left milieu has the lowest totals on all three milieu criteria, and the Right milieu has the highest totals on the first and third criteria (totals for the four milieux in the listed order, for the three criteria are: 14,19,18,19; 13,23,19,15; 15,17,17,20). The Left milieu has 12 out of 21 predicted "1s," but the Right milieu has only six of the predicted "4s." Predictions on the Least Deviant and Most Heterogeneous milieux were even less successful.

Another way to test the hypothesis by means of these rankings is to take the Least Deviant level of association as a norm and ascertain on how many dimensions the Left group has stronger associations and the Right group, weaker associations. The Left churches show stronger associations five out of seven times on all three milieu criteria. The Right churches, however, have weaker associations than the norm only three, one, and three times, respectively; while they are stronger in association four, six, and four times on the three criteria selections.

These results clearly point to a revision of the hypothesis. The milieu of a local church is clearly associated with a dimensionality patterning within the members of that church. If the church is homogeneously "right" or "left," its members will have more congruence between the dimensions of their religiosity. Conversely, more dissonance will be found in the dimensional patternings within members of the heterogeneous or pluralistic churches (where the association level was below that of the Least Deviant norm ten out of twenty-one times).

With present information, there is no way of knowing whether the greater congruence within the members of the homogeneous extremes is the result of some kind of conditioning or socializing process or simply the result of self-selection. But this finding does converge with our earlier description of the polarization found within the overall denomination regarding social action. This is reflected here in the large negative gamma ($-.43$) found for the association of Dimensions 1 and 2 within the most Right group of churches selected by the Self-Ascription Index.

INDIVIDUAL INTEGRATION AS THE RESULT OF RELIGIOSITY

We are at last in a position to raise what is clearly the most intriguing question of all: Does religion make a difference? Some readers may, in earlier sections dealing with personal and social morality, have been wondering "What do any of these matters have to do with religion?" Such a query, while predictable, would not have been wholly accurate, since a number of the "matters" were in fact beliefs and religious practices. But we are now concerned to reverse the query, asking "Does religion have anything to do with these matters?" More specifically, does the church as a religious institution have any role in shaping the beliefs and values and styles of persons, or are the churches simply loci for the assemblage of already like-minded persons? This is an especially relevant inquiry in the case of the Unitarian Universalists, since so many of them are converts and since so many of these converts indicate that they adopted their present basic values before they became Unitarian Universalists. In the light of this, it would be quite reasonable to argue that the patterns of UU religiosity, such as the value-consensus found within the post-traditional group, are simply an effect of nonreligious factors within the culture, but that Unitarian Universalism, as a religious movement, has no causal role in the development of such values. In other words, the commonality of religiosity found within many of the churches and subgroups of the UUs is a result of self-selection rather than a result of any kind of religious socialization that can be attributed to the churches.

Strictly speaking, the only way of determining this would be to study the same individuals, at different points in time as related to their exposure to Unitarian Universalist religiosity, attempting somehow to rule out the effect that any extraneous conditions might have upon the production of any changes that were discovered. This kind of research has yet to be done. In the meantime, we may very roughly approximate it with a simulated panel study. In the first place, let us limit our focus to the converts since we may more readily determine the starting point of their "socialization" into UU religiosity. Then, since we know that age has a considerable effect upon religiosity, let us further limit our attention to those converts between the ages of 35 and 54. Using two years of membership as the dividing point, we will thus contrast new and old UUs in terms of their respective religiosity integrations. This information, (which may be compared to the overall denominational pattern shown in Table 8.4) is presented in Table 8.7, where the gamma statistic indicating dimensional integration is shown in parentheses for the "older" members.

Let us first approach this information in terms of the congruence model, which is actually a unidimensionality model in terms of the concepts that have been used in the empirical studies of religious groups. This would lead us to expect increasing association between dimensions as a result of denominational experience (in fact, congruence would be reflected in the disappearance of all dimensionality). Using a difference of .05 in gamma as a criterion, the strength of association increases only three times, decreases twelve times, and is unaffected thirteen times. Clearly, the length of church membership makes a difference in religiosity—but not in the direction of unidimensionality.

If, however, we take a more neutral approach and assume that every variety

TABLE 8.7

Socialization into UU Religiosity: Dimensional Associations Measured by Gamma for Converts, Age 35-54, with Less than Two Years Membership and (More Than Two Years)

Dimension[a]	Dimension							
	1	2	3	4	5	6	7	8
1. Personal beliefs, styles, and values	1.00	-.04 (-.28)	-.16 (-.10)	-.04 (-.04)	.23 (.10)	.28 (.14)	.21 (.11)	-.23 (-.17)
2. Social-ethical values (28)		1.00	.36 (.20)	.15 (.09)	.20 (.12)	.14 (.05)	-.12 (-.11)	.08 (.03)
3. Church sociality values and participation (29)			1.00	.36 (.33)	.16 (.13)	.13 (.25)	-.23 (-.30)	.11 (-.03)
4. Psychological development values (31)				1.00	.18 (.15)	.25 (.26)	-.12 (-.11)	.12 (.03)
5. Aesthetic-reflective-worship values (8)					1.00	.27 (.22)	-.13 (.12)	-.08 (-.02)
6. Educational function of the church (30)						1.00	.05 (-.04)	.07 (-.02)
7. The church as source of personal friendships (45)							1.00	-.04 (-.01)
8. Intrasectarian affirmations (44)								1.00

[a]Dimensions represented in this table by highest-loading items from factor analysis. Identifications in parentheses refer to item numbers of Table 2.6. For Dimension 1, the Self-Ascription Index has been used. It is based upon items 35 and 10, which are second and sixth, respectively, in loading Dimension 1.

of religiosity (including the UU variety) has its own particular patterning of dimensionality, we would describe satisfactory socialization as occurring when the associations of patterns of new members move toward the patterns of older members, which in turn move toward the patterns of the overall group. In almost every case this is occurring here, with the important qualification that the overall group patterning contains an abnormally high proportion of relatively new convert patterns.

The clearest change is the increased association (−.04 to −.28) between Dimensions 1 and 2; between personal beliefs and values, on the one hand, and social values. In the preceding section of this chapter, we saw this to be one of the relationships most sensitive to the milieu of the local church. The data of Table 8.7, based upon 68% of the converts, further confirm that the major impact of the Unitarian Universalist experience is in strengthening this relationship between the personal and social. In stating this, however, we must remember the important limitation in this kind of analytic procedure. We have not actually followed individual UUs throughout several years of their UU experience and studied their religiosity at each stage. Instead we have assumed that changes in the subgroups were not to be accounted for by defection on any particular ideological basis.

SUMMARY

In the light of the several analyses we have made, what can now be said regarding the integrative role of religion—at least of the Unitarian Universalist form of religion? If we center our focus upon those dimensions of individual personality relating to religious beliefs and practices, personal moral values, and social moral values (Dimensions 1 and 2 of our religiosity model), we can clearly say that integration of these personality aspects occurs.

If we also intend by "integration" the inclusion into some social subgroup on the basis of having come to share its values, we must also conclude that integration is a result of UU religiosity.

For the future, we need to explore other levels of integration as they may be related to religiosity. What does integration mean in relationship to the natural world, for instance, or the immediate family or community, or the artifactual world of science and technology, or the global (or even cosmic) population? Integration may not always be deemed a value, but it provides an ideal analytic focus.

Chapter 9

POSTTRADITIONALITY IN PERSPECTIVE

We now need to back away from the specific analyses of the Unitarian Universalists and see what all this means in terms of the larger world. Where does this group fit into Western culture, religiously? How significant are trends within this group in understanding other religious groups?

BACK TO PRESUPPOSITIONS

At the beginning of this book, two presuppositions were argued. On the one hand, the claim was made that empirical study of religion would add to our knowledge of an important aspect of human life, and that the techniques of survey research could fruitfully be used. It was also contended that using a sufficiently large sample would not only give precision of generalizability but would also permit analysis of a number of other fruitful elements. In the examination of the effects of religious background in this study, for instance, this has been amply borne out.

In the narrow statistical sense, of course, the increase of sample size brings a reduction of sampling error. Beyond that, it brings the statistical parameters of significance between subgroups down to a size where we are less likely to omit findings because they did not meet stringent criteria. It also permits more straightforward analysis of more elements without introducing mathematical assumptions which necessarily distort while rendering the data more tractable. For instance, in many cases we were able to proceed by simple crosstabulations and contingency tables simply because of the sample size. With a smaller sample, some of these associations could only have been understood by the introduction of assumptions of linearity of the data, etc. which are a high price for the discussion of data.

Our second presupposition was a plea for methodological openness regarding the nature of "religion." If we really know in advance what it is, study is unnecessary. If we do not fully know, as we argued in Chapters 1 and 2, then it becomes crucial that we do not let ideological assumptions inhibit our research. For instance, the assumption of the centrality of supernaturalism or belief-structures in any and all religions would have ruled out serious study of the Unitarian Universalists.

THE VIABILITY OF UNITARIAN UNIVERSALISM

In the brief sketching of methodological assumptions at the beginning of the book, an evolutionary framework was used which made "viability" a key concept. In the evolutionary sense, this refers to the ability of individuals to survive up to the breeding age. If we apply the metaphor to religions, it means that there are significant differences between cults that last for only a few years and those that are able to reproduce and sustain themselves throughout several generations of men.

For this very reason, we must be careful in generalizing from the Unitarian Universalist data. The most consistent and clear contrast we have found has been between the converts to this religion and the faithful, born UUs. We have stressed the adjective faithful, since the most cursory examination of past figures of denominational size will convince us that the great majority of those born into this group have not been "faithful," that is to say, they are no longer around. No doubt the total denomination would be different if more of them retained their birthrights. But we cannot specify the direction of change.

What is apparent is that the 90% convert rate is singular for any established group. We have not found many evidences of assimilation. In fact it would appear that the converts are assimilating the birthrights.

But this proportionality of old and new members makes it doubtful that many of the processes observable within Unitarian Universalism are generalizable to other, more normal, religious groups.

THE VIABILITY OF POSTTRADITIONALITY

Let us look more closely now at posttraditionality, which we have found to be the dominant characteristic of the overall Unitarian Universalist denomination today, as well as the overwhelming characteristic of the UU converts. If we return to our beginning metaphor, that the modern Unitarian Universalists are converts in "the stepfathers' house," the generalization that was just made regarding the nonpresence of assimilation within Unitarian Universalism means that the newly adopted members of the family are not taking over the faith of the stepfathers. Nevertheless, it is quite clear that these converts have not only come to Unitarian Universalism with a faith of their own but that they have, together, intensified certain aspects of this faith during their period of membership. As we saw in Chapter 8, there has been a measurable increase in the coherence of the various dimensions of their religiosity as a result of their length of membership. Instead of speaking, therefore, of assimilation, we can describe this process as one of "socialization," indicating that the qualities of the total group have an impact upon the individual members over a period of time.

It will be fruitful to look at the process of religious posttraditionality as being both a precursor and exhibiting many parallels to the dramatic emergence of a "youth culture" in the 1960s in American society. Theodore Roszak, one of the ablest observers of this scene, has dubbed this the "counter culture" (1968). Carefully delineating the interwoven effects of technocracy and abundance in relation to the variety of value patterns and lifestyles that now exist in American society, Roszak clearly, if critically, sides with the "young centaurs" in their struggle against the "defending Apollos" of society. Despite the nonhistorical excesses of some journalists in dealing with the counter culture, it is quite clear that it did not appear from nowhere. In fact, some of the closest students of the rebellious young have insisted that the college radicals show a close continuity with their own family patterns and that their own rebellion is directed not so much against their own fathers and mothers as against certain elements in the dominant culture which they learned to question at home (Flacks, 1967). With this in mind, it is worth examining more closely the patterns of posttraditional religiosity on the assumption that we may be dealing with some of the adult and family values that have created and supported the counter culture.

The Psychological Basis of Posttraditionality

There is a clear sense in which the posttraditional UUs are religious "dropouts" in relation to the Jewish and Christian outlooks that dominated the Western culture in its formative periods. Furthermore, it may be noted that their dropping out is an active rather than a passive process. They have identified themselves with a presumably new and different form of religion and, in their own labeling of that religion and in their desire for its future direction, clearly indicated their wish to be affiliated with something other than Judaism or Christianity.

It would be a mistake to focus upon the dropping-out process however, and ignore the likelihood of it being accompanied by a "dropping-in" process. When a new religious affiliation has occurred, it would seem quite clear that this is the case. Thus the Self-Ascription Index that we have been using throughout this

book to delineate the Unitarian Universalist spectrum has really a double
meaning when we turn to those persons that it designates as "left." Their
negation of Christianity is readily apparent, but it is also the case that their
affirmation has an equally clear patterning.

The Value Basis of Posttraditionality

We have consistently seen the ways in which the posttraditional UUs, in
contrast to their more conservative coreligionists, share a higher consensus on
their value commitments. Many of these values, such as the common concern for
the implications of science and knowledge, can be traced all the way back to the
Greek sources of Western culture. Others, such as the stress upon individualism
and tolerance, are more characteristic of the left-wing of the sixteenth-century
Reformation, and especially of the eighteenth-century Enlightenment. Some of
the posttraditional values are, on the other hand, quite modern in origin.

The innovative aspects of posttraditional religiosity

The posttraditionals consistently prefer that their religious experience furnish
them with "intellectual stimulation." The more traditional functions of Western
religion, such as ritual and worship and celebration, seem considerably less
important to them. If we interpret this in the light of the suggestive dictum of an
anthropologist of religion, Anthony Wallace, that ritual is "communication
without information," then it would appear that the posttraditionals desire a
religion wherein the stress on information is high (1968). This same concern for
ideas, for the expansive stimulation of newness, appears in the concerns of the
posttraditionals that their religion should be exploring the sciences as well as
other religious traditions.

The therapeutic aspects of posttraditional religiosity

Philip Rieff, in describing the world since Freud, has suggested that the older
culture of "commitment" has been challenged by a new culture of "the therapeutic" where men turn their attention to more immediately realizable goals and
strivings and insist that the gratifications of these goals shall be experienceable in
a personal sense, and in this present world (1966). Bearing in mind that this
search for pleasurable personal experience may be more the effect of Sigmund
Freud than his real intention, it would appear that the posttraditional UUs, in
their concern for personal psychological development and in their relatively high
concern for artistic and aesthetic experiences, are embodying this therapeutic
aspect of modernity. The depth of this commitment may be further measured
by the striking parallelism in their desires for themselves and their own children
in regard to experiences of psychological development. The older culture, one
suspects, would have been far less explicit in this and, indeed, would probably

have insisted that there are certain things that children must pedagogically experience, whether their parents continue to seek similar experiences or not.

The privatization aspects of posttraditional religiosity

We have used the term "privatism" to refer to one element involved in "doing your own thing," namely, the element that logically extends the same rights to one's neighbors. It goes without saying that the Unitarian Universalists, on the level of traditional theological beliefs, have long been committed to privatism. Their consistent refusal to permit the application of creedal statements attests to this. On the level of personal moral values it would appear that privatism is a relatively newer thing, in fact an attitude that distinguishes between the born UUs and their converts. The consistently-expressed values of the posttraditionals in regard to a variety of sex questions illustrate their privatism. In almost every case, their response was that the individual or individuals involved should be permitted to do what they desire to do. We have suggested that this dimension of personal morality reflects the assessments that are made of kinds of behavior that basically have no larger social impact. Clearly, the posttraditional UUs are not privatistic in regard to racism, or sexism, or war, or poverty—kinds of behavior in which there are clear victims. In those cases, they appear quite ready to level moral criticism at the victimizers.

The unisexual aspects of posttraditional religiosity

Finally, we must remark the striking convergence of the posttraditional UU men and women on questions of value in contrast to the sharply gender-related separation of the conservative UU men and women. This was true in regard to a number of sex and family values reflecting the personal aspect of morality and was also found to be true on items of social morality dealing with racism and conscientious objection. This aspect of posttraditionality may be one of the most significant religious innovations of all. The Western religious tradition has been notoriously ambivalent on the issue of violence, for instance, with women typically adhering to the "Christian" values of gentleness and men embracing more violent values in the name of Christian "realism." In posttraditional religiosity, it would appear that there is not only an elimination of these gender-related distinctions but also a common movement toward those gentler values traditionally embodied only by women.

Why Do They Go to Church?

None of the value aspects that we have just outlined, or, for that matter, none of the specific values that led to these generalizations, are unique to Unitarian Universalists, whether conservative or posttraditional. Beyond the obvious sense in which every individual has his own personal structuring of values, and many groups have a peculiar way of structuring their common values, there is no research evidence to indicate that other individuals or even groups outside of the American churches might not be indistinguishable from the posttraditional Unitarian Universalists.

Nevertheless, beyond all of these specific values and general clusters of value that the posttraditional UUs share, there is one additional value that characterizes them and distinguishes them from their more secularized colleagues: they go to church. Since most of them are converts, we can look for specific reasons for this behavior over and above the common church-going pattern of this social class within American culture. On the basis of our examinations of the data as well as the general history and present patterns of the Unitarian Universalist movement, several generalizations regarding the functions of the posttraditional church seem in order. The functions in our list are again by no means unique to this group, although several of the more traditional church functions, such as missions and evangelism, necessarily will not appear.

The support function

Without doubt, the participation in a community of like-valued persons serves to support these values within the individual. The more marginal these values are within the larger community, the more likely this is to be true. But there is certainly no way of knowing whether a person with similar values who did not join or remain in one of these churches would show greater shifting of values without the supportive community of such a church. In the absence of firm evidence, we can simply note the generally-expressed feeling that this is the case.

The socialization function

Not only does the local church tend to serve as a community of value-support for its members, but it also is to some extent a value-generating institution in the sense that persons interiorize new values in the process of discussion. The important place given by Unitarian Universalists to the writing, debating, and passing of resolutions on matters of social policy reflects this function.

The symbolizing function

On an overt level, the religiosity of many of the posttraditional UUs would appear to be devoid of symbolization. Their churches are characterized by the absence cf crosses and more obvious religious symbolism. In some cases, substitute symbols have been created—circles, candles, flaming chalices. Even in their absence, however, we can note that the act of church-going is itself ritualistic and symbolic. There is, thus, a group-symbolization going on in the lives of the posttraditonal UUs that distinguishes them from their more secular neighbors.

The transgenerational function

The posttraditional UUs have a very explicit commitment to the communication of their religious and social values to their own children. The high value that they place upon religious education indicates their judgment that such communication would not occur effectively without the church. Inferentially, we may assume that the common ordering of educational priorities in curriculum that the posttraditionals exhibit for adults as well as children indicates their commitment to a transgenerational communication that moves both ways along the age scale. Equally inferentially, the relatively lesser gap in values between younger and older posttraditionals as compared to more conservative Unitarian Universalists indicates the efficacy of this transgenerational communication function for them.

The transcultural communication function

In several ways the data have indicated the affinities that the posttraditionals feel for some religious traditions outside of Western culture. This not only explains the curricular place that they would accord to studying such traditions but indicates some of the basis for their generally-expressed internationalism and for the internationalist aspect they would push for their religious denomination.

THE SIGNIFICANCE OF POSTTRADITIONALITY

By now it is surely clear that the most significant fact of Unitarian Universalist religiosity is the dominance of posttraditionality. The central element in the UU experience is the conversion experience, if we remember the necessary qualifications to that term. The UU convert, unlike the convert traditionally associated with revivalistic Protestantism, apparently does not experience the intense emotional crisis that leads to an instant affiliation with the new religious group. Nor does he typically move from an intensified awareness of "sinfulness" to a new and relief-bringing affect of repentence. Nor does he experience the intense alienation from his former surroundings and neighbors and the necessary support of his new religious community. He is, indeed, a convert, in the sense that he has moved from his childhood position to a radically different institutional affiliation. But, in terms of the time span usually involved in this pilgrimage, the conversion is slow and growing rather than sudden. And in terms of the various shapers of the processes that eventually lead to the institutional conversion, these are typically not religious but secular. Above all, the university seems to function as the central agency in what must be called a deconversion process. Whatever posttraditional religious impact the Unitarian Universalist churches may have on the wider culture, they are numerically too few to explain the deconversion process. For the same reason, we must assume that many more Americans have experienced a similar deconversion.

In the posttraditionality of the Unitarian Universalists that we have been analyzing, this deconversion has been found to be closely and powerfully associated with the shift to a large cluster of personal and social values and lifestyles. On the basis of several strands of indirect evidence, we have been led to accept the respondents' claims that they had embraced these values before embracing Unitarian Universalism. For convenience in understanding this, we may think of three distinct phases. Phase 1 is the deconversion stage, the dropping-out of the older religious identification. Phase 2 is the assimilation and integration of the new clusters of values required by this new self-identification. We could expect these newly assimilated values to be closely related to the alternative values existent within the individual's context at the time of deconversion. Deconversion within the university would be an exposure to different sets of alternative values than deconversion within the factory. Phase 3 occurs when, and if, for some reasons, these new identification-values become institutionally grounded.

In the case of the UU converts, Phase 3 reflected affiliation with a liberal church. Clearly, however, Phase 3 is not inevitable. There are, no doubt, far more Americans living comfortably with Phase 2 than there are Unitarian Universalists on the whole continent. It is also quite possible that the institutional affiliation of Phase 3 may indeed be a reaffiliation with the institution of one's childhood. In the case of many Roman Catholics today, this would seem to be the case. We might also assume this to be the case with the high percentage of less-than-orthodox Congregationalists that Glock and Stark discovered.

Is it conceivable that other churches and religious institutions might become as predominantly posttraditional as the churches comprising the Unitarian Universalist Association? This is a matter of pure conjecture, of course, but any such eventualities will be clearly related to the openness of such groups toward divergent new membership, to the perceived flexibilities of their own attitudes toward their historic traditions, and to the attractiveness that they actually hold for potential converts. It may also be suggested that religious institutions have two doors, one marked "In" and the other marked "Out." If too many people enter who are too different, some of the original members may choose to exit by the other door. As we have noted, many of the persons who were born in Unitarian Universalist churches are clearly no longer there. Whether this is related to the upsurge of posttraditionality within the churches of their childhood is an interesting research problem, but any suggestions at this point along this line would be sheer guesswork.

From the foregoing, it is clear that that fact of posttraditionality and religious deconversion has wide-ranging cultural significance. At the very least, our study of the Unitarian Universalists has shown us that loss of faith is in no sense related to loss of values. Indeed, the more the deconverted move toward a posttraditional form of religiosity, the more their new values become integrated. Thus we may regard the kind of posttraditional religiosity that is emerging among the UUs as one, known, outcome of a very widespread religious deconversion within Western culture. While there is no guarantee that all of the deconverts within our society will move either toward value integration or, more specifically, toward integration around liberal clusters of values, we can at least observe that some do.

APPENDICES

Appendix A

SAMPLING, WEIGHTING, DATA COLLECTION AND ANALYSIS

As indicated in the preface, the data used in this book grew out of a study commissioned by the Committee on Goals of the Unitarian Universalist Association. In 1965, the Board of Trustees of the denomination appointed this short-term committee to create some broad proposals for long-range planning. The fourteen members of this committee met on and off for two years and issued their report. In the course of preparing that report, it became clear that a projection of long-range goals required a better understanding of the current situation, and a research project was outlined which received its basic underwriting and primary financing from the Board of Trustees.

The aim of this project was to sketch a profile of the "typical Unitarian Universalist," to measure any regional differences that might exist within the denomination, and to ascertain if there were any noteworthy differences between existing churches that had been experiencing rapid growth and ordinary churches. A contract was made with the National Opinion Research Center of the University of Chicago to provide overall consultative and professional services. The project director was Robert B. Tapp (who was also chairman of the Committee on Goals), and NORC's Survey Research Service Director, Paul B. Sheatsley, acted as consultant. Under the terms of this contract, NORC would, as an independent research agency and in cooperation with the project director, evaluate for the Committee on Goals and the Unitarian Universalist Association the sampling technique, the data collecting procedures, and the results relating to the three areas of the original proposal. After this phase of the analysis had been completed, the data would remain available to the project director for a period of two years from the completion of the contract. After that time, NORC, as a nonprofit research agency, would be free to make further scientific use of the data. NORC was selected because of its wide experience with survey research, its willingness to engage in a limited consultative role, and because it was felt that an outside agency of this standing would guarantee, both actually and psychologically, the validity of the results.

SAMPLING PROCEDURES

Since the study was concerned with both individuals and churches, sampling was stratified by types of churches. The first stratum of "growth churches" was comprised of those twenty-two churches which had experienced the highest rate of membership growth from the merger in 1961 through the latest figures for 1965. Ten churches were randomly drawn from this stratum. The remaining 681 churches, hereafter called "ordinary" churches, were sampled on a proportional-to-size basis to form the second stratum. The third stratum comprised the 401 "fellowship groups" which were listed in the 1966 *Directory* of the Unitarian Universalist Association. These were lay-led groups which were hypothesized to be quite distinct in composition. Some of them were spin-offs from established churches where population shifting had occurred, some of them were small groups in communities that could not support a professionally-led church, some were incipient churches, and a few were larger groups with a commitment to nonprofessional leadership. A random sample of 51 fellowships was chosen from this third stratum. Before any of this sampling was done, groups were excluded which were in inactive status, or operated only during the summer, or were legally "federated" or in some other way linked with another denomination.

Because of interest in the three types of churches reflected in this stratification, and a secondary interest in the possibilities of geographical differentiations, an intentionally large initial sample was drawn. If all the groups in this sample had agreed to cooperate, the official denominational figures showed a potential of 36,219 respondents. Should this large number have been realized, additional subsampling would have been performed within individual groups. As it turned out, however, 80 groups returned questionnaires by the processing deadline, and all data in this book are based upon this obtained sample of 12,146 completed questionnaires. Thus, 30 of the 110 groups in the original sample are not represented in the study. Some of these groups participated in the process but were unable to return their questionnaires before the processing deadline, and other arrangements were made to provide them with local results.

Among the churches that declined to participate in the survey, a variety of reasons were given. Several had just completed local surveys of their membership for local purposes, such as preparation for financial campaigns or self-study prior to calling a new minister. One of these churches reported that the self-study process had been so "divisive" that it would be years before they would try it again, if ever.

Table A.1 presents information on the stratification of the sample. It will be seen that 80% of the growth churches cooperated, 70% of the ordinary churches, and 73% of the fellowships. These responses are sufficiently close to indicate, at least in terms of the stratification, that no systematic biases were introduced in the data-gathering process. It was not possible to determine what other factors might have been operative within the 30 additional societies which were in the invited sample. The wide range of explanations just given, however, makes it not unreasonable to assume that no systematic distortions occurred as a result of this response-by-group rate.

The membership figures for the invited sample in Table A.1 are compiled from denominational records. On the basis of such figures, the apparent return rate for individuals in each stratum is disturbingly low. Church and denominational statistics are, however, notoriously inaccurate and typically err toward overstatement. As packets of questionnaires arrived from participating churches, it became clear that Unitarian Universalists were no exception. Each participating church, having agreed to solicit all its "legal adult members," had been supplied with questionnaires for its denominationally-reported "official" membership, plus an additional 10% to cover new members.

In order to arrive at a more realistic return rate, each group was later asked to furnish a figure for the number of actual questionnaires it had mailed to its members. These figures were consistently lower than the official membership figures. In a number of cases, explanations were volunteered; influenced, no doubt, by the postal costs involved, mailing lists had been winnowed to exclude inactive, absentee, or noncontributing members. As an illustration of this process, one church which listed 700 official members, sent out 400 questionnaires, and returned 300 of these completed. Since the person who did not receive a questionnaire cannot realistically be considered a nonrespondent, the return rates upon which the study proceeded were computed from these "mail-out" figures. For growth churches, there was a 67% return; for ordinary churches, 47%; and for fellowships, 69%.

More subtle factors come into play when we consider the adequacy of the response rates. If we were trying to predict, say, voting behavior, such response rates from registered voters would obviously be quite unsatisfactory. In this case, however, we are dealing with a voluntary organization whose members freely join and leave. In such organizations, the impact that a particular individual makes is a function of many things, including the amount of time, commitment, and money that he contributes. It may be reasonable to assume that the willingness to complete a questionnaire is an indirect measure of the willingness

TABLE A.1
Nature of Sample by Type of Church[a]

Type of church	UUA		Sample				
			Invited societies		Cooperating societies		
	Number of societies	Number of members	Number	Members	Number	Respondents	Weighted respondents
Growth churches	22	10,638	10	6,281	8	2,513	10,762
Ordinary churches	681	144,915	49	26,316	36	7,866	142,746
Fellowships	401	17,106	51	3,622	36	1,767	17,250
Total	1,104	172,659	110	36,219	80	12,146	170,758

[a]Membership figures are based on the 1966 Unitarian Universalist Association *Directory*. Federated, inactive, and summer churches were excluded before sampling.

to commit at least time to the purposes of the church. Therefore, especially in trying to understand the present or predict future conditions within a church, the responses of those who have filled in questionnaires may be more indicative than the unknown responses of those who fail to do so.

WEIGHTING

A weighting system was created to equalize the return rates for each of the 80 groups and also to compensate for the stratification of the sampling. This weighting, devised by Seymour Sudman, NORC's Director of Sampling, resulted in the generation of an integer weight to be assigned to all members of each one of the groups. The multiplier effect of weighting is indicated in the last column of Table A.1 and the last two columns of Table A.2. While the system was devised to produce that set of smallest integers accounting both for stratification and response rates, it will be noted that the "weighted respondents" correspond almost exactly to the official membership figures for each stratum. This coincidence, needless to say, is of no statistical consequence. Except for comparisons between individual churches, most of the tables in this book utilize this weighting scheme. The symbol "Nwt" indicates that weighted respondents have been used whereas the conventional symbol "N" indicates the use of unweighted respondents.

The weighting system makes the independent assumptions that in the case of the 80 churches the individual responses would not have been different had the rate for that church been identical to the average response rate for all churches, and that respondents in each of the three strata are represented proportional to the share of that stratum within the UU population (and not within the sample).

REGIONAL BREAKDOWNS

Given the New England origins of both Unitarianism and Universalism in America, and a widespread stereotype within denominational circles that the churches in this original area remained quite conservative while an increasing liberalism could be perceived as one moved westward, it seemed desirable to ascertain the possible effects of regionalism. To some extent, it was possible to do this despite the geographical grid of 23 districts that had been created in the process of merging these two denominations. Rather than attempt to impose some artificial regional structure upon the total population, four selected "regions" were constructed for purposes of analysis. The results of this procedure are shown in Table A.2. The four districts comprising the New England region embrace (with the exception of Maine) what is both conventionally and within Unitarian and Universalist circles called New England. The Ballou Channing District, named for founding Universalist and Unitarian leaders, extends south

TABLE A.2

Distribution of Sample by Selected Regions

Region	UUA			Sample			
	Number of societies	Members	Percent of UUA	Number of societies	Number of members	Number of respondents	Weighted respondents	Percent of weighted respondents
Canada[a]	47	6,037	4	8	2,381	1,141	15,439	9
Pacific[b]	92	15,663	9	9	2,777	1,422	17,772	10
Midwest[c]	212	32,488	19	16	4,592	2,309	38,721	23
New England[d]	215	40,948	24	10	2,469	844	29,364	17
Other	538	77,523	44	37	10,735	6,430	70,512	41

[a]All groups in Canadian districts plus two groups from the Midwest, as noted below.

[b]Pacific Central and Pacific Southwest districts.

[c]Central Midwest, Rocky Mountain, Michigan-Ohio Valley, and Prairie Star districts, minus one Canadian group from each of the last two.

[d]Ballou Channing, Central Massachusetts, Connecticut Valley, Massachusetts Bay districts.

from the Massachusetts Bay area to the Rhode Island shore. The Midwest region embraces four districts whose perimeter is almost identical to the old Unitarian "Western Conference." In earlier times, that area was viewed as the seedbed of "liberalism" (which, in this context, meant a humanistic religion hostile to the liberal Christianity of the New England Unitarians). The Pacific region, embracing three districts, represents an area thought in more recent times to be the most "liberal" within the denomination.

Although the denomination in 1966 made no clear distinction between United States and Canadian members, it appeared useful, for analytic purposes, to observe this national breakdown. Since two of the groups within the artificial Midwest region were Canadian, they were, in all tabulations reflecting the selected regions, shifted to the more appropriate Canadian designation.

As already indicated, the size of the sample and the varied regional densities of this denomination made a total regionalization indefensible. Therefore the "Other" category shown on tables in this Appendix (which includes groups in cities as disparate as New York City, New Orleans, and Denver) is not regarded as conceptually meaningful and has not been included in any of the regional breakdowns in tabular presentations in the main body of this book.

Table A.3 shows the types of churches in the sample design as reflected in the weighted respondents located in each region. It will be noted that there were no New England growth churches in the survey. Thus the New Englanders, with few fellowships, are predominantly in ordinary churches. In the case of the Canadians, a high number of growth churches were in this region, as reflected in the 11% of the weighted respondents in this stratum. The Pacific region has a disproportionate number of fellowships and this is reflected in the 20% of their weighted respondents in this stratum. In the Midwest region, a normal proportion of growth churches exists and a somewhat below-normal proportion of fellowships.

TABLE A.3
Church Type by Region[a]

	Region					Total sample
Type	Canada	Pacific	Midwest	New England	Other	
Growth	11	7	6	0	8	6
Ordinary	78	74	89	99	78	84
Fellowship	11	20	5	1	14	10

[a]Nwt=170,758; figures are percentages.

DATA COLLECTION

The ministers or lay presidents of each of the 110 fellowships and churches in the sample received a letter from the chairman of the Committee on Goals, outlining the project, stressing its importance to the future life of the denomination, and urging cooperation. The limited initial funding of the project made it necessary to ask the churches to share in the costs of the survey, and this stipulation no doubt had some effect on the decision of individual groups to cooperate. Each church in the sample was asked to mail a questionnaire to every adult member, and to include a stamped envelope for its return. They were also to agree to handle whatever follow-up mailing was necessary to maximize the return rate. The sharing of survey expenses amounted to a commitment by the groups of 20 cents postage per member, plus materials and secretarial time to supervise the mailing. As an inducement both to cooperate and to make more useful the information that would be gathered, each participating church was promised a breakdown of its local finding. This letter is reproduced here.

MEADVILLE THEOLOGICAL SCHOOL
OF LOMBARD COLLEGE
Affiliated with The University of Chicago
5701 WOODLAWN AVENUE, CHICAGO 60637

ROBERT B. TAPP
  Professor of Philosophy of Religion

April 14, 1966

Dear

I need your help in a project that should prove of great significance for the future of liberal religion.

Last year, the UUA Board of Trustees appointed a Committee on Goals to study long-range goals and make recommendations to the denomination. As the Committee discussed its job, it became increasingly clear that we lacked any trustworthy knowledge of present Unitarian-Universalist beliefs and practices. We therefore proposed, and found financing, for a questionnaire-type survey of the movement. This study will be conducted by the National Opinion Research Corporation and will conform to the best practices in sampling and analysis. Several months of intensive preparation have gone into the questionnaire, which is now at the printers.

For valid results, we must study about 10% of our churches and fellowships. Technically, the sample has been drawn "proportional to size," and your group is one of those selected. The reliability of the study obviously will be weakened unless we can convince each of the selected groups to cooperate.

The procedure is as follows. When we receive the enclosed air mail post card from you, we will furnish questionnaires for all your adult members, with a suggested plan for mail distribution via your office. Your members will return their completed questionnaires to you, for forwarding to me in a single packet. We want to achieve as close to 100% participation by individuals in the selected churches and fellowship as possible, and will provide a plan for follow-through and check-off by your office.

The questionnaire has proved quite stimulating within those groups where it has been pre-tested, and we think your members will share this feeling. We will send you the tabulations for your own group. The national tabulations will be incorporated in the final report of the Committee on Goals to the 1967 General Assembly.

Research on such a scale, however necessary and desirable, is expensive. With available denominational funds, we can only accomplish it by a great amount of volunteer labor and by distributing some of the costs to the participating churches. Specifically this will involve "in-and-out" postage from your office to your members ($ .20, or less if you use a bulk mailing permit) plus the cost of any follow-up mailings to achieve complete participation. Plus the return of the completed set to Chicago (at book rate).

While I cannot distribute questionnaires until the actual study begins, I can assure you that it is a comprehensive instrument designed to prove a wide variety of personal and social beliefs and attitudes as well as such factors as religious background and present expectations. The resultant profiles will be of tremendous value to our continental movement, as well as to the participating churches and fellowships. While furnishing individual tabulations to the participating groups will add to the cost, we are doing it to make full participation more likely. I hope you will agree that this value will more than offset the postage and labor costs of the study that we are asking your church to share.

Will you, therefore, use whatever channels may be necessary to approve participation and let me know via the enclosed card? You will receive questionnaires and further details by return mail.

Hopefully,

Robert B. Tapp
Chairman, Committee on Goals

Each of the twenty-three district executives received a copy of this letter, along with a personal letter from the committee chairman explaining the significance of the project, listing the churches within his district that were in the sample, and enlisting his help in gaining full support from these groups.

As affirmative replies were received from the selected churches, sufficient questionnaires were shipped to cover 110% of the *Directory*-listed adult membership. Local groups were reminded of their agreement to mail the questionnaires to their members, including a stamped return envelope. They were also asked to write their own covering letter, stressing the importance of full participation, assuring their members that the code numbers on the questionnaire were for check-off purposes only, and that the questionnaires would only be examined by NORC after the code numbers had been destroyed.

After two months, a second letter, reproduced here, was sent to ministers or presidents who had not yet responded to the invitation.

June 27, 1966

Dear Mister   :

The Committee on Goals of the Unitarian Universalist Association is carrying out a continental questionnaire study of present beliefs, values, and attitudes to assist us in our task of choosing between alternative long-range plans for our movement.

Last April you received a letter from me outlining this project (copy enclosed) and indicating that your group had been chosen in our sample of more than one hundred churches and fellowships. We have not yet heard from you, and are anxious to have your participation. Unless we can have complete coverage, the study will lose validity.

Would you kindly take this up with the appropriate persons and let me know? I hope you will say Yes and advise me of your present legal adult membership so that I can rush the questionnaires and instructions to you.

Sincerely,

Robert B. Tapp, Chairman
Committee on Goals

After an additional month, if there was still no reply from the minister of a local church, a third letter was sent to the lay president (chairman) of the church.

**MEADVILLE THEOLOGICAL SCHOOL
OF LOMBARD COLLEGE**
Affiliated with The University of Chicago
5701 WOODLAWN AVENUE, CHICAGO 60637

ROBERT B. TAPP
Professor of Philosophy of Religion

July 29, 1966

Dear Mister   :

    The Committee on Goals of the Unitarian Universalist Association is making a questionnaire study of more than 100 churches and fellowships to assist us in proposing some long-range plans for the denomination. Your church was one of those chosen in the sample and we have not yet heard from you.

    I am enclosing copies of the earlier letters which went to your minister. As I explained there, the validity of our study will be weakened unless all of the chosen churches participate. Would you kindly check into this and let me know as soon as possible. I realize this is a bad season to mail things to our members but hope you can find some way to say Yes.

Sincerely,

Robert B. Tapp, Chairman
Committee on Goals

RBT:sf

Encl. April 14 letter with postcard
       May 31 letter with label
       June 30 letter with postcard

Due to a variety of delays and the fact that many churches were closed during the summer, data-processing had to be postponed and this provided the opportunity for one more appeal to groups not yet participating. Letter number four was sent simultaneously to ministers and chairmen of such churches.

MEADVILLE THEOLOGICAL SCHOOL
OF LOMBARD COLLEGE
Affiliated with The University of Chicago
5701 WOODLAWN AVENUE, CHICAGO 60637

ROBERT B. TAPP
Professor of Philosophy of Religion

September 14, 1966

Committee on Goals

Unitarian Universalist Association

To Ministers and Board Chairmen:

As you may recall, the Committee on Goals last spring undertook a questionnaire study of the religious beliefs and attitudes of individual Unitarian Universalists. In proposing alternative long-range goals for the denomination, we felt it essential to gain a clear picture of where we are now.

Your group was selected as part of the sample unit of more than one hundred churches and fellowships. Almost all of the sample have now mailed out their questionnaires and returned them to us, and we are now processing the data.

Your group was one of the few that at that time said No or failed to respond. A number of unforeseen delays on this end have postponed the final shaping of our study and I am therefore writing you once more in the hope that you might be induced to participate in the project this fall. We could then include information on your members in our final report. Obviously this will greatly increase the accuracy and validity of our understanding of the present nature of religious liberalism.

A number of the already-participating churches have written of the excitement and stimulation generated locally by the questionnaire. At a later date, each group will receive breakdowns on its own membership which should prove highly useful in local programming.

If you can find a way to now say Yes (via the enclosed card), we will ship you the questionnaires and detailed instructions. Briefly, your share of the costs (as outlined in an April 14 letter from me) comes to "in and out" postage for your legal adult membership (10¢ each way), envelopes, and the cost of shipping the collected questionnaires in a bundle to the National Opinion Research Center in Chicago.

May I hope that the new church year and your present local situation will enable you to become part of the study?

Sincerely,

Robert B. Tapp
Chairman, Committee on Goals

RBT:1fl

At the same time, letter number five was sent to the District Directors indicating the presence of such churches in their districts.

MEADVILLE THEOLOGICAL SCHOOL
OF LOMBARD COLLEGE
Affiliated with The University of Chicago
5701 WOODLAWN AVENUE, CHICAGO 60637

ROBERT B. TAPP
Professor of Philosophy of Religion

September 15, 1966

Dear   :

This is a brief progress report on our Questionnaire Study. Thanks to your excellent help, almost all of the churches and fellowships have agreed to participate, and a majority have already sent the completed questionnaires to the National Opinion Research Center.

I am enclosing a copy of a letter I have just sent to the ministers and board chairmen of groups that either said No last spring or failed to respond in any way. I have listed below any groups in your district that received this letter.

I am also enclosing, for your information, a letter sent to all churches after they have shipped their questionnaires.

Again--with thanks,

Robert B. Tapp, Chairman,
Committee on Goals

Letters were sent, at this time, to participating churches asking for more accurate information on the number of questionnaires actually mailed to members. The text of this letter, number six, appears here. Similar information was subsequently obtained from churches participating after this date. These revised figures were used in computing return rates.

**MEADVILLE THEOLOGICAL SCHOOL
OF LOMBARD COLLEGE**
Affiliated with The University of Chicago
5701 WOODLAWN AVENUE, CHICAGO 60637

ROBERT B. TAPP
Professor of Philosophy of Religion

Committee on Goals
Unitarian Universalist Association

September 14, 1966

To Churches and Fellowships who have participated in the Questionnaire
Study:

We have now received the questionnaires from most of you, and the
return-percentage from local groups has generally been excellent. As you
have probably surmised, initial delays on printing and distribution from our
end and the intervention of summer have slowed our time-schedule. However, this can be used to provide us with an even more accurate picture
for our final report.

Have you received additional questionnaires from your members
since your bulk shipment to Chicago? Would a card from you to those
who did not return their questionnaires improve the percentage? Or even
a "last call" via your local newsletter? Naturally we can rush additional
questionnaires if they are needed.

You should also know that a number of persons added "notes to the
minister or fellowship president" on their questionnaires. Due to the
promised anonymity, the questionnaires cannot, of course, be returned
to you. You may want to mention this in your next newsletter. One member even used the questionnaire to offer a special gift to his church! For-
tunately, National Opinion Research Center happened to spot this and relay
the information to the minister.

One final and crucial matter. There have been a number of wide
discrepancies between membership figures in the Yearbook, the figures
indicated in your April request for questionnaires, and the numbers of
questionnaires that you reported having actually mailed out when you sent
the shipping card to me. This makes for statistical chaos on this end,
since it affects each group's calculated return rate and therefore the
reliability and validity of all of our results!

Will you, therefore please check into this and return the enclosed card
to me as soon as possible?

Thanks again,

Robert B. Tapp, Chairman,
Committee on Goals

Send the questionnaires to:

Unitarian Universalist Association
National Opinion Research Center
6030 South Ellis
Chicago, Illinois 60637

RBT:lfl

All questionnaires received by December 1, 1966 were included in the final processing.

THE QUESTIONNAIRE

As indicated in the preface, the impetus for the questionnaire study on which this book is based was the need for information experienced by a denominational committee on long-range planning. After two years of deliberations, that committee presented its report to the Board of Trustees of the Unitarian Universalist Association, which published the report in April, 1967, and included an appendix giving the distribution of responses to the items of the questionnaire. Those tables, which also indicate the nonresponse percentages for each item, are reproduced here as Appendix B.

In a real sense, the questionnaire was the work of many hands. While the final inclusion and exclusion of items as well as wording is the responsibility of the author, the members of the Committee on Goals spent many hours helping define the scope of the inquiry. Above all, Professor Ralph Conant and the Reverend Paul Carnes must be cited for their central roles. Denominational officials were solicited with reference to their particular interests, and a number of items included in the final version stem directly from their counsel. In this connection, particular mention should be made of Homer A. Jack, Leon C. Fay, and Royal Cloyd. In addition, a number of the academic colleagues listed in the Acknowledgements made valuable suggestions on the shaping of questions.

The questionnaire was pretested with the members of the First Universalist Church of Chicago, the Glenview Illinois Unitarian Fellowship, and the Unitarian Universalist students of Meadville/Lombard Theological School, an affiliate of the University of Chicago. Among other things, this pretesting sanctioned the use of relatively sophisticated terminology in some of the wording and led to the decision not to repeat items throughout the questionnaire as a means of increasing reliability. It also ruled out some items on which near unanimity was found within this population (for instance, opposition to capital punishment).

The final version of the questionnaire began with personal beliefs and attitudes, included a number of items on social beliefs and attitudes, contained a section on local church, society, fellowship, a section of denominational attitudes, and concluded with personal data.

Finally, it may be noted that none of the invited churches saw the questionnaire until they had agreed to participate. This "sight unseen" basis prevented the bias that would have been introduced had the leadership of any particular church declined the invitation on the basis of any of the questionnaire items. To be sure, as indicated by the nonresponse rates printed for each item in Appendix B, individuals rejected various items, and an unknown number of persons in effect rejected the whole set of items by failing to return their questionnaires.

Some concluding reflections may be of value to others conducting similar kinds of research. The various follow-up procedures, including the intervention of district directors, reduced to six the number of groups that did not respond in any way. The final letter, however, addressed to the lay-leader rather than minister of nonresponding churches, did not increase participation. In retrospect, it would have been preferable to have sent the initial mailing to both the minister and the leading layman rather than just to the minister. In several cases, for instance, it turned out that the minister had made a negative decision on his own regarding the survey. When this had happened, local problems might have arisen in any attempt to reverse that decision. One minister who had not responded to the several invitations described the procedure of writing his board chairman as an attempt to go "behind his back."

The decision to preserve individual confidentiality seems to have been a correct one, especially in view of the extent of personal information elicited, including financial data. In most of the cooperating churches, the requested covering letter assuring such anonymity was written and sent by the minister or lay-leader. Only in a few cases was the agreement to confidentiality not observed. Some of these churches, apparently not willing to wait for the results, did their own tabulations before forwarding the questionnaires. Despite these deviations from the agreed procedures, no complaints on administration reached the project director. Nor, since such deviations would have occurred after the completion of the questionnnaires, is there any reason to believe that these local practices had any effect upon the information given.

The research design also specified that the identity of the participating groups would be known only to the project director and to NORC. Many participating local churches made their own profiles available to their membership, but these local breakdowns were not completed until several months after the publication of the continental percentages. Any such local indications of having participated in the sample were, of course, with the rights of the individual churches. An amusing by-product of the anonymity of the groups in the sample was a letter released to a Boston newspaper by seventeen New England ministers. They stated that questionnaires had not been distributed in their churches and that the published results were "not representative" of them or their churches. Obviously the results were representative insofar as the sampling was representative, and what they intended to assert was that their responses distributed at one end of the continental range of responses (at the conservative end, it would appear).

DATA ANALYSIS

Preliminary analysis was made of the first 4300 questionnaires that had been received. This tentative information enabled the Committee on Goals to make a first draft of its report in the fall of 1966. The results of that analysis correspond so closely to the final percentages that there is no reason to suppose that external events during the several months in which the questionnaires were completed by different groups had any significant effect upon the results. This comparison also suggests that there were no major differences between the groups that responded early to the invitation and those that responded only after considerable prodding. There was, unfortunately, no way of assessing the total impact of noncooperation by local groups upon the final results.

These first-level analyses of the preliminary and continental samples, and the church-type and regional breakdowns, were made by NORC. The results for individual churches were produced by Data/Text software at the University of Chicago's Computation Center, yielding printout that could be readily understood by laymen with minimal instruction.

TESTS OF SIGNIFICANCE

In view of the size of the sample, even without weighting, the traditional tests of significance based upon the distribution of chi-square are of little value and, therefore, probability levels are not indicated on the tables of this book. Any inferences made from this data in the text, however, are based upon the criterion levels of $p \leqslant .001$ for the weighted continental sample, $p \leqslant .01$ for the regional and type-of-church breakdowns, and $p \leqslant .05$ for the unweighted individual churches.

Kruskal and Goodman's gamma is used as the statistic of association when the relationship of variables is summarized. This statistic can vary from +1.00 to −1.00. The value of gamma, apart from sign, indicates the strength of a relationship, and the sign indicates the direction of the relationship. Gamma was developed to explore relationships between ordered, qualitative variables. It has the additional advantages of being unaffected by assumptions regarding symmetry or differences in the numbers of individuals on different tables, being minimally affected by differences in the numbers of rows and columns in a contingency table, and providing a direct measure of proportional reduction of error.

QUESTIONNAIRE, WITH WEIGHTED FREQUENCY DISTRIBUTIONS

The questionnaire appears here with the original cover page and with the original items printed as consecutively-numbered tables showing the frequency distributions in percentages. The "n-r" at the bottom of each table indicates the percentage of respondents failing to respond to that item. In percentaging actual responses, nonrespondents were excluded from the percentage base and the weighting system described in Appendix A was used.

The order and wording of the items are the same as in the questionnaire as administered. The five groupings used as subheadings and in item-numbering also appeared on the questionnaire.

THE QUESTIONNAIRE

Information and Instructions to Respondents
(reprinted from page 1 of actual questionnaire)

In 1965, the Board of Trustees of the Unitarian Universalist Association created a Committee on Goals to examine some long-range planning possibilities for our denomination. It quickly became clear to us that we needed fuller knowledge of the *present* before we could speak effectively of alternatives for the *future*. No study of our total membership has ever been made!

221

The Trustees therefore agreed to finance such a study, and we turned to the National Opinion Research Center at the University of Chicago for guidance. Given our budget limits, a pre-coded questionnaire, self-administered by all the adult members of a sample of churches and fellowships, seemed the answer. If we can achieve full participation from the more than one hundred churches and fellowships in the sample, the study will prove of tremendous value.

The questionnaire is *not* to be signed. It contains a number of questions dealing with theological-philosophical beliefs as well as personal and social values. While the questionnaire looks (and is) long, almost all questions can be answered by circling a code number next to the alternative which is most similar to your opinion. Many individuals as well as pre-test groups have tried to word the choices so as to include most of us, most of the time. Please answer *every* question (unless instructions state otherwise), and return the questionnaire *promptly* in the envelope provided.

Let me assure you that the Committee on Goals does not intend to make recommendations by computer. The continental results will be a part of our report to the 1967 General Assembly, but we shall be putting before the denomination several alternative long-range goals that seem best to us, not just easiest or most popular.

In making this questionnaire, we have not used any fixed definition of the meaning of "religion." We are simply assuming that the Unitarian Universalist Association is a religious organization which is made up of churches and fellowships. Perhaps we should also add that the Committee on Goals is deeply committed to the principles of individual freedom of religious belief, and sees this study as a way of making more effective the organizations that advance this freedom.

Special note to members of fellowships: The use of "church" in this questionnaire is intended to cover any local group, including fellowships. Therefore, please answer these questions by reference to your own group. You may wish to skip those few questions, dealing with ministers, that have been marked by an asterisk.

PERSONAL BELIEFS AND ATTITUDES

TABLE 1

P-1.   Which one of the following statements comes *closest* to expressing your beliefs about God? (Circle one.)

"God" is a supernatural being who reveals himself in human experience and history 2.9

"God" is the ground of all being, real but not adequately describable 23.1

"God" may appropriately be used as a name for some natural processes within the universe, such as love or creative evolution 44.2

"God" is an irrelevant concept, and the central focus of religion should be on man's knowledge and values 28.0

"God" is a concept that is harmful to a worthwhile religion 1.8

n-r = 2.7

TABLE 2

P-2. Which of the following describe the purpose or function that prayer fulfills for *you?* (Circle all that apply.)

Communion with God 12.4

Petition (for self) 7.5

Intercession (for others) 9.0

Meditation 39.0

Autosuggestion 8.6

Communion with inner self 31.3

Other (describe in margin) 2.6

I do not find the term useful 33.6

n-r = 1.2

TABLE 3

P-3. How frequently do you pray? (Circle one.)

Often 11.6

Occasionally 24.6

Seldom 27.8

Never 36.0

n-r = 2.0

TABLE 4

P-4. Which one of these statements comes *closest* to your feeling about the relation of modern science to human values? (Circle one.)

Science can help us choose one value over another 41.6
Science is ethically neutral, and we must choose values on some other basis 55.7
Other (describe in margin) 2.7
n-r = 3.5

TABLE 5

P-5. How do you think modern science affects religious beliefs? (Circle one.)

Science strengthens liberal religion 79.4
Science has little effect on liberal religion 19.1
Science weakens liberal religion 1.5
n-r = 2.8

TABLE 6

P-6. How important to you are the following aspects of attending church service? (Circle one on each line.)

	Very Important	Somewhat Important	Not Important
Intellectual stimulation	74.4	23.1	2.5
Fellowship	45.2	47.0	7.8
Celebrating common values ..	30.0	49.4	20.6
Group experience of participation and worship	24.3	43.3	32.5
Personal reflection	49.3	37.9	12.8
Music – aesthetic satisfaction	31.3	47.9	20.8
Motivation to serve others	32.7	47.2	20.1

n-r = 3.9

TABLE 7

P-7. How has your membership in a Unitarian Universalist Church affected your basic system of values? (Circle one.)

Provided me with an essentially new value system 11.8
Supported my previous value system 76.7
My basic values are not closely related to my religion .. 6.9
Other (describe in margin) 4.6
n-r = 3.5

TABLE 12

P-12. Man's potential for "love" can overcome his potential for "evil."

Agree 89.5
Disagree 10.5

n-r = 11.3

TABLE 13

P-13. In the last hundred years, historical scholars have made a number of varied estimates of Jesus. Indicate your reactions to the ones below by circling the appropriate number on each line.

	Strongly Agree	Agree	Disagree	Strongly Disagree	Don't Know
Jesus was essentially in the tradition of the Jewish prophets	14.0	49.2	12.9	1.8	22.1
Jesus, breaking with Judaism created a new religion	6.7	37.0	33.3	8.5	14.5
Jesus' belief in the end the world so affected his teachings that their value for modern man is limited	4.8	18.4	42.6	14.0	20.1
Jesus' teachings are as true and useful now as then...................	16.2	51.6	20.2	3.8	8.2
Jesus thought of himself as a Messiah or Christ	7.3	31.2	26.7	9.0	25.7
After Jesus' death the church created the idea of his divinity	30.5	50.9	7.4	1.2	10.0
Trustworthy historical records are so scanty that we can really know little about Jesus	21.1	52.5	17.6	1.7	7.2
Jesus may never have lived	3.5	15.7	46.9	22.6	11.2

n-r = 3.7

TABLE 8

P-8. Would you personally define your own religion as "Christian?"

Yes 43.1

No 56.9

n-r = 3.4

TABLE 9

P-9. Is immortality, in the sense of a continued personal existence of the individual after death, part of your belief system?

Yes 10.5

No 89.5

n-r = 3.4

Listed below and on the next page are some belief statements that have been current among religious liberals. Please indicate in each case whether, *on balance*, you agree more than disagree, or disagree more than agree.

TABLE 10

P-10. There is a power that works in history through man that transforms evil into good.

Agree 41.1

Disagree 58.8

n-r = 4.6

TABLE 11

P-11. There has been progress in the history of human civilization.

Agree (ANSWER A) 95.2

Disagree (GO TO P-12.) 4.8

A. IF AGREE: Circle the code numbers next to the *three strongest* supports for your belief in an over-all progress.

Growth of science and knowledge 88.5

Increase in moral sensitivity 44.0

Emergence of a world community 50.8

Elimination of poverty and disease 37.2

Increasing rationality of man 39.1

Increase of leisure time 14.2

Other (describe in margin) 2.9

n-r = 2.5

TABLE 14

P-14. P ase indicate how close, religiously, you feel to each of the following groups. (Circle one on each line.)

	Very Close	Some-what Close	Some-what Distant	Very Distant	Don't Know
Methodists	1.9	18.6	35.1	36.4	7.9
Congregationalists	6.0	37.5	25.1	17.4	13.9
Episcopalians	1.4	12.4	31.0	49.1	6.1
Roman Catholics	.7	4.3	13.8	79.0	2.2
Fundamentalists	.8	2.4	5.1	76.9	14.7
Quakers	17.0	45.1	15.3	12.6	10.0
Lutherans	.8	5.7	27.1	56.7	9.7
Christian Scientists	1.1	9.7	20.9	60.7	7.5
Ethical Culturists	16.9	23.8	6.9	12.2	40.1
Orthodox Jews	.7	6.2	24.2	57.8	11.2
Reform Jews	14.3	44.3	19.4	11.9	10.2
Muslims	.4	3.9	13.0	49.8	32.8
Buddhists	2.9	19.4	18.6	29.6	29.5

n-r = 4.5

SOCIAL BELIEFS AND ATTITUDES

TABLE 15

S-1. For the social problems listed below, please indicate how important it is to you that liberal religion (in the local church or denomination) be involved in education and action. (Circle one on each line.)

	Very Important	Somewhat Important	Not Important
Alcoholism	34.2	48.4	17.4
Drug addiction	39.4	45.2	15.4
Gambling	15.4	35.8	48.8
Juvenile delinquency	68.5	27.8	3.7
Mental illness	57.0	34.1	8.9
Organized crime	32.2	42.6	25.2
Poverty	60.9	32.8	6.3
Racial integration	69.7	24.7	5.6
Sexual morality	39.4	41.3	19.3

n-r = 3.2

TABLE 16

S-2. Which one of the following statements best describes the policy you would prefer the United ˆtates to follow in Viet Nam? (Circle one.)

U. S. military pressure on the Communists should increase, including if necessary the bombing of Hanoi and even the bombing of the atomic factories of China 9.2

U. S. military and other means should be continued to stop communist aggression in South Viet Nam, but we should be careful not to extend the war 31.8

The U. S. should take further initiatives to end the war, such as another pause in the bombing of North Viet Nam or the encouragement of a transition or coalition regime in South Viet Nam, including the N.L.F. 33.6

The U. S. should pull its armed forces in Viet Nam back to coastal enclaves 3.6

The U. S. should withdraw militarily from South Viet Nam 21.7

n-r = 5.0

TABLE 17

S-3. If a person of draft age is opposed to certain wars (such as Viet Nam) rather than to all wars, do you think he should or should not be eligible for classification as a conscientious objector? (Circle one.)

Should be eligible 40.3
Should not be eligible 46.0
Don't know 13.6

n-r = 2.2

TABLE 18

S-4. Which of these statements comes closest to your feelings about non-violent civil disobedience? (Circle one.)

I approve of civil disobedience when laws are unjust 62.3
I disapprove of civil disobedience under any
circumstances 28.3
Other (describe in margin) 9.4

n-r = 4.6

TABLE 19

S-5. If you were a member of the pulpit committee seeking a minister for your church, which of these statements would best describe how you would feel about a Negro candidate? (Circle one.)

His race might hamper his effectiveness 26.6

His race would make little difference in his effectiveness 62.5

His race might improve his effectiveness 10.9

n-r = 2.2

TABLE 20

S-6. If you were a member of the pulpit committee seeking a minister for your church, which of these statements would best describe how you would feel about a woman candidate? (Circle one.)

Her sex might hamper her effectiveness 47.2

Her sex would make little difference in her effectiveness 47.6

Her sex might improve her effectiveness 5.2

n-r =2.2

TABLE 21

S-7. If you faced a serious personal emotional problem, what would be the likelihood of your turning to the following sources of help? (Circle one on each line.)

	Very Likely	Likely	Unlikely	Very Unlikely
Friends	23.9	33.6	29.9	12.6
Minister	19.6	39.4	29.5	11.4
Psychotherapist or psychiatrist	36.0	31.3	20.5	12.3
Other physician	14.6	35.1	33.4	16.9
Marriage or family counselor	11.2	28.5	36.2	24.2
Lawyer	3.8	13.8	41.3	41.1
Family	30.9	28.5	22.6	18.0

n-r = 3.6

TABLE 22

S-8.   If your marriage ran into serious difficulties, what would be the likelihood of your turning to the following sources of help? (Circle one on each line.)

	Very Likely	Likely	Unlikely	Very Unlikely
Friends	14.0	24.2	38.2	23.5
Minister	24.0	37.2	26.4	12.4
Psychotherapist or psychiatrist	26.4	29.7	27.6	16.2
Other physician	7.8	23.8	42.4	26.0
Marriage or family counselor	35.8	33.6	17.5	13.1
Lawyer	8.1	22.7	38.3	30.8
Family	19.3	24.9	29.4	26.4

n-r- = 7.4

One of the most important yet difficult areas of moral beliefs concerns sexual behavior. The next six questions explore some of the most controversial topics. Please circle the one alternative that comes *closest* to your feelings.

TABLE 23

S-9.   What do you think should be grounds for divorce? (Circle one.)

If one partner to a marriage wishes a divorce, he or she should be able to obtain it without any legal obstacles .. 17.4

If the partners are incompatible and both wish to end the marriage, they should be able to do so 67.1

If the other partner has practiced mental or physical cruelty, a divorce should be granted 9.6

Only if the other partner has deserted, is mentally ill, or has engaged in adultery or criminality should a divorce be granted 5.4

There are no valid grounds for divorce 6

n-r = 3.8

TABLE 24

S-10.   Please indicate whether or not you think it should be possible for a pregnant woman to obtain a *legal* abortion under each of the following circumstances. (Circle one on each line.)

	Yes	No
A. If there is a strong chance of serious defect in the baby?	97.0	3.0

TABLE 24 — continued

B. If she is married and does not want any
more children? 61.8   38.2

C. If the woman's own health is seriously
endangered by the pregnancy? 99.0   1.0

D. If the family has a very low income and
cannot afford any more children? 75.6   24.4

E. If she became pregnant as a result of rape 97.3   2.7

F. If she is not married and does not want to
marry the man? 71.9   28.1

n-r = 3.1

TABLE 25

S-11. Sexual intercourse between unmarried persons: (Circle one.)

Is never justifiable 20.0

Is justifiable for engaged couples 5.8

Is justifiable if there is mutual affection 18.0

Should be left to free choice 55.6

Should be encouraged 6

n-r = 3.5

TABLE 26

S-12. Extra-marital sexual intercourse: (Circle one.)

Is never justifiable 43.4

Is justifiable if marriage partner agrees 18.3

Should be left to free choice 38.0

Should be encouraged 3

n-r = 4.3

TABLE 27

S-13. Homosexuality: (Circle one.)

Should be discouraged by law 7.7

Should be discouraged by education, not by law 80.2

Should not be discouraged by law or education 12.0

Should be encouraged 1

n-r = 3.6

TABLE 28

S-14. Do you approve or disapprove of making contraceptive information and devices or pills available to each of the following *if they want them?* (Circle one on each line.)

	Strongly Approve	Approve	Disapprove	Strongly Disapprove
Married persons	91.5	8.2	.2	.0
Engaged couples	56.4	29.4	10.6	3.6
Any adult	50.8	32.9	11.3	4.9
Any young person	26.9	27.9	28.8	16.4

n-r = 3.1

LOCAL CHURCH, SOCIETY, FELLOWSHIP

TABLE 29

L-1. How active has your participation generally been in your local church?

Very active 21.6
Moderately active 39.5
Slightly active 29.2
Inactive 9.6

n-r = 2.1

TABLE 30

L-2. Listed below are some major emphases of local churches. Please indicate whether each is very important, somewhat important, or not important in terms of what you feel your local church's emphases *should be*. (Circle one on each line.)

	Very Important	Somewhat Important	Not Important	Can't Decide
Public worship	36.2	38.4	23.5	1.8
Social action	48.4	43.7	6.5	1.4
Fellowship among members	51.4	45.0	3.2	.4
Religious education	70.4	25.6	3.4	.7
Personal development	53.0	38.6	6.5	1.9
Ministerial leadership	56.5	35.6	6.1	1.8
Lay leadership	33.7	54.8	8.9	2.5
Adult programs	41.9	50.8	5.8	1.5

n-r = 2.7

TABLE 31

L-3. Now please indicate whether each of these is very important, somewhat important, or not important in terms of what you feel your local church's emphases *now are*. (Circle one on each line.)

	Very Important	Somewhat Important	Not Important	Can't Decide
Public worship	40.7	42.0	14.7	2.7
Social action	38.1	46.7	13.2	2.0
Fellowship among members	42.1	49.7	6.5	1.6
Religious education	63.7	30.5	4.0	1.8
Personal development	21.1	49.4	23.0	6.5
*Ministerial leadership	52.9	35.2	8.3	3.6
Lay leadership	32.3	53.0	10.5	4.2
Adult programs	32.2	52.9	12.1	2.8

n-r = 4.8

TABLE 32

L-4. Do you define your local church as "Christian?"

Yes	40.5
No	59.4

n-r = 3.6

TABLE 33

L-5. Would you say that others in your community generally regard your local church as "Christian?"

Yes	43.7
No	56.3

n-r = 6.3

TABLE 34

L-6. Would you describe your local church as strong, average, or weak?

Very strong	13.8
Strong	41.8
Average	33.6
Weak	9.7
Very weak	1.1

n-r = 2.7

TABLE 35

L-7. *In your experience with your present minister, how would you evaluate his skills and preparation in the following areas? (Circle one on each line.)

	Very Strong	Strong	Average	Weak	Very Weak
Preaching	40.7	33.9	19.8	4.6	.9
Counseling	21.8	33.7	32.6	9.1	2.9
Social Action	39.4	35.0	19.4	4.5	1.6
Religious Education	27.2	38.0	27.1	6.1	1.6
Dealings with people	31.0	31.2	23.6	9.5	4.6

*Omit if you are a member of a fellowship.

n-r = 12.0

TABLE 36

L-8. If you were on a pulpit committee to select a new minister, how important would his skills in each of the following areas be for you?

	Very Important	Somewhat Important	Not Important
Preaching	74.2	23.8	1.9
Counseling	58.2	38.8	3.0
Social Action	44.7	46.7	8.6
Religious education	59.0	36.9	4.1
Dealings with people	84.1	15.4	.4

n-r = 2.2

TABLE 37

L-9. Do you approve or disapprove of our churches using the following methods to deal with controversial social issues? (Circle one on each line.)

	Strongly Approve	Approve	Disapprove	Strongly Disapprove
Discussion meetings	68.5	30.4	.8	.2
Sermons	51.1	41.9	5.6	1.4
Public stands by a committee	21.0	45.8	26.8	6.4
Public stands by congregation	27.8	45.9	20.7	5.5
Public stands by minister	32.8	49.3	13.9	4.0
Participation in demonstrations by minister	22.5	45.2	21.3	10.9
Participation in demonstrations by members	28.1	48.7	16.0	7.2

n-r = 3.1

TABLE 38

L-10. Of your three closest friends, how many are members of your local church?

None	46.3
One	21.2
Two	13.9
Three	9.7
Don't have three close friends	8.9

n-r = 2.4

TABLE 39

L-11. Within our churches we frequently use the labels "liberal" and "conservative." Below, please make a check mark in whichever of the six places between liberal and conservative best describes the position of the person or group in the statement.

[Since a majority, on almost every item, used only the first two boxes, figures given are for percentage checking box 1 — closest to "liberal."]

Your own position on social issues and values:	29.0
*Your present minister's position on social issues and values:	49.8
The position of the governing body or board of your local church on social issues and values:	18.8
The denomination's position on social issues and values:	28.0
Your own position on theological issues and values:	52.0
*Your present minister's position on theological issues and values:	51.8
The position of the governing body or board of your local church on theological issues and values:	28.1
The denomination's position on theological issues and values:	30.2

n-r = 4.7

*Fellowship members were instructed to omit this.

TABLE 40

L-12. How would you describe the social status of *most* of the other members of your local church?

Lower than mine	4.3
About the same as mine	81.1
Higher than mine	14.6

n-r = 2.4

DENOMINATIONAL

TABLE 41

D-1. Which one of the following best describes where you would prefer the Unitarian Universalist Association to be theologically ten years from now? (Circle one.)

Closer to liberal Protestantism 6.4
Closer to the ecumenical movement within Christianity 4.8
Closer to an emerging, universal religion 36.7
Closer to a distinctive, humanistic religion 52.0

n-r = 3.4

TABLE 42

D-2. The Unitarian Universalist merger of 1961 led to the creation of 23 districts, each staffed by a district executive. In the case of your church, how has this affected your relationship to the continental denominational movement?

Related us more closely to the denomination 10.5
About the same 18.4
Weakened our relationship with the denomination 1.2
Don't know 69.9

n-r = 2.6

TABLE 43

D-3. How has the creation of districts affected the relationship of your local church to other liberal churches in your area?

Strengthened our ties 13.2
About the same 20.0
Weakened our ties 6
Other (describe in margin) 5
Don't know 65.6

n-r = 2.6

TABLE 44

D-4. How do you feel about the Unitarian Universalist fellowships?

They are most useful as they develop into churches 54.9
They will help us develop a religious organization that
   no longer needs to depend upon professional ministers 12.5
Don't know 32.6

n-r = 3.9

TABLE 45

D-5. By resolutions and reports, the Unitarian Universalist Association stimulates discussion and moves toward some consensus. How do you feel about such efforts toward consensus and common public statement in the following areas? (Circle one on each line.)

	Strongly Approve	Approve	Disapprove	Strongly Disapprove
Consensus on social issues	29.7	55.5	11.6	3.2
Consensus on denominational goals	27.4	64.8	6.5	1.3
Consensus on theological issues	17.0	52.9	23.9	6.2

n-r = 6.1

TABLE 46

D-6. Would you approve or disapprove *if* each of the following changes in emphasis were made in our *church school* curriculum? (Circle one on each line.)

	Strongly Approve	Approve	Disapprove	Strongly Disapprove
More stress on Unitarian Universalist past and present	22.3	62.9	13.9	.9
More stress on Judeo-Christian traditions	9.9	51.3	35.1	3.7
More stress on the Bible	8.9	33.3	47.4	10.4
More stress on non-Western religions	10.2	65.8	22.4	1.6
More stress on personal psychological development	33.5	53.1	12.5	.9
More stress on religious implications of science and modern knowledge	34.6	56.6	8.0	.8
More stress on social problems of modern world	41.2	50.5	7.6	.7
More stress on creative and artistic activities	26.2	54.3	17.9	1.6

n-r = 6.5

TABLE 47

D-7. Would you approve or disapprove *if* each of the following changes in emphasis were made in our *adult program* materials? (Circle one on each line.)

	Strongly Approve	Approve	Disapprove	Strongly Disapprove
More stress on Unitarian Universalist past and present	21.6	60.4	16.9	1.1
More stress on Judeo-Christian traditions	7.7	43.8	42.9	5.6
More stress on the Bible	6.9	29.2	50.8	13.2
More stress on non-Western religions	13.1	63.1	22.1	1.7
More stress on personal psychological development	36.7	51.8	10.6	.8
More stress on religious implications of science and modern knowledge	39.2	53.8	6.2	.8
More stress on social problems of modern world	46.6	46.8	6.0	.6
More stress on creative and artistic activities	25.9	54.1	18.0	2.0

n-r = 6.9

TABLE 48

D-8. Our denomination now operates in a number of areas of social controversy. Do you approve or disapprove of including each of the following in planning denominational activities for the next five years? (Circle one on each line.)

	Strongly Approve	Approve	Disapprove	Strongly Disapprove
Peace activities	42.5	43.6	10.8	3.1
Civil rights (race relations)	46.6	44.0	6.8	2.5
Civil liberties	46.4	46.4	5.4	1.8
Church-state relations	27.5	54.1	15.8	2.6
Service committee work abroad	32.3	57.6	9.1	1.0
Service committee work at home	38.1	58.4	3.0	.5
Legislative activity (U.N. and Washington offices)	30.2	52.1	14.5	3.2

n-r = 4.6

PERSONAL DATA

TABLE 49

PD-1. How long have you been a Unitarian or Universalist?

0-2 years 16.0
3-10 years 40.1
11 or more years 33.2
I was born a Unitarian Universalist 10.6

n-r = 2.0

TABLE 50

PD-2. What was your own religious preference before joining a Unitarian Universalist Church?

Does not apply; have always been
Unitarian Universalist 11.7
Liberal Protestant 37.1
Fundamental Protestant 6.2
Liturgical Protestant (Lutheran, Episcopal)............... 7.9
Catholic (Roman or Eastern Orthodox) 3.3
Reform Jewish 1.9
Conservative or Orthodox Jewish 5
Other (describe in margin) 3.9
No organized religion 27.6

n-r = 3.1

TABLE 51

PD-3. What was your family religion during your childhood?

Unitarian, Universalist 12.1
Liberal Protestant 27.9
Fundamental Protestant 20.7
Liturgical Protestant (Lutheran or Episcopal)........... 11.7
Catholic (Roman or Eastern Orthodox) 6.2
Reform Jewish 2.4
Conservative or Orthodox Jewish 1.9
Mixed (Catholic/Non Catholic) 1.8
Mixed (Jewish/Non-Jewish) 7
Other (describe in margin) 5.3
No organized religion 9.4

n-r = 3.4

TABLE 52

PD-4.   During which of the following stages of life did the values of
liberal religion *first* become personally meaningful for you?

Grade school 7.7
High school 19.0
College and/or before marriage 28.5
Early married 15.1
Early parenthood 16.8
Later maturity 13.0

n-r = 3.4

TABLE 53

PD-5.   During which of the following stages of life did the values of
your *previous* religion *cease* to be meaningful for you?

Does not apply; no previous religion 8.6
Does not apply; born Unitarian Universalist 11.2
Grade school 9.3
High school 25.6
College and/or before marriage 26.0
Early married 9.4
Early parenthood 4.2
Later maturity 5.6

n-r = 7.6

TABLE 54

PD-6.   What is your sex?

Male 43.7
Female 56.3

n-r = 1.9

TABLE 55

PD-7.   What is your age?

Under 25 .... 3.3
25-34 .... 18.9
35-44 .... 33.0
45-54 .... 21.2
55-64 .... 12.0
65 and over 11.6

n-r = 1.7

TABLE 56

PD-8. What is your marital status?

Single, never married	8.9
Married, never divorced	72.1
Divorced and remarried	8.2
Divorced or separated	5.2
Widowed	5.5

n-r = 1.9

TABLE 57

PD-9. How many children do you have? (IF NONE, ENTER ZERO.)

Number

0	18.6
1	13.1
2	30.4
3	23.4
4	10.5
5	3.0
6	.6
7	.2
8	.2
9	

n-r = 3.1

TABLE 58

A. *IF ANY CHILDREN:* How many of your children are now in church school or LRY

Number

0	37.2
1	16.1
2	24.7
3	14.5
4	5.9
5	1.2
6	.2
7	.2
8	
9	

n-r = 25.1

TABLE 59

PD-10. Where do you now live?

Large city (100,000 population or more) 41.6
Suburb near a large city 37.3
Small or middle-sized city or town, under 100,000 popula-
tion and not a suburb of large city 17.3
Open country (not a farm) 3.1
Farm 8

n-r = 2.0

TABLE 60

PD-11. How long have you lived in the community served by your
present local church?

0-5 years 27.5
6-10 years 20.2
Over 10 years 52.3

n-r = 2.4

TABLE 61

PD-12. What was your total family income before taxes last year?

Under $3,000 .... 3.2
$3,000-$4,999 .... 5.5
$5,000-$7,499 .... 12.5
$7,500-$9,999 .... 16.2
$10,000-$14,999 .... 32.8
$15,000-$24,999 .... 22.1
$25,000 or more 7.6

n-r = 5.3

TABLE 62

PD-13. What is the occupation of the main earner in the family?

Manual labor or personal service 1.5
Skilled labor or trade 6.2
Sales or clerical 8.7
Managerial or business owner 17.0
Professional: teaching 13.0
Professional: science or engineering 25.8
Professional: other (describe in margin) 26.5
Student 1.2

n-r = 9.4

TABLE 63

PD-14. Which of these describes the main earner's employer?

A private enterprise 44.3
A non-profit organization 14.1
Some level of government 25.4
Self-employed 12.6
Not employed 3.5

n-r = 6.4

TABLE 64

PD-15. *ANSWER IF YOU ARE NOT THE MAIN EARNER IN YOUR FAMILY:* What is *your* occupation?

Housewife, not employed outside the home 66.6
Manual labor or personal service 1.0
Skilled labor or trade 1.4
Sales or clerical 6.0
Managerial or business owner 1.8
Professional: teaching 9.9
Professional: science or engineering 1.4
Professional: other (describe in margin) 7.2
Student 4.6

n-r = 41.0

TABLE 65

PD-16. What was the last year of school *you* completed?

8th grade or less 1.2
Some high school 4.2
High school grade 11.1
Some college 23.4
College graduate 34.7
Hold graduate degree 25.4

n-r = 2.4

TABLE 66

PD-17. What was the last year of school *your father* completed?

8th grade or less 27.1
Some high school 14.8
High school graduate 18.3
Some college 14.2
College graduate 14.6
Hold graduate degree 11.0

n-r = 5.5

TABLE 67

PD-18. To which of the following organizations, if any, do you belong? (Circle all that apply.)

NAACP or Urban League	9.7
CORE or SNCC	4.3
ACLU	12.5
Memorial Society	16.0
Planned Parenthood Association	10.7
League of Women Voters	11.3
U.N. Association	8.6
SANE or UWF	5.4
Other (describe in margin)	15.7
None	45.3

n-r = 9.0

TABLE 68

PD-19. Which policital party do you generally support?

IF YOU LIVE IN U.S.A.:	Democrat	56.3
	Republican	33.8
	Other describe in margin)	3.7
	None	6.2
IF YOU LIVE IN CANADA:	Conservative	4.5
	Liberal	35.3
	New Democratic (NDP)	53.0
	Social Credit	.4
	Other (describe in margin)	1.6
	None	5.2

n-r = 2.9

TABLE 69

PD-20. *IF YOU LIVE IN U.S.A.:* For whom did you vote in the last
presidential election?

Goldwater	18.0
Johnson	73.2
Someone else	1.3
Did not note	7.5

TABLE 69 (Continued)

IF YOU LIVE IN CANADA: For which party did you vote in the 1965 national election?

Conservative	5.6
Liberal	37.1
New Democratic (NDP)	51.0
Social Credit	.3
Other (describe in margin)	.3
Did not vote	5.7

n-r = 2.9

TABLE 70

PD-21. What political party did your parents generally support?

IF U.S.A.:	Democrat	37.0
	Republican	48.6
	Other (describe in margin)	1.7
	Politically divided	9.0
	None	3.7
IF CANADA:	Conservative	27.6
	Liberal	36.3
	New Democratic (NDP)	12.6
	Social Credit	.4
	Other (describe in margin)	5.1
	Politically divided	9.9
	None	8.1

n-r = 6.4

Appendix C

ITEMS USED IN FACTOR ANALYSIS

Number	Item[a]
1	Which one of the following statements comes closest to expressing your beliefs about God? (supernaturalist/atheist—5)
2	How frequently do you pray? (often/never—4)
	How important to you are the following aspects of attending church service:
3	Intellectual stimulation (very important/unimportant—3)
4	Fellowship (very important/unimportant—3)
5	Celebrating common values (very important/unimportant—3)
6	Group experience of participation and worship (very important/unimportant—3)
7	Personal reflection (very important/unimportant—3)
8	Music—aesthetic satisfaction (very important/unimportant—3)
9	Motivation to serve others (very important/unimportant—3)
10	Would you personally define your own religion as "Christian?" (yes) no—2)
11	Is immortality, in the sense of a continued personal existence of the individual after death, part of your belief system? (yes/no—2)

Number	Item[a]
12	There is a power that works in history through man that transforms evil into good. (agree/disagree—2)
13	Man's potential for "love" can overcome his potential for "evil." (agree/disagree—2)
	For the social problems listed below, please indicate how important it is to you that liberal religion (in the local church or denomination) be involved in education and action.
14	Drug addiction (very important/unimportant—3)
15	Gambling (very important/unimportant—3)
16	Poverty (very important/unimportant—3)
17	Racial integration (very important/unimportant—3)
18	Which one of the following statements best describes the policy you would prefer the United States to follow in Viet Nam? (escalate/withdraw—5)
19	If a person of draft age is opposed to certain wars (such as Viet Nam) rather than to all wars, do you think he should or should not be eligible for classification as conscientious objector? (eligible/ineligible—2)
20	Which of these statements comes closest to your feelings about nonviolent civil disobedience? (approve/disapprove—2)
21	What do you think should be grounds for divorce? (one party wish/no grounds—5)
	Please indicate whether or not you think it should be possible for a pregnant woman to obtain a legal abortion under each of the following circumstances.
22	If she is married and does not want any more children? (agree/disagree—2)
23	Sexual intercourse between unmarried persons (never justifiable/should be encouraged—5)
24	Extramarital sexual intercourse (never justifiable/should be encouraged—4)
	Do you approve or disapprove of making contraceptive information and devices or pills available to each of the following if they want them?
25	Any young person (strongly approve/strongly disapprove—4)
26	How active has your participation generally been in your local church? (very active/inactive—4)

Number	Item[a]
	Listed below are some major emphases of local churches. Please indicate whether each is very important, somewhat important, or not important in terms of what you feel your local church's emphases *should be*.
27	Public worship (very important/unimportant—3)
28	Social action (very important/unimportant—3)
29	Fellowship among members (very important/unimportant—3)
30	Religious education (very important/unimportant—3)
31	Personal development (very important/unimportant—3)
	Do you approve or disapprove of our churches using the following methods to deal with controversial social issues?
32	Participation in demonstrations by minister (strongly approve/ strongly disapprove—4)
	Within our churches we frequently use the labels "liberal" and "conservative." Please make a check mark in whichever of the six places between liberal and conservative best describes the position of the person or group in the statement.
33	Your own position on social issues. (liberal/conservative—6)
34	Your own position on theological issues and values (liberal/conservative—6)
35	Which one of the following best describes where you would prefer the UUA to be theologically ten years from now? (closer to liberal Protestantism/closer to humanistic religion—4)
	Would you approve or disapprove if each of the following changes in emphasis were made in our *adult program* materials?
36	More stress on the Bible (strongly approve/strongly disapprove—4)
	More stress on personal psychological development (strongly approve/strongly disapprove—4)
37	Our denomination now operates in a number of areas of social controversy. Do you approve or disapprove of including each of the following in planning denominational activities for the next five years?
38	Peace activities (strongly approve/strongly disapprove—4)
	In the last hundred years, historical scholars have made a number of varied estimates of Jesus. Indicate your reactions to the ones below.

Number	Item[a]
39	Jesus was essentially in the tradition of the Jewish prophets (strongly agree/strongly disagree—4)
40	Jesus, breaking with Judaism, created a new religion (strongly agree/strongly disagree—4)
41	Jesus' belief in the end of the world so affected his teachings that their value for modern man is limited. (strongly agree/strongly disagree—4)
42	Jesus' teachings are as true and useful now as then (strongly agree/strongly disagree—4)
43	Jesus thought of himself as a Messiah or Christ. (strongly agree/strongly disagree—5)
44	After Jesus' death the church created the idea of his divinity (strongly agree/strongly disagree—5)
45	Of your three closest friends, how many are members of your local church? (0/3—4)

[a]The paraphrased extremes and the number of ordered responses for each item are indicated in parentheses.

Appendix D

TABLES TO ACCOMPANY CHAPTER 8

TABLE D.1

Dimensional Associations, Measured by Gamma, for Most Left Churches
Selected by Three Milieu Criteria

Church number	Association of Dimension 1 with Dimension:						
	2	3	4	5	6	7	8
	Milieu criterion: self-ascription						
29	−0.33	−0.31	0.03	0.03	0.28	0.26	−0.08
10	0.07	−0.01	−0.25	0.11	0.12	0.50	−0.01
103	−0.13	0.32	−0.02	0.11	0.39	0.45	−0.63
106	−0.27	−0.17	−0.02	0.09	0.26	0.31	0.17
43	0.07	−0.08	0.14	0.11	0.37	0.26	−0.12
31	−0.45	0.09	−0.30	0.05	0.28	0.06	−0.20
86	−0.40	−0.71	0.11	0.33	1.00	0.64	−0.60
89	0.39	0.27	−0.30	0.24	−0.24	0.60	−0.27
	Milieu criterion: racial integration						
29	−0.33	−0.31	0.03	0.03	0.29	0.26	−0.08
74	0.03	−0.79	0.22	−0.05	−0.48	0.29	0.48
103	−0.13	0.32	−0.02	0.11	0.39	0.45	−0.63
56	−0.19	0.02	−0.02	0.17	0.25	−0.06	−0.21

TABLE D.1 (continued)
Dimensional Associations, Measured by Gamma, for Most Left Churches
Selected by Three Milieu Criteria

Church number	Association of Dimension 1 with Dimension:						
	2	3	4	5	6	7	8
	Milieu criterion: racial integration						
93	−0.33	−0.	1.00	1.00	−0.50	−1.00	−1.00
97	0.06	0.12	−0.00	0.44	−0.18	0.22	−0.41
59	−0.50	−0.19	−0.35	−0.26	−0.17	0.09	−0.32
2	−0.13	0.01	0.00	0.16	0.21	0.28	−0.20
	Milieu criterion: psychological development						
70	0.68	−0.40	0.33	0.03	−0.02	0.60	−0.83
86	−0.40	−0.71	0.11	0.33	1.00	0.64	−0.60
92	−0.30	−0.37	−0.43	−0.26	−0.00	−0.18	0.68
106	−0.27	−0.17	−0.02	0.09	0.26	0.31	0.17
103	−0.13	0.32	−0.02	0.11	0.39	0.45	−0.63
32	−0.53	0.17	−0.25	0.04	0.35	−0.16	−0.12
78	−0.31	0.55	−0.01	0.21	0.13	−0.24	−0.35
87	−0.38	0.29	0.14	0.07	0.18	−0.15	0.03
41	−0.19	−0.21	−0.18	0.12	0.18	0.23	−0.27
13	−0.08	−0.28	0.24	−0.11	0.22	0.44	0.24

TABLE D.2
Dimensional Associations, Measured by Gamma, for Least Deviant Churches
Selected by Three Milieu Criteria

Church number	Association of Dimension 1 with Dimension:						
	2	3	4	5	6	7	8
	Milieu criterion: self-ascription						
38	−0.28	−0.19	−0.24	0.30	−0.10	0.08	−0.26
26	−0.02	0.54	0.09	0.57	0.28	−0.34	−0.22
9	0.09	0.22	0.16	−0.04	0.17	−0.01	−0.10
56	−0.19	0.02	−0.02	0.17	0.25	−0.06	−0.21

TABLE D.2 (continued)
*Dimensional Associations, Measured by Gamma, for Least Deviant Churches
Selected by Three Milieu Criteria*

Church number	Association of Dimension 1 with Dimension:						
	2	3	4	5	6	7	8
	Milieu criterion: self-ascription						
54	−0.17	0.01	−0.21	0.24	0.13	0.16	−0.09
42	−0.22	−0.07	0.16	0.10	0.33	0.15	−0.19
21	−0.33	−0.19	−0.08	0.17	−0.01	0.01	−0.23
98	−0.56	0.30	0.06	0.41	0.28	−0.14	0.09
5	−0.19	−0.07	−0.19	0.02	−0.06	0.12	−0.15
52	−0.25	0.03	0.04	0.13	0.25	0.06	−0.28
	Milieu criterion: racial integration						
11	−0.26	−0.09	−0.24	0.14	0.00	0.24	−0.33
19	−0.16	−0.18	−0.05	0.09	0.15	−0.17	−0.11
5	−0.19	−0.07	−0.19	0.02	−0.06	0.12	−0.15
107	0.29	0.11	0.24	−0.29	−0.01	0.36	0.12
30	−0.11	−0.09	−0.05	0.09	0.16	−0.01	−0.12
3	−0.13	0.07	−0.16	0.01	−0.01	0.09	−0.17
79	−0.39	−0.23	0.44	0.09	0.19	0.45	−0.54
27	−0.21	−0.11	−0.01	−0.17	0.14	0.06	−0.11
7	−0.25	0.14	−0.12	0.05	0.19	−0.08	−0.01
22	−0.08	0.04	0.41	0.00	0.44	−0.20	−0.43
	Milieu criterion: psychological development						
97	0.06	0.12	−0.00	0.44	−0.18	0.22	−0.41
42	−0.22	−0.07	0.16	0.10	0.33	0.15	−0.19
55	0.09	0.15	−0.01	0.07	0.06	−0.03	−0.27
57	−0.28	−0.03	−0.02	−0.13	0.22	0.22	−0.09
5	−0.19	−0.07	−0.19	0.02	−0.06	0.12	−0.15
21	−0.33	−0.19	−0.08	0.17	−0.01	0.01	−0.23
8	−0.13	0.12	0.11	−0.02	0.34	0.11	−0.03
11	−0.26	−0.09	−0.24	0.14	0.00	0.24	−0.33
6	−0.06	0.00	0.15	0.14	−0.01	0.03	−0.27
14	−0.22	−0.01	0.11	0.25	0.18	0.07	−0.34

TABLE D.3

Dimensional Associations, Measured by Gamma, for Most Heterogeneous Churches
Selected by Three Milieu Criteria

| Church number | Association of Dimension 1 with Dimension: | | | | | | |
	2	3	4	5	6	7	8
	Milieu criterion: self-ascription						
44	−0.52	0.06	−0.13	0.35	0.14	−0.28	−0.37
48	−0.50	−0.02	−0.12	0.42	−0.10	−0.30	−0.00
41	−0.19	−0.21	−0.18	0.12	0.18	0.23	−0.27
7	−0.25	0.14	−0.12	0.05	0.19	−0.08	−0.01
53	−0.27	0.19	−0.08	0.12	0.13	−0.00	−0.17
2	−0.13	0.01	0.00	0.16	0.21	0.28	−0.20
24	−0.19	0.20	−0.10	0.14	0.31	−0.03	−0.25
92	−0.30	−0.37	−0.43	−0.26	−0.00	−0.18	0.68
14	−0.22	−0.01	0.11	0.25	0.18	0.07	−0.34
	Milieu criterion: racial integration						
44	−0.52	0.06	−0.13	0.35	0.14	−0.28	−0.37
95	0.40	−0.37	−0.16	−0.61	0.35	0.83	−0.40
35	−0.26	0.25	0.09	0.51	0.50	−0.11	−0.02
28	−0.11	−0.03	0.08	0.19	0.31	−0.10	0.04
32	−0.53	0.17	−0.25	0.04	0.35	−0.16	−0.12
13	−0.08	−0.28	0.24	−0.11	0.22	0.44	0.24
10	0.07	−0.01	−0.25	0.11	0.12	0.50	−0.01
38	−0.28	−0.19	−0.24	0.30	−0.10	0.08	−0.26
72	0.13	−0.22	−0.03	−0.07	0.13	0.20	0.06
85	−0.36	0.20	0.42	−0.22	−0.33	−0.17	−0.25
	Milieu criterion: psychological development						
71	0.02	−0.14	0.23	0.35	0.19	0.19	0.27
65	−0.18	−0.10	−0.05	0.47	−0.11	−0.17	−0.33
58	−0.20	−0.05	−0.12	0.04	0.14	0.00	0.31
74	0.03	−0.79	0.22	−0.05	−0.48	0.29	0.48
56	−0.19	0.02	−0.02	0.17	0.25 ·	−0.06	−0.21
31	−0.45	0.09	−0.30	0.05	0.28	0.06	−0.20
52	−0.25	0.03	0.04	0.13	0.25	0.06	−0.28
17	−0.34	0.14	0.10	0.08	−0.07	−0.10	0.01
9	0.09	0.22	0.16	−0.04	0.17	−0.01	−0.10
68	−0.59	0.27	0.59	−0.42	−0.12	−0.08	−0.08

TABLE D.4
Dimensional Associations, Measured by Gamma, for Most Right Churches
Selected by Three Milieu Criteria

	Association of Dimension 1 with Dimension:						
	2	3	4	5	6	7	8
Church number	Milieu criterion: self-ascription						
45	0.10	0.	0.40	0.85	0.12	−0.66	−0.58
47	−1.00	0.06	−0.38	0.25	−0.73	0.63	−1.00
49	−0.62	−0.39	−0.33	−0.13	−0.05	0.19	−0.10
35	−0.26	0.25	0.09	0.51	0.50	−0.11	−0.02
99	−0.57	0.36	−0.08	−0.92	0.31	0.53	−0.33
30	−0.11	−0.09	−0.05	0.09	0.16	−0.01	−0.12
46	−0.12	0.13	−0.06	−0.07	0.17	−0.10	−0.14
32	−0.53	0.17	−0.25	0.04	0.35	−0.16	−0.12
84	−0.66	−0.18	−0.25	0.02	0.25	−0.44	0.29
33	−0.56	−0.19	−0.20	0.25	−0.06	0.20	−0.06
	Milieu criterion: racial integration						
47	−1.00	0.06	−0.38	0.25	−0.73	0.63	−1.00
49	−0.62	−0.39	−0.33	−0.13	−0.05	0.19	−0.10
86	−0.40	−0.71	0.11	0.33	1.00	0.64	−0.60
78	−0.31	0.55	−0.01	0.21	0.13	−0.24	−0.35
46	−0.12	0.13	−0.06	−0.07	0.17	−0.10	−0.14
96	−0.33	0.66	0.09	−0.33	0.45	0.03	−0.46
84	−0.66	−0.18	−0.25	0.02	0.25	−0.44	0.29
98	−0.56	0.30	0.06	0.41	0.28	−0.14	0.09
83	−0.59	−0.04	0.09	−0.05	0.33	−0.35	−0.16
99 ·	−0.57	0.36	−0.08	−0.92	0.31	0.53	−0.33
	Milieu criterion: psychological development						
93	−0.33	−0.00	1.00	1.00	−0.50	−1.00	−1.00
45	0.10	−0.00	0.40	0.85	0.12	−0.66	−0.58
99	−0.57	0.36	−0.08	−0.92	0.31	0.53	−0.33
10	0.07	−0.01	−0.25	0.11	0.12	0.50	−0.01
82	−0.60	−0.20	0.07	0.36	−0.14	−0.14	−0.39
105	−0.36	−0.52	−0.08	−0.22	−0.36	−0.13	0.05
95	0.40	−0.37	−0.16	−0.61	0.35	0.83	−0.40
101	0.20	1.00	−0.68	0.32	−0.37	0.21	−0.23
84	−0.66	−0.18	−0.25	0.02	0.25	−0.44	0.29
100	0.03	−0.14	−0.20	0.12	0.02	0.43	−0.53

REFERENCES

Abelson, R. P., Aronson, E., McGuire, W. J., Newcomb, T.M., Rosenberg, M. J., & Tannenbaum, P. H. (Eds.), *Theories of cognitive consistency: a sourcebook.* Chicago: Rand McNally, 1968.

Bartlett, L. *Bright galaxy.* Boston: Beacon Press, 1960.

Bellah, R. N. Religious evolution. *American Sociological Review,* 1964, **29**, 358-374.

Bogue, D. J. *The population of the United States.* Glencoe: The Free Press, 1959.

Campbell, T. C. & Fukuyama, Y. *The fragmented layman.* Philadelphia: Pilgrim Press, 1970.

Cassara, E. *Universalism in America: a documentary history.* Boston: Beacon Press, 1971.

Demerath, N. J. III, *Social class in American Protestantism.* Chicago: Rand McNally, 1965.

Dittes, J. E. Research on variables in religion. In E. Aronson & G. Lindzey (Eds.), *Handbook of social psychology* (Revised Edition). Reading, Mass.: Addison-Wesley, 1969, **V**, 602-659.

Dittes, J. E. Two issues in measuring religion. In M. P. Strommen (Ed.), *Research on religious development.* New York: Hawthorn Books, 1971. Pp. 78-106.

Faulkner, J. E. & De Jong, G. F. Religiosity in 5-D: an empirical analysis. *Social Forces,* 1966, **XLV**, 246-254.

Festinger, L. *A theory of cognitive dissonance.* Evanston: Row, Peterson, 1957.

Flacks, R. The liberated generation: an exploration of the roots of student protest. *Journal of Social Issues,* July 1967, **23**, 52-75.

Flacks R. Young intelligentsia in revolt. *Transaction,* June 1970, 7, 46-55.

Fromm, E. *Psychoanalysis and religion.* New Haven: Yale University Press, 1950.

Fukuyama, Y. *The parishioners: a sociological interpretation.* New York: The Research Department of the United Church Board for Homeland Ministries, 1966.

Gilkey, L. *Naming the whirlwind: the renewal of God-language.* Indianapolis: Bobbs-Merrill, 1970.

Glock, C. Y. Religion and the integration of society. *Review of Religious Research,* 1960, 2, 49-61.

Glock, C. Y. & Stark, R. *Religion and society in tension.* Chicago: Rand McNally, 1965.

257

Glock, C. Y., Ringer, B. B., & Babbie, E. R. *To comfort and to challenge.* Berkeley: University of California Press, 1967.

Hadden, J. K. *The gathering storm in the churches.* New York: Doubleday, 1969.

Howe, D. W. *The Unitarian conscience.* Cambridge: Harvard University Press, 1971.

Humphreys, L. C. Factor analysis. *International Encyclopedia of the Social Sciences,* 1968, New York: Macmillan and Free Press, 1968. V, 281- 287.

Hutchinson, W. R. *The transcendentalist ministers; church reform in the New England renaissance.* New Haven: Yale University Press, 1959.

Keniston, K. *Young radicals.* New York: Harcourt, Brace, and World, 1968.

King, M. B. Measuring the religious variable: nine proposed dimensions. *Journal for the Scientific Study of Religion,* 1967, **6,** 173-190.

King, M. B. & Hunt, R. A. Measuring the religious variable: amended findings. *Journal for the Scientific Study of Religion,* 1969, **8,** 321-323.

Kloetzli, W. *The city church: death or renewal.* Philadelphia: The Muhlenberg Press, 1961.

Kluckhohn, F. R. & Strodtbeck, F. L. *Variations in value orientations.* Evanston: Row, Peterson & Co., 1961. P. 341.

Lazerwitz, B. A comparison of major United States religious groups. *Journal of the American Statistical Association,* 1961, **56,** 569-574.

Lenski, G. *The religious factor* (Revised Edition). New York: Anchor Books, 1963.

Luckman, T. *The invisible religion.* New York: Macmillan, 1967.

Lyttle, C. H. *Freedom moves west: a history of the Western Unitarian Conference, 1852-1952.* Boston: Beacon Press, 1952.

Morris, C. *Varieties of human value.* Chicago: University of Chicago Press, 1956.

Newsweek, I-believe-with-reservations. *Newsweek,* 1946, **28,** 78.

Niebuhr, H. R. *The social sources of denominationalism.* New York: Henry Holt, 1929.

Parke, D. B. *The epic of the Unitarianism; original writings from the history of liberal religion.* Boston: Starr King Press, 1957.

Pearsons, Stow. *Free religion, an American faith.* New Haven: Yale University Press, 1947.

Rieff, P. *The triumph of the therapeutic.* New York: Harper & Row, 1966.

Robinson, E. A. *American Universalism, its origins, organization and heritage.* New York: Exposition Press, 1970.

Rossi, A. S. Abortion laws and their victims. *Transaction,* September-October 1966, **3,** 7-12.

Rossi, A. S. Public views on abortion. In A. F. Guttmacher (Ed.), *The case for legalized abortion now.* Berkeley: San Diablo Press, 1967. Pp. 26-53.

Roszak, T. *The making of a counter culture.* Garden City: Anchor Books, 1969.

Scott, C. L. *The Universalist church of America, a short history.* Boston: Universalist Historical Society, 1957.

Simpson, G. G. *This view of life.* New York: Harcourt, Brace & World, 1964.

Smith, W. C. *The meaning and end of religion.* New York: Macmillan, 1963.

Spilka, B. Research on religious beliefs: a critical review. In M. P. Strommen (Ed.), *Research on religious development.* New York: Hawthorn Books, 1971. Pp. 485-520.

Spoerl, D. T. The values of Unitarian-Universalist youth. *Journal of Psychology,* 1961, **51,** 421-437.

Stark, R. & Glock, C. Y. *American piety.* Berkeley: University of California Press, 1968.

Tapp, R. B. A look at Unitarian Universalist goals. *Christian Century,* 1967a, **LXXXIV,** 515-18.

Tapp, R. B. Toward a new liberal theology. *Journal of the Liberal Ministry,* Spring 1967b, 7, 47-53.

Tapp, R. B. Empirical study of the posttraditionally religious. Paper presented to the annual meeting of the American Academy of Religion, Chicago, October 20, 1967.

Unitarian Universalist Association. *The free church in a changing world.* Boston: Unitarian Universalist Association, 1963.

Verba, S., Brody, R. A., Parker, E. P., Nie, N. H., Polsby, N. W., Ekman, P. & Black, G. S. Public opinion and the war. *American Political Science Review,* 1967, **LXI**, 317-333.

Wallace, A. F. C. *Religion: an anthropological view.* New York: Random House, 1966.

Whitman, L. B., Keating, B. J., & Matthews, R. W., (Eds.). *United Presbyterian national education survey.* United Presbyterian Church: Board of Christian Education, 1966.

Wilbur, E. M. *A history of Unitarianism.* 2 vols., Cambridge: Harvard University Press, 1949-1952.

Wright, C. *The beginnings of Unitarianism in America.* Boston: Beacon Press, 1955.

Yinger, J. M. *The scientific study of religion.* New York: Macmillan, 1970.

INDEX

Abortion, attitudes toward, 86-88
Adult programs,
 emphasis on, 132, 133
 satisfaction with, 161, 163
Advertisement, 148-149
Aesthetic satisfaction, as church attendance
 value, 74
Affiliation, 200
 distinguished from identification, 14
Age,
 gaps on dimensions of religiosity, 175-
  176
 as source of self-ascription, 106, 107,
  130
 of Unitarian Universalists, 7, 8
Alienation, 125
 mobility and, 125-127
American Civil Liberties Union, member-
 ship in, 97, 99
American Ethical Union, 63
American Humanist Association, 63
American Unitarian Association, 137, 153
 founding of, 5
Arius, view of Trinity, 69
Arminius, human freedom and, 75
Artistic activities, in religious education,
 134,135
Assimilation, 194-195
Atheism, 54-55
Attitudes, *see also* Beliefs
 church participation and, 32

Authority, moral, 81-82
Autosuggestion, as function of prayer, 72

Behavior dimension, 37-38
Belief(s), 29, 30, 34, 37, 43, 45, 48, 75, 77
 age, gender and class gaps on, 176, 177-
  178
 associations of, 179, 190
 devotional orientation and, 31
 about Jesus, 64-70, 76
 organizational involvement and, 31
 related to self-ascription, 53-61
 religious knowledge and, 31
Bible, in religious education, 14, 134, 135
Buddhists, religious distance from, 62-63
Bultmann, Rudolf, 68, 70

Calvinism, 75
Catholics, *see* Roman Catholics
Children, effect on self-ascription, 120, 130
 church school and, 120-121
Christianity, 65
 relationship to Judaism, 65-66
Christian label, applied to Unitarian Uni-
 versalists, 135-137, 157
Christian Scientists, religious distance from,
 62
Church, 174
 distinction between sect and, 26

261